"This is a highly significant, vital book. Appropriate modern spirituality requires the interaction of the critical prophetic voice calling for incisive response to suffering and corruption, together with bodhisattva openness and commitment informed by deep awareness of interconnectedness. For the best in our American founding values to survive, and even for our human world to survive and thrive amid its current dangers, this intersection of the prophetic call and bodhisattva grounding in community and meditative awareness will be essential."

—**Taigen Dan Leighton**, author of *Zen Questions*

"There can be no real peace without justice!" announces Berrigan, the prophet. "But there can be no real justice without compassion!" responds Thich Nhat Hanh, the bodhisattva. In this book, Strain the scholar enables us all to enter and carry on this engaging and so urgent conversation."

—**Paul F. Knitter**, Union Theological Seminary

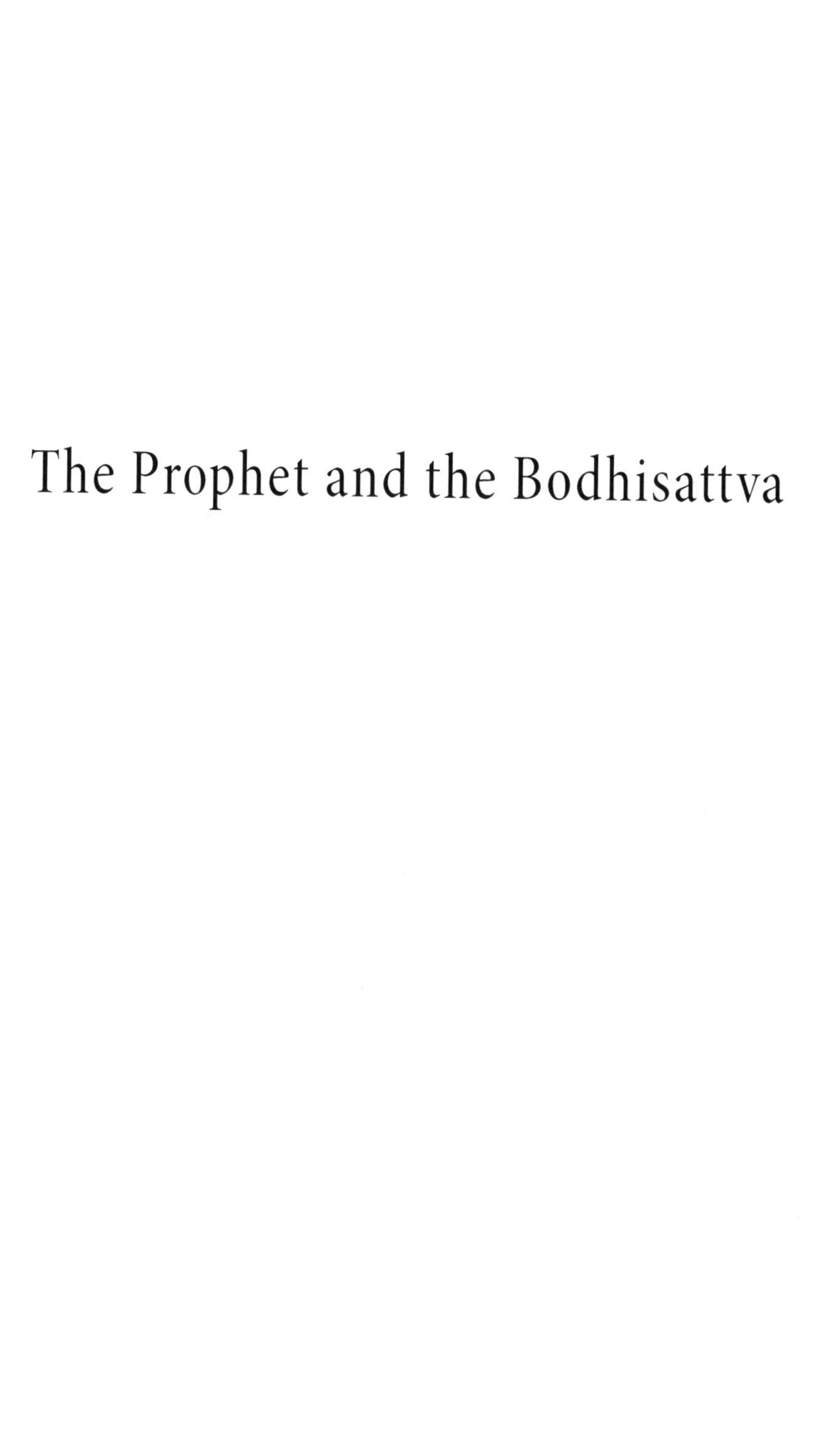

The Prophet and the Bodhisattva

The PROPHET and the BODHISATTVA

Daniel Berrigan, Thich Nhat Hanh, and the Ethics of Peace and Justice

CHARLES R. STRAIN

WIPF & STOCK · Eugene, Oregon

THE PROPHET AND THE BODHISATTVA
Daniel Berrigan, Thich Nhat Hanh, and the Ethics of Peace and Justice

Wipf & Stock
An Imprint of Wipf and Stock Publishers
199 W. 8th Ave., Suite 3
Eugene, OR 97401

www.wipfandstock.com

ISBN 13: 978-1-62032-841-5

Manufactured in the U.S.A.

With gratitude to my teachers and mentors:

William G. Storey

Hugh T. McElwain

Richard J. Meister

CONTENTS

ACKNOWLEDGMENTS

I AM GRATEFUL TO my many teachers and mentors as I have struggled with issues of peace and justice over decades. Kristen Tobey, Thomas O'Brien, and Paul Knitter provided advice and encouragement when this book was in its proposal stage. Frida Furman, Jack Lawlor, Michael Baxter, and David Wellman read different chapters and gave them a careful review. Liam Heneghan helped with sources for chapter 7. James Block not only gave chapter 6 a careful going over, but without years of team-teaching our "Transforming Empire" course together, that chapter would have been inconceivable. Thanks to Sister Jane Gerard, CSJ, for her indispensable assistance in preparing the manuscript and to Ian Petchenik for invaluable technical assistance. Aaron Bobrow-Strain has led me on an almost two-decades-long journey exploring borders and boundaries. Daniel William Strain inspired me to look seriously at the issue of climate change. I am deeply appreciative of Dianne Hanau-Strain for her patience and support throughout this long process. Parts of various chapters were presented at conferences of the Peace and Justice Studies Association. DePaul's University Research Council awarded me a research leave, which enabled me to finish this project.

Introduction

THE BLESSING OF ELDERS

AT THE VERY BEGINNING of his deeply moving book *Living Buddha, Living Christ*, on the inner connections of Buddhism and Christianity, Thich Nhat Hanh tells the story of a Christian theologian who introduced an ecumenical conference by admonishing the participants not to make "a fruit salad" of their traditions. "When it came my turn to speak," Thich Nhat Hanh continued, "I said 'Fruit salad can be delicious! I have shared the Eucharist with Father Daniel Berrigan, and our worship became possible because of the sufferings we Vietnamese and Americans shared over many years.'"[1]

For his part, Berrigan, in his foreword to a play by Thich Nhat Hanh, repeats the story of five students in the School of Youth for Social Service that Thich Nhat Hanh founded in Vietnam. These students had worked tirelessly to aid the refugees of war but they were taken from their beds and murdered (all but one!) because both sides in that conflict abhorred their nonviolent service. The play was written so that the savor of these salutary lives would not be erased in bloody death. Berrigan comments that the dead youth "cross the waters in our direction. They come toward us, and their speech is all of forgiveness, of hope, and joy. . . . Are you saying to us, Thich Nhat Hanh, that the Vietnamese dead will come back to us who murdered them? Will come, not as ministers of vengeance, but sacramental presences, angels, spirits of new creation?"[2]

At first glance both stories are acts of transgression—of ecclesial prohibitions, of war's psychic mine fields, of death's own chasm. Read mindfully, they speak volumes of how rootedness in tradition uncovers what

1. Nhat Hanh, *Living Buddha*, 1.
2. Berrigan, foreword to *Love in Action*, 6–7.

Thich Nhat Hanh calls the "interbeing" of all things living and dead. As acts of transgression, both stories reflect a way of being religious that I will call "prophetic." As dissolving boundaries through loving kindness, both stories exemplify what I will call the "bodhisattva path."

Both Berrigan, now over ninety years old, and Thich Nhat Hanh, well into his eighties, have been actively seeking to create a peaceful and just world for almost fifty years. Both are prolific writers; in volume after volume they explore the anatomy, the beating heart, of their respective religious ways of living and acting ethically. In a time of war they came to know one another, to listen deeply and to speak thoughtfully with one another. When we read *The Raft Is Not the Shore*, the 1974 conversations in France between Berrigan and Thich Nhat Hanh, what most impresses is the ease of their sharing, the absence of any defensiveness or one-upmanship. Solidly grounded in their own traditions, they trade insights, savoring the wisdom that the other has to offer. Throughout this work I hope to emulate this spirit of radical openness.

"It is the blessing of elders that keeps the movement going from generation to generation," Ched Myers says in his appreciation of the life and work of Daniel Berrigan.[3] This saying is not a truth that can be held self-evident. In fact, much of our experience would seem to refute it. What movement, we may ask? And why bring up the distant past? To the first question, the answer is emphatic: Both Berrigan and Thich Nhat Hanh have persevered for decades in building communities of love and resistance to bridge the generations. To the second question, William Faulkner once provided the clearest answer: The past is not dead; it is not even past.

Thich Nhat Hanh and Father Daniel Berrigan are my elders. Their blessings have shaped my life. In their cases, old age has burst its seams in a torrent of writings—each in itself a rite of passage for the reader. Yet serious engagement with this Buddhist and this Christian has its hazards. "Present tense afire" is how one writer describes Berrigan; this phrase could equally and aptly apply to Thich Nhat Hanh.[4]

MORAL AGENT AS A CLASSIC

The crucible of war tempered the characters of both Daniel Berrigan and Thich Nhat Hanh, and gave definitive shape to each man's life as a moral agent. The claim of this book is that each of them is a "blessing." But what do we mean by that vague term, particularly when we attend to both their

3. Myers, "Way the Book Invites," 86.
4. Wylie-Kellermann, "Taking the Book," 87.

spiritual practice and their authorship as a unified moral agency? What Taigen Dan Leighton suggests about the various bodhisattvas who populate the Mahayana Buddhist pantheon in his important work, *Faces of Compassion: Classic Bodhisattvas and Their Modern Expression*, can also be applied to the prophets as spiritual types.

> Each reveals an overall character and style that practitioners may identify or align with at different times or phases of their practice. . . . All of these bodhisattvas have their own psychological approach and strategy toward practice and their own function as spiritual resources.[5]

Imagine that each prophet and each bodhisattva represents a different wavelength of light. To say that Daniel Berrigan and Thich Nhat Hanh are for me the "blessing of elders" is to say that each one's very particular and specific radiation of light has been refracted and reflected in my own life. But in a more complicated way, their own light is itself a refraction-reflection of their engaged reading of, respectively, the prophets and bodhisattvas of their traditions. Stated bluntly, Daniel Berrigan and Thich Nhat Hanh are modern embodiments of classic forms of moral life and agency.

In a recent essay, David Clairmont suggests how we might view persons as moral and religious classics.[6]

> To expand the notion of classic to include persons would mean focusing not primarily on their highest achievements (i.e., as embodiments of ideals of excellence or as paragons of virtue) but rather as exemplifications of moral struggle toward visions of the good within the reality of human limits. . . . On this understanding persons become classics to each other with each attempt to live a moral life in response to the teachings of their own traditions thereby calling other persons to acknowledge their lives as projects both morally and epistemologically incomplete, in the process of purification and transformation. Despite this incompleteness, such lives nonetheless point beyond themselves.[7]

What is clear in this definition is that a classic is not an antique, something—or, in this case, someone—relegated to an imagined pristine past. Persons as moral classics "point beyond themselves" and do so in and

5. Leighton, *Faces of Compassion*, 27.

6. Clairmont, "Persons as Religious Classics," 687–720. An extended analysis of Clairmont's complex argument is not to my purpose here. Rather I hope to shed light on his intriguing suggestions by applying the method.

7. Ibid., 712–13.

through their own incompleteness. Echoing David Tracy, Clairmont argues that classics convey an "ethical demand" for genuine conversation and interpretation.[8] In Tracy's words, the key to the interpretation of a classic is the recognition of it as an event, a claim exerted in the present.[9] The classic calls forth an engaged reader, that is, one in whom the work and works of the classic person are both refracted and reflected.[10]

If we see a classic in this sense as an event, we can come to a more unified understanding of Berrigan's actions and Thich Nhat Hanh's practice and of their outpouring of profoundly transformative texts. One interpretation of both men might be that their decisively moral impact was during the Vietnam War (and, perhaps in Berrigan's case, the Plowshares action in 1980)—an event that has long receded. This certainly would ignore the moral coherence of what has followed in each man's life work. Such an interpretation also ignores the way in which the act of writing is a moral act, spiritually shaped, and launched, an act whose reverberations continue. Shaped by these reverberations, the engaged reader, too, becomes responsible for acting.

BLUE CLIFF MONASTERY 2009, SAIGON 1963

When I ask acquaintances if they've ever heard of Thich Nhat Hanh, more frequently than I can count they mention reading *Being Peace* or *The Miracle of Mindfulness*. They fit easily into a new category of spiritual seekers called "nightstand Buddhists."[11] Their *Thay* ("teacher," as disciples refer to Thich Nhat Hanh) utters words, as simple as a pebble falling in water.

> Breathing in, I calm my body
> Breathing out, I smile
> Dwelling in the present moment
> I know that this is a wonderful moment.[12]

The Thay I know and love is different. I am at a retreat in the autumnal Adirondacks in 2009. Thich Nhat Hanh is leading a walking meditation to the crest of a hill. He stops and we gather in a loose circle while he sits and slowly, silently drinks a cup of tea. But his face is drawn, haggard. He looks every bit his age of eighty-two, a man who has just survived a two-week

8. Ibid., 711.
9. Tracy, *Analogical Imagination*, 235.
10. On the role of a reader of classics, see ibid., 100–103, 115–16, and 136n8.
11. Tweed, "Night-Stand Buddhists," 71–90.
12. Nhat Hanh, *Being Peace*, 15.

ordeal in the hospital. These eyes see through the murky depths to which the pebble has sunk.

For those of us who survived the Vietnam War—and many born thereafter—two images are inscribed in our collective memory. The first is of a young girl, stripped naked by napalm, running, arms akimbo, her mouth frozen forever in a scream. The second is of a monk sitting preternaturally calm engulfed in flames, self-immolated. Thich Nhat Hanh's response to the latter event was captured in a poem that he wrote in 1963, "The Fire That Consumes My Brother."

> The fire that burns him
> burns in my body.
> And the world around me
> burns with the same fire
> that burns my brother.
>
> He burns. . . .
>
> Deeply wounded, I remain here . . .
> I will not betray you—
> are you listening?
> I remain here
> because your very heart
> is now my own.[13]

The self-immolation of Thich Quang Duc in June of 1963 followed by those of two other monks in August provoked Thich Nhat Hanh into action, appealing to the UN to intervene in support of persecuted Buddhists in Vietnam. Thich Nhat Hanh's book, *Vietnam: Lotus in a Sea of Fire*, published in 1967, was a summons to action in ways that rejected the ideological chasm separating Left and Right and the military divide between North Vietnam and South Vietnam. While the book was a guide to peaceful protest, Thich Nhat Hanh himself was the lotus sitting calmly in the sea of fire. Like the Bodhisattva, Avalokiteshvara, he listened to the cries of millions of dying Vietnamese and thousands of Americans.

> The storm screams with your cries.
> Hearing you,
> each cell in me, O my brother,
> burns with tears."[14]

13. Nhat Hanh, "Fire that Consumes My Brother," 48–49.

14. Ibid.

Reading *Vietnam: Lotus in a Sea of Fire* in the late '60s changed everything for me. Thich Nhat Hanh's voice was tempered by the sufferings of his people under the French, the Japanese, then the French again, and finally by civil war and America's involvement. His was a counter-narrative to the propaganda of both sides of the conflict. It provided a historical anchor to otherwise abstract moral principles that had led me to oppose the war. I sensed in it something rare and wonderful: a person crying out for peace from the very heart of war, a voice without rage, words that did not traffic in the labels of good and evil. His prose grounded my own commitment to nonviolent resistance. Years later, when I found *Being Peace*, it was like finding a path again after blundering unguided through a forest.

In a story that Thich Nhat Hanh wrote to commemorate the self-immolation in 1962 of his student, Nhat Chi Mai, fire is transformed into quenching rain. A great white bird, which spends its days flying slowly and quietly meditating on the nature of time and eternity, awakens one day to the anguished cry of birds and the smell of smoke as fire engulfs the ancient forest. The bird dips its huge wings in water and shakes them over the fire.

> It was not enough. . . . Why was there no rain . . . ? The bird let forth a piercing cry. The cry was tragic and passionate and was suddenly transformed into the rushing sound of a waterfall. All at once, the bird felt the fullness of its existence. . . . Without anxiety, the bird plunged into the forest fire like a majestic waterfall."[15]

The bird; Nhat Chi Mai; Avalokiteshvara—the bodhisattva who hears the cries of the world—as well as the Vietnamese monk who tells the story become one.

CHICAGO 1990s, CATONSVILLE 1968

In the 1990s, Daniel Berrigan came to DePaul University to teach for a term on three different occasions. I treasure our meetings as much for Daniel's silent presence as for his austere speech. On the wall of my office hangs a woodblock print—a gift of my wife from the early years of our marriage. Carved from a scrap piece of wood, the figure of a prophet is tall and gaunt. The head is forcibly bent by a kind of radiance that invades the space of self-possession. The rays stream through the figure and out of the hands. When last I saw him, Daniel Berrigan physically resembled the carving, only the rays did not impinge from without, if they ever did. They appeared to come

15. Nhat Hanh, *Love in Action*, 149–51.

from somewhere within. Daniel's dark eyes in their hollowed sockets focused on some inner place where self had been displaced—except, that is, when with a wry grin those eyes lit up.

In his autobiography, *To Dwell in Peace*, Berrigan reflects on the turning point in his life, the pivot: "I speculate at times . . . what might have happened to us had there been no civil rights movement and no war in Vietnam . . . ? As though one were to ask . . . something absurdly unanswerable . . . like, What if we had not been born at all? I had been born; one began from that and because of the war, I had been born again; and one must begin from that."[16]

There is a photo of Daniel and his brother Philip in priestly garb standing over a smoldering pile of draft files in Catonsville, Maryland, in May of 1968, matches in hand. Their faces are solemn; their action liturgical. In contrast to Thich Nhat Hanh's poem, fire is not the emblem of war's pitiless destruction. Metaphorical convergence sparks a deeper divergence. No bird quenches the fire; rather, phoenix hope rises from the flames. "The act was pitiful, a tiny flame amid the consuming fires of war. But Catonsville was like a firebreak, a small fire lit, to contain and conquer a greater. . . . A new fire, new as a Pentecost, flared up in eyes deadened and hopeless. . . . 'Nothing can be done!' How often we had heard that gasp: the last of the human, of soul, of freedom. Indeed, something could be done; and was. And would be."[17]

At more than forty years' remove, it is hard to imagine unless you lived through it how significant was the subsequent picture of Berrigan in handcuffs flashing the peace sign. The civil rights movement had accustomed the American population to witnessing acts of civil disobedience. This was different: The country was at war and these were priests! Their action, for us Catholics, was deeply sacramental; the fiery symbol was visceral in its impact. An era was over, the era in which American Catholics, as members of a minority under suspicion of foreign allegiance, compensated by strenuously proclaiming their patriotism.

What Berrigan was to write three decades later about one of his spiritual ancestors—Jeremiah—could equally be said of him: "The fury of Yahweh burns in him; he has swallowed fire." And yet Jeremiah remained "his own man, not to be . . . consumed . . . , even by the holiest of fires."[18] And so Berrigan prays to Christ, "our avatar of hope,"

16. Berrigan, *Dwell in Peace*, 167.

17. Ibid., 220–21.

18. Berrigan, *Jeremiah*, 34.

whose heart   in spite of all
hopes on for us   in spite of us—
rain   rain on us . . .
your wildfire   storm of hope[19]

But there is another side to the prophet on fire. There is the Berrigan who treasures community as deeply as does Thich Nhat Hanh, who finds the kingdom of God *here and now* as surely as his Buddhist friend. One poem—as spare as it is elegant—lays bare the prophet's soul. It is entitled "Eucharist."

7 a.m. trial day,
courtesy of Warden Foster,
the San Jose vineyards
and a common baking shop

we took
in a workman's cracked cup
at a slim table

prisoners' pot luck.[20]

As in a Zen haiku, it is all there. A community of resistance and suffering. A simple act of compassion. The Word made real, in a cracked cup.

THE PROPHET AND THE BODHISATTVA

This book puts to the test two assumptions, first, that "the prophet" and "the bodhisattva" are two distinct forms of religious and ethical practice and, second, that these are complementary forms of practice that need each other. It will then show how the inspiration of the prophet and the bodhisattva can foster the development of a social ethics that builds upon the strengths of each. Finally, it will provide a pragmatic test for this social ethics by treating two issues of great moral concern.

To be sure, I am not interested in isolating two ideal types; rather, I submit that we can learn a great deal about the springs of moral vision and action from a living prophet and a living bodhisattva. This is especially true when, as in the cases of Berrigan and Thich Nhat Hanh, the living exemplar has also reflected and written at length about the way of being religious and ethical that he embodies. So the first and most important task, taken up in part 1, is to listen deeply to the words of the prophet and the words of the

19. Berrigan, *Testimony*, 227.

20. Berrigan, "Eucharist," 124–25.

bodhisattva. Chapters 1 and 2 of the book focus in large part on Berrigan's reflection on the Hebrew prophets and Thich Nhat Hanh's reflection on bodhisattvas of the Mahayana Buddhist tradition. Religious ethics, I believe, can best be done by steeping oneself in the practice of those who incarnate distinctive forms of engaged spirituality.

With what sword can you cut through a moral fog? Chapter 1 takes up the issue of the prophet's approach to such a moral imperative. It does so with careful attention to Berrigan's midrash on the prophets, his outpouring of a series of commentaries on the Hebrew prophets. As with a set of nested Russian dolls, we wrestle with Berrigan, the prophet, who wrestles with the Hebrew prophets who wrestle with Yahweh. Classic works by Abraham Heschel and Walter Brueggemann will assist us in our effort to understand Berrigan's lacerating prose.

Chapter 2 traces the experience of "the bodhisattva in hell" through Thich Nhat Hanh's poetry. It then examines Thich Nhat Hanh's work of building sanghas around the globe, communities engaged in the practice of "being peace." Thich Nhat Hanh's commentaries on the *Lotus Sutra* and the *Avatamsaka Sutra* will be our guides in understanding the nature and function of the bodhisattva as an emblem of engaged spirituality.

Two objections, coming from somewhat oblique angles, can be raised about this endeavor. Berrigan's close friend, William Stringfellow, railed against those who called Berrigan a prophet. He thought it a way of dismissing Berrigan by elevating him above the level of ordinary humans. We know how this works—Martin Luther King Jr., for example, has been so elevated as virtually to disappear into the stratosphere. My response to Stringfellow is simple: I will stick closely to Berrigan's and, for that matter, Thich Nhat Hanh's own words in evoking their respective visions and I will deal with them seriously, albeit with critical honesty, in trying to construct a social ethics that draws upon both Buddhist and Christian sources. Moreover, elements of both men's visions remain so disconcerting to me—and I hazard to most of us—that any attempt at hagiography would inevitably miscarry.

The second objection comes from Thich Nhat Hanh himself. On a retreat in Plum Village, Thich Nhat Hanh's monastery in southern France, Robert King came to Thich Nhat Hanh asking for an interview, explaining that he was writing a book about Thich Nhat Hanh's friendship with Thomas Merton. The response that King received was blunt. "Why do you want to write a book about Merton and me?" Thich Nhat Hanh asked. "You should write a book about your own practice."[21] Undoubtedly Thich Nhat Hanh

21. King, *Thomas Merton and Thich Nhat Hanh*, 1.

would say the same about this endeavor. My response would echo King's: This book *is* about my own practice—to which I must add, *such as it is.*

These contemporary guides will take us only so far. Most of us do not live the celibate life of priest or monk. Unlike both men, our lives are more cobbled together than lived with utter consistency. More to the point, we live our lives embedded in social institutions: families and cities, universities and corporations, churches and sanghas, above all the nation state. Truth be told, we live not only in the world but more *of* the world than we care to admit even to ourselves.

Institutions—think of the automotive and oil industries, insurance firms, agribusiness, banks, and brokerage houses—shape us, constrain and mold us to their liking. It is by no means clear what use we are to make of the prophet and the bodhisattva. Certainly the austerity of a monastery or a prison cell does not attract many of us. We lack the courage to live that simply, and the spiritual core to live freely under such constraints. If we are to follow the paths laid out by our elders, what do we do with our embedded lives?

The dilemma was brought home to me during lunch with Daniel Berrigan some years ago during one of his periodic semester sojourns at DePaul. I tried to explain to him why I had moved into higher education administration working with the chief academic officer whose vision of an engaged university offered the possibility of a transformed institution cutting across the grain of the American empire. I explained how we were developing service learning programs to link the university's academic mission with its Vincentian mission to serve the urban poor. Daniel, to put it bluntly, was not buying it. He said little and his silence spoke volumes. "Peacemaking is hard, / hard almost as war. / The difference being one / we can stake life upon / and limb and thought and love. . . ."[22] Nothing short of this would move the prophet. Nothing less does he demand of us. Yet I have persisted working within my chosen institution to create educational programs that foster peace and social justice. Before we can transform our institutions, we must think through, must sift what is just and what is not in their collective thrust. We must imagine a path of transformation, as did the Buddha, but now in a social register. Are we (am I?) simply wandering in the wilderness, failing to acknowledge that we have long ago lost our way? How can we craft an ethics of social responsibility that will guide us in reshaping these institutions, in creating the architecture of peace and justice?

Chapter 3 is the first of three chapters in part 2 that take up these challenges by distilling a more systematic ethics from the ways in which

22. Berrigan, "Peacemaking Is Hard," 100.

Berrigan and Thich Nhat Hanh in their lives and in their writings *perform* their moral and religious visions. Chapter 3, in particular, examines the theses of two scholars, Damien Keown and Peter Gathje, that, respectively, Buddhist ethics in general and the ethics of the Berrigan brothers are species of virtue ethics. What sorts of virtuous lives are we called to by the prophet and the bodhisattva? In the case of Berrigan, I will argue that virtuous living only begins with laser surgery on our moral cataracts. The moral fog that we live under is our own clouded vision. In the case of Thich Nhat Hanh, the moral life entails repairing and reweaving a fragile web.

Both Daniel Berrigan and Thich Nhat Hanh have presented their moral visions in a cascade of genres—poetry, drama, journals, and scriptural commentaries to name a few. How do we make sense of such a wild proliferation? Chapter 4 takes a novel approach to grasping the social ethics of the prophet and the bodhisattva. It argues that social location can be an important clue to Daniel Berrigan's and Thich Nhat Hanh's social ethics. Moreover, each location calls forth a distinctive form of engagement. Thich Nhat Hanh's social location is the sangha, and the form of engagement is building community through the *practice of being peace*. Daniel Berrigan's social location is at the cutting edge of the peace movement and the form of engagement proper to that location is *symbolic acts of resistance*. Speaking from my own social location in an institution of higher learning, I will discuss how we can move from their distinctive forms of engagement to *a praxis of just peacemaking*. Since action always involves power, we will ask how these forms of engagement measure up to Reinhold Niebuhr's analysis of the ambiguity of power in his classic work *Moral Man and Immoral Society*.

Chapter 5 is the last of the three approaches to the ethics of the prophet and the bodhisattva. It recognizes that, in our time, any social ethics needs to be grounded in a theory of justice. Yet both the prophet and the bodhisattva challenge social theories that pit social justice against "charity" as a defective form of social engagement. Both Berrigan and Thich Nhat Hanh, to the contrary, see a much more dialectical relation between compassion and justice. Such an enhanced model of justice will also go beyond liberal individualism's purely procedural understandings of justice to discuss what Catholic social teaching refers to as "integral development." Chapter 5 will argue that Martha Nussbaum's "capability theory" of justice best addresses these concerns of the prophet and the bodhisattva. Finally chapter 5 will ask what sort of praxis is congruent with this theory of justice and what might be vehicles for carrying it forward as well.

Chapters 6 and 7, comprising part 3 of this book, test the fruitfulness of the hybrid social ethics that is developed in the previous three chapters in relationship to two pressing issues: (a) the new American militarism, its imperial overreach, and the need for an ethics of resistance, and (b) the need for an ecological ethics that addresses both climate change and issues of environmental justice. Both Berrigan's and Thich Nhat Hanh's actions and writings on war and peace may be relegated by some to a previous era. Chapter 6 demonstrates their continuing relevance by juxtaposing their body of work to current debates regarding America's imperial mission, debates in which the lines between conservatives and liberals are frequently blurred. Part of this debate is over the proper role and limits of the American military as discussed by historians like Chalmers Johnson and political theorists like Andrew Bacevich. How, the chapter asks, can we incorporate the prophetic critique of the idolatry of the nation state in Berrigan's ethics of resistance and Thich Nhat Hanh's injunction not to cling to any ideology into these profoundly moral appraisals of America's role in the world? Is there any possible meeting ground, this chapter will ask, between the Niebuhrian realism of these critics of imperial hubris and the pacifism of the prophet and the bodhisattva? I will argue that the praxis of just peacemaking requires some broader coalitions to end the empire's endless wars than most forms of peace activism in the American context are inclined to accept.

Chapter 7 takes up two interlocking issues, namely climate change and environmental justice. Buddhism, in particular, has been frequently and superficially defined as a "green religion." Chapter 7 goes beyond such facile characterizations to ask what virtues flow from the bodhisattva's practice that can alter our relationship with the biosphere. Climate change, however, poses a challenge to any virtue ethics because of the immediacy of the crisis. How must we act, Taigen Dan Leighton asks, when our planet is on fire?[23] Clearly a prophetic voice is called for to confront us with—in Dr. King's potent phrase—"the fierce urgency of Now." Climate change is occurring simultaneously with another global phenomenon, the aspiration of poor peoples and countries to escape the iron traps of poverty, hunger, disease and the unnecessary denial of a life worthy of the name human. It is also clear that climate change is affecting and will affect most those poor peoples who have made the least contribution to greenhouse gas emissions. Liberation theology introduced to the category of structural vilence. In examining the issue of environmental justice, chapter 7 will draw upon a relatively new category in the lexicon of environmental justice, that of "slow violence."

Finally, the conclusion brings us full circle. I ask what sort of praxis might flow from reflections on the prophet and the bodhisattva for those

23. Leighton, "Now the Whole Planet," 187–93.

who are involved, as I am, as professionals working within highly developed institutions. Must we end up with the prophet in jail? Must one live a life of voluntary poverty with the bodhisattva? What, then, of the institutions themselves (think of universities, churches, law courts, the health care system)? Do they follow their given course relentlessly while we choose whether or not to opt out of them?

In a most telling, if mildly voiced, criticism, Thich Nhat Hanh suggests, "America is somehow a closed society." Closed, that is, to the immensity of suffering in this world. As an antidote, he offers this "mindfulness training," this spiritual exercise: "Aware that looking deeply at the nature of suffering can help us develop compassion and find ways out of suffering, we are determined not to avoid or close our eyes before suffering."[24] In part in response to this injunction, I have been taking DePaul students and faculty since 1994 to the United States-Mexico border where we study firsthand the impact of globalization on the lives of poor people. On one such trip, one student said that her "eyes had been peeled to the back of her head." If the bodhisattva listens to the cries of the world, the prophet is in the business of peeling back our closed eyes. Either way we are then left with the task of finding our way within a world of immense suffering.

24. Nhat Hanh, *Being Peace*, 93.

Part I

THE PROPHET AND THE BODHISATTVA

1

THE PROPHET

God's Agony Made Flesh and Word

The way I see the world is strictly illegal
to wit, through my eyes[1]

—Daniel Berrigan, "Prophecy"

In *Isaiah: Spirit of Courage, Gift of Tears*, Daniel Berrigan writes of his boyhood experience during the Great Depression, following in his father's footsteps as he plowed a field. The whole world, the boy thought, must be like this, pregnant with new life. "I had," the man reflects, "much to learn." Before many more springs, four of his brothers went off to fight a World War and "life came to this. As long as swords were drawn, we humans lost our bearings. . . . The social fabric was torn; the war ended through abominable deeds, mass murder." And then? "My lifetime was to be a perpetual war time."[2]

THE LIFE OF THE PROPHET

Daniel Berrigan was born on May 9, 1921, the fifth of six sons born to Thomas and Frida Berrigan. Raised in rural Minnesota and upstate New York by a fearsome and frustrated father, and a nourishing and protective mother, Berrigan's progress toward a calling to join the Society of Jesus was,

1. Berrigan, "Prophecy," 230.
2. Berrigan, *Isaiah*, 15–17.

for the times, conventionally Catholic—except, that is, for the presence of Dorothy Day's *Catholic Worker* newspaper in their home and his mother's hospitality to passing strangers in the midst of the Great Depression. In August of 1939, with Europe on the cliff edge of war, Berrigan joined the Society of Jesus. The Jesuits took Berrigan in hand, cultivated his sharp mind and bent his spirit to long discipline. Bright though he was, the young priest, ordained in 1952, still had much to learn. Reflecting on a stint as a chaplain to GIs in Germany in 1954, Berrigan confesses to being completely oblivious to the nuclear standoff, East and West poised for mass murder at that very place.[3] "It is small comfort to dredge up one's memories," he writes in his autobiography, *To Dwell in Peace*, "and come on a moral blank screen. . . . What an unfinished human I was."[4]

Introduction to the worker priests of France, eventually Vatican II, the civil rights movement but, above all, his friendship with the two icons of late twentieth-century Catholicism, Thomas Merton and Dorothy Day, along with the constant prodding of his younger brother Philip, would remold the young Jesuit. Like Saint Augustine, Berrigan would lament "how long, too, the clumsiness and groping, false starts and cowardice, the good, bad and indifferent in the human meld." And yet: "I think my soul was moving in a contrary wind."[5]

The war in Vietnam made of that wind a howling gale. But here, too, Berrigan moved in fits and starts: creating Clergy and Laity Concerned about the War in Vietnam with Rabbi Abraham Heschel and Reverend Richard Neuhaus; supporting student activists at LeMoyne College and later at Cornell University. "The damned war! It was a creeping miasma, an irresistible current; it swept along, in its filthy wake, nearly everyone and everything . . . and because I was objecting to the war, I must be treated like a deserter."[6] Running afoul of the arch-patriot, New York's Cardinal Spellman, Berrigan was sent into Latin American exile in Autumn 1965.

Reflections that were published as *Consequences, Truth And . . .* show Berrigan struggling through a dark night and wrestling with the Church's unjust exercise of its authority. This exile—"the wrong place, with the wrong work"—challenged him to surmount despair, "the point at which one can do nothing—the point of truth." Finally, in a Lima slum Berrigan discovered that truth. "Understand . . . that you are led here for this purpose: to know in such a place as perhaps nowhere else that a future is being formed for you

3. Daniel Berrigan, *No Bars to Manhood*, 6.

4. Berrigan, *Dwell in Peace*, 137.

5. Ibid., 137–39.

6. Ibid., 181.

and others. In these people, in the few that share their fate, a new exodus is under way."[7] Berrigan was recalled to the States after a five-month exile. He continued his antiwar efforts by working with students as a chaplain at Cornell University and flying with Howard Zinn to Hanoi in February 1968 for the transfer of a few American prisoners.

As we saw in the introduction, the burning of draft files in May 1968 in Catonsville, Maryland, was the pivotal experience in Daniel Berrigan's life. His earlier involvements were all rehearsals for the drama that lay ahead. Brother Philip had already burned draft files in Baltimore and he invited Daniel to repeat the action with others at Catonsville. "A sense . . . of immense freedom," Daniel recalled of his decision, "as though in choosing, I could now breathe deep, and call my life my own. A sense, also, of the end of a road, or a fork, or a sudden turn and no telling what lay beyond. . . . And no looking back."[8]

Burning files of the Selective Service System using a homemade concoction of napalm resonated because it was solemnly liturgical, even sacramental. The Catonsville Nine (Brother David Darst, John Hogan, Thomas Lewis, Marjorie Bradford Melville, Thomas Melville, George Mische, and Mary Moylan, as well as Daniel and Philip) had gone beyond words to convey a more visceral truth. "Our instructor in these [symbolic acts]," Daniel was to write much later, "is Jeremiah himself—bearing the yoke, breaking the jar, witnessing the vision of the basket of figs, the signs of drought, the vine devoid of grapes. Each of these bespeaks a nonviolent effort of conscience. . . . They challenge the tyranny implicit in 'things as they are.'"[9]

Given the ritual character of the event, it made perfect sense that Berrigan later transformed the official trial transcript into an award-winning play in which the Catonsville Nine proclaim:

> Our apologies   good friends
> for the fracture of good order the burning of paper
> instead of children   the angering of the orderlies
> in the front parlor of the charnel house
> We could not   so help us God   do otherwise
> For we are sick at heart our hearts
> give us no rest for thinking of the Land of Burning Children.
> . . .
> All of us who act against the law
> turn to the poor of the world   to the Vietnamese

7. Berrigan, *Consequences, Truth*, 114, 122.
8. Berrigan, *Dwell in Peace*, 217.
9. Berrigan, *Jeremiah*, 133–34.

to the victims to the soldiers who kill and die
for the wrong reasons for no reason at all
because they were so ordered by the authorities
of that public order which is in effect
a massive institutionalized disorder
We say: killing is disorder
life and gentleness and community and unselfishness
is the only order we recognize.
. . .
We have chosen to say
with the gift of our liberty
if necessary our lives:
the violence stops here
the death stops here
the suppression of the truth stops here
this war stops here
Redeem the times!
The times are inexpressibly evil.
. . .
And yet and yet the times are inexhaustibly good
solaced by the courage and hope of many
The truth rules Christ is not forsaken
In a time of death some men and women
the resisters those who work hardily for social change
those who preach and embrace the truth
such men and women overcome death
their lives are bathed in the light of the resurrection
the truth has set them free.[10]

A few words of commentary may help us to grasp what is going on in this dramatic inversion of the ritual of crime and punishment. In times of crisis, Victor Turner argues, those who engage their times seize "roots not straws." The roots that Turner has in mind are "root paradigms," the religiously symbolic equivalent in humans as cultural beings to DNA in humans as biological beings. Drawing his examples from historical agents ranging from Thomas Becket to the Mexican priest-revolutionary Miguel Hidalgo, Turner argues that paradigms have the power to shape freely chosen actions into a patterned whole, into a convincing narrative. At their most profound, paradigmatically generated actions restore a primal experience of community by cutting through the tangled knots of self-interest and by breaking or suspending the structures that establish hierarchical separation.[11] In

10. Berrigan, *Trial of Catonsville Nine*, 93–95.

11. Turner, *Drama, Fields, and Metaphor*, 66–68.

Berrigan's paradigm the officially established order is "institutionalized disorder." The prophet suffers—"no rest for thinking of the Land of Burning Children"—mindful of the suffering that the so-called order perpetuates. If a genuine order is to be restored, the prevailing public order must be disrupted. More precisely, disruption is simply the opening act in a drama called "redeeming the times." Against the "nuclear liturgies" of death is set the pattern of self-sacrificing resistance, a countervailing ritual that is seemingly violent, certainly clumsy and patently offensive to the orderly flow of systematic killing. Out of resistance comes a restoration of "life and gentleness and community . . . the only order we recognize."

Before jail, Berrigan went underground, popping up at peace rallies and then disappearing to the consternation of the FBI. What was happening in the depths of his spirit was more important than the cat and mouse game, for Berrigan's travelling companion was John of the Cross—the journey was through a long night and the way unknown. Stepping back to view the disease whole, the corrupting imperial power of which Vietnam was "only a tick on the rhino's hide," was to enter a long night. "How [to] build a life worthy of human beings in the darkness?"[12] In the deepest sense the last forty plus years have only continued this journey. "The not knowing," Berrigan at his most Zen-like says, "became a parable of existence itself; and in a darksome way underscored the need for integrity. One was in the dark—as to the worth, result, impact, political wisdom of what one was about. . . . Now and again came a sense of a providential, caring God. The inkling was seldom consoling . . . a God of Job."[13]

As the Vietnam War wound down, the Cold War heated up, along with proxy wars in Africa, Central America, and, eventually, in Afghanistan. Indeed, through the 1980s, the nuclear arms race would run wild. Released from prison, but in no wise repentant, the Berrigans turned their attention toward America's vast arsenal of nuclear weapons, which Daniel called "a demonic anti-sacrament." "The moral fog was indivisible: all one. Some breathed shallow, others deep. But we were all enveloped in the same miasma, a machine that was churning out moral impenetrability."[14]

Given his early experience tilling the soil, it is not surprising that Berrigan and his fellow conspirators turned to Isaiah 2:4, "They shall beat their swords into plowshares," to devise a sacrament of resistance as much to heal the "nuclear winter" in our souls as to dent the armament of genocide. On September 9, 1980, eight men and women entered a G.E. factory in King of

12. Berrigan, *Dark Night of Resistance*, 14–15, 43.

13. Berrigan, *Dwell in Peace*, 247–48.

14. Ibid., 345.

Prussia, Pennsylvania, where the Mark 12A nuclear missile reentry vehicles were manufactured. Armed with hammers and bottles of their own blood, they moved quickly into the heart of the labyrinth and proceeded to hammer away at the nose cones of missiles destined to carry nuclear warheads. The "Plowshares Movement" was born. Daniel recalls:

> Hammers and blood. The blood, we thought, was a reminder of our common life, our common destiny, the bloodline that joins us to one another, for good or ill. The blood, as Exodus reminds us, is a sign of life, and therefore of the Lifegiver, and therefore sacred. A sign also of covenant, a common understanding, that the blood of Christ, once given, forbids all shedding of blood. "This is the new covenant in My blood, given for you." A gift, a wellspring of justice and peace.[15]

In that one phrase, "the blood of Christ, once given, forbids all shedding of blood," Berrigan conveys the kernel of his ethics and the command that compels him to act. There is in the more than one hundred Plowshares actions that were to follow an effort to clear the moral air. But given an all-enveloping moral miasma, the task has proved to be as overwhelming as lifting a fog by waving one's arms.[16]

During their trial, the Plowshares Eight attempted to invoke international law as it emerged at Nuremburg after World War II, laws that prohibit preparation for genocide or mass murder and that require citizens to intervene to halt crimes against humanity.[17] "We eight have been trying to take responsibility for [these murderous weapons]," Berrigan declared at the trial, "to call them by their right name, which is murder, death, genocide, the end of the world."[18]

Appeals of the guilty verdict for the Plowshares action dragged on through the decade of the '80s until a judge released the eight with "time served." One of the more recent Plowshares actions involved a group of five, ranging in age from sixty to eighty-three, who trespassed into the Trident submarine base at Kitsap-Bangor, Washington, in November 2009.[19] The

15. Berrigan, *Testimony*, 7, 18–19.

16. Berigan, *Dwell in Peace*, 345.

17. Nepstad, *Religion and War Resistance*, 78–79; Nepstad provides a history of the movement.

18. Daniel Berrigan as quoted in ibid., 80.

19. Bryan Farrell, "Disarm Now Plowshares Receive Sentencing," *Waging Nonviolence*, March 29, 2011, n.p, http://wagingnonviolence.org/2011/03/disarm-now-plowshares-receive-sentencing/. Astonishingly the Jesuit Bill Bischel acted with the official sanction—commission would be the appropriate term—of his provincial superior who hoped that Bischel's action might inspire younger Jesuits who might be "hearing God's

base houses more nuclear warheads than the combined total of England, France, China, Israel, India, Pakistan, and North Korea. The destructive power of the Trident fleet is twenty-four thousand times that of the bomb dropped on Hiroshima. "Is anyone paying attention?" Sr. Anne Montgomery asks. "The only hope is that we can all wake up from the dream of a secure 'way of life' at whatever cost to others . . . and to listen to our hearts, not our fears."[20] For Berrigan this "dark night of resistance" requires a spiritual discipline, placing the outcome of our actions in God's hands. Yet "not merely the outcome, but each step takes on the dignity of an end in itself and must be carefully weighed and judged as such."[21]

To Dwell in Peace, Berrigan's autobiography, was written when he was only sixty-six. In the more than two decades that have followed, Berrigan has continued to engage in acts of nonviolent resistance, but not of the high-stakes order of Catonsville and King of Prussia. Indeed, it is in his writings, especially in the incandescent commentaries on the prophets, that Berrigan has concentrated his agency. These works, as I hope to demonstrate, are moral acts of the highest order.

THE PROPHET'S MIDRASH ON THE PROPHETS

Beyond his more than four decades of activism on behalf of peace, Daniel Berrigan has written a prodigious series of commentaries on books of the Hebrew and Christian scriptures. His own words are a profound testimony

still distant, disturbing call to prophecy against the violence and war." See the press release from November 2, 2009, at http://www.jonahhouse.org/archive/Disarm_Now_Plowshares/pressrelease.htm. See also Patrick Lee to Bichsel, 23 October 2009, at http://www.jonahhouse.org/archive/Disarm_Now_Plowshares/bichselmissioning.htm.

20. Montgomery, "Is Anyone Paying Attention," November 28, 2010, n.p., http://disarmnowplowshares.wordpress.com/2010/11/28/. Follow-up actions by nonviolent activists have included symbolic shutdowns of the entrance to the naval base. The most recent Plowshare action occurred in July 2012, when Greg Boertje-Obed, Michael Walli, and Sr. Megan Rice entered a High Energy Uranium Manufacturing Facility in Oak Ridge, TN, poured human blood on the cornerstone, raised banners, spray painted a denunciation of the production of nuclear weapons, and offered bread and roses to the guards. In May 2013, the three were convicted of "interfering with or obstructing the national defense and depredation of government property." This is designated as a "federal crime of terrorism." Conflation of nonviolent civil disobedience with an act of terrorism is a sign of how far a national security state will go to force its citizens into submission. See "Judge Issues Rule 29 Decision," posted by TNPlowshares, October 9, 2013, n.p., http://transformnowplowshares.wordpress.com/2013/10/09/judge-issues-rule-29-motion/.

21. Berrigan, *Dwell in Peace*, 336.

to the costs of this work, costs far beyond the energy devoted to intellectual labor.

> For the last twenty-five years I studied and wrote on the Hebrew Bible, publishing studies of the major and minor prophets. Each was the fruit of days of reflection offered across the country, and courses taught at universities. Revise, sweat, burn midnight oil. There was no end of it. I was pursued by a demon or a fireball. Or writing was an exorcism. I struggled to rid the text of rhetoric, puffing, self-justification, *parti pris*. How [to] let words, images, events, parables, speak for themselves? It was purgatorial.[22]

In carrying out this task, Berrigan clearly immersed himself in relevant scholarship, but he gives short shrift to those biblical scholars whom he refers to as "cautious taxidermists." Their crime? "They forbid utterly the rabbinical method of midrash. Safe, sure, and ultimately deadly . . . , it was as though the Christian testament cast no light on the ancient texts."[23] Berrigan recognizes, however, that he is by no means immune to this scholarly disease. Words, all too easily, become a cocoon protecting the writer from hearing God's own word.[24] As the prophets wrestled with their visions and their God, Berrigan wrestles with them in a no-holds-barred clash of minds and hearts. The metaphor that comes to mind is of flint striking steel. The steel is the prophet's uncompromising commitment to the God of Exodus and the God of the Sinai Covenant. The flint is Berrigan's equally uncompromising commitment to the nonviolent God of Jesus.[25]

The flint strikes the steel in blow after blow as Berrigan struggles with the texts, passage after passage. The result: sparks fly. The tinder, if you will allow this pursuit of metaphor, is the reader who willingly lays bare her heart. We should expect from such a clash neither a systematic theology nor a blueprint for social transformation. Berrigan repeatedly exhibits a

22. Berrigan, *Testimony*, 33. The actual publication of his reflections, however, came in a five-year burst of creativity: *Minor Prophets, Major Themes* in 1995; *Isaiah: Spirit of Courage, Gift of Tears* in 1996; *Ezekiel: Vision of the Dust* in 1997; and, then, *Jeremiah: The World, the Wound of God* in 1999. I will concentrate my analysis principally on these four books. In another burst of creativity, Berrigan published the "prequel" to the prophetic literature, *Exodus: Let My People Go* in 2008 and then waded neck deep into the biblical mire out of which, lotus-like, he emerged publishing works on the books of Kings (*The Kings and Their Gods: The Pathology of Power*, 2008) and on Deuteronomy (*No Gods but One*, 2009). Each of these works exhibits the same disciplined, verse-by-verse labor with the text punctuated by bursts of poetic insight.

23. Berrigan, *Testimony*, 33.

24. Berrigan, *Exodus*, 2.

25. Myers, "Way the Book Invites," 90–91. Myers's analysis of Berrigan's method of biblical interpretation has been most helpful to me.

disciplined freedom—the discipline of following the tracks of the text, the freedom to take issue with the Israelite prophets every bit as much as they criticized the erstwhile prophets whose words rang false to their committed ears. Quoting Walter Wink, for example, Berrigan calls the book of Hosea an "apostate text," one of the "texts of terror that dehumanize women."[26] Berrigan's critical freedom goes so far as to take issue with the god of Exodus—a lower-case god, and, to Berrigan's mind, deservedly so. The god of Exodus issues "a mandate that can only be termed murderously pharaonic. Let the children die! What difference, all said, between the two Faustian decrees, between the death of Hebrew male infants and the death of Egyptian first born? Are we to abominate the former, and celebrate the latter? The mind boggles."[27] The ultimate larceny of the god of Exodus is to expunge from all memory the Egyptians's story, the kind of story a father might tell a child who survived the "night of blood." The true wandering in the wilderness traverses a moral wasteland "in this deity, in ourselves." Exodus demands enactment but it requires critical readers as well who will go counter to the text and thereby reclaim its original intent so that "the Bible may prove of service to ethical maturity in the world."[28]

Berrigan, the poet, takes license in his translations of the biblical texts. Nowhere is this more apparent than in his rendition of central passages in his beloved Isaiah. Reworking Isaiah 30:1–18, Berrigan excoriates the *realpolitik* of the national security state. Yahweh speaks:

> Cursed be the rebellious,
> devious plans in place,
> crime upon crime!
> This plan, that pact,
> security here, advantage there!
> . . .
> Write this down, Isaiah
>   Seal it close,
>   My words languish, lost, dead
> by a dead sea.
> . . .
> This people—
>   to what
>   compare them?
>   a firm-seeming wall

26. Berrigan, *Minor Prophets*, 14, 22. For a critical analysis of the prophets' metaphors from a feminist standpoint, see O'Brien, *Challenging Prophetic Metaphor*.

27. Berrigan, *Exodus*, 49.

28. Ibid., 81–82, 118.

a mortal crack runs through.
It sways, it heaves and buckles
and falls asunder!

This people—clay,
a pot of faulted clay—
shattered.
        Shards
useless at the hearth,
worthless at the well!
. . .
Very well then,
unpeaceable, distrustful ones!

Hear what comes of this
haste, waste, misapprehension—

nothing, and less—
catastrophe, defeat.
. . .
your armies dissolve
like mist in midair!
Look what is left to you;
    a tattered pennant
    on a hilltop hanging
    like a hanged
    head, disconsolate—
    in stale air stalemated
    signifying
    nothing.

    And yet
    despite all—
    mine, my people!

    Write this, Isaiah:
    "I condemn you to—
    hope!"[29]

Notice here that it is not a people who is cursed but the "devious plans" of a national security state. Not Yahweh's mighty arm that crushes Israel. Rather Isaiah is made to say, "Hear what comes of this." The karmic crack

29. Berrigan, *Isaiah*, 74–76.

that precedes the fall runs deep under the pillars of the state. Do we then, full though we are of sound and fury, signify nothing? Hardly. Yahweh counts our every tear, writes our name in the palm of her hand, beckons us to soar:

> Little one, arise,
> drink the rainbow,
> sing a new song, schooled
> by larks and nightingales!
> . . .
> trust, hope in Yahweh—
> be renewed, dream eagles,
> on high
> mount, drink the sun![30]

Larks and nightingales join with Isaiah's eagle in a hymn of rebirth and transcendence. But transcendence is never without cost.

> My servant!
> a victim
> borne to the abattoir,
> . . .
> It was for us, the lost,
> for us she suffered.[31]

Berrigan' translations soar while the commentator takes upon himself the heavy yoke of the text. In the earliest rabbinic midrash we are told, "The focus of interest is on individual verses of scripture, and interpreting those verses in the order in which they appear forms the organizing principle of sustained discourse."[32] This discipline, however, is not on behalf of biblical literalism; it is rather a "retelling of scriptural stories in such a way as to impart to those stories new immediacy."[33] But Berrigan's style of commen-

30. Ibid., 111–12.

31. Ibid., 140. The distinction between Isaiah and Second Isaiah is acknowledged, the latter penning "a magnificent extended midrash on great-great-great grandfather Isaiah." Ibid., 99. Yet it is the unified sweep of the text that ignites the poet. In places the scriptural text is pared to the bone; in others, as with the larks and nightingales, the poet lets loose the reins of imagination. And what, finally, are we to make not with the association of the servant with Easter dawn, a conventional Christian interpretation, but the reference to the servant as "she"? Despite the fact that a text like the book of Isaiah was composed over four hundred years, Marvin Sweeney argues that prophetic texts should be seen as coherent literary wholes which synthesize as many as ten subgenres. Sweeney, *Prophetic Literature*, 16, 33–37.

32. *Dictionary of Judaism in the Biblical Period*, s.v. "midrash."

33. Ibid. A more postmodern understanding of midrash sees it as a response to "a gap or tear or hole or discontinuity of some kind; a wound, a silence or absence or lack."

tary alters the genre. He is not making a creative application of the text to contemporary issues. Rather the context of imperial war invades the text. Berrigan's style, argues Bill Wylie Kellermann, mimics prophetic discourse. Fragments are laid out on the page. "And in between, in the gaps and the cracks there is—what? sighs too deep for words . . . ? The wrestling with God or doubt or death? The movement of history?"[34] Midrashim nestle inside each other like Russian dolls. Deutero Isaiah's midrash on Isaiah. Berrigan's midrash on both. Yet the metaphor is too placid. "Isaiah becomes something other than an unattainable icon. He becomes the measure of our own possibility. . . . The coal is lifted from the fire and held to his lips. Thus the fire of godliness is passed on and on. A community, a circle about the fire is not merely warmed by the fire, but touched by the fire, marked indelibly."[35]

In this passage we get a sense of why laboring with the prophetic texts was such a harrowing experience for Berrigan. We urban folk have lost the original meaning of harrowing which, as my dictionary has it, is to break clods or remove weeds using a heavy frame with iron teeth. Berrigan suggests that in doing midrash, we come upon "one or two commanding texts," words that set "the human in motion." The command is simply "do it." The scores of Plowshares actions collectively became a midrash on Isaiah 2:1–4.[36]

Both the metaphor of flint/steel and the interpretive category of midrash should alert us: Berrigan is not involved in any quest for the historical Isaiah, the historical Jeremiah, or the historical Ezekiel. He wrestles with the author who appears in the text. Walter Brueggeman, summarizing nearly a quarter century of scholarship on the prophets in his own classic text, *The Prophetic Imagination*, argues that what our context demands "is to take the prophetic texts as text and not as 'personality.'" The latter method yielded a confrontational model, pitting the prophet against the establishment, a strategy that today is "largely ineffectual posturing." In line with contemporary scholarship, Brueggemann stresses that prophets were not isolated "loners," they emerged within subcommunities of resistance.[37] Four traits distinguish these groups: First, "there is a *long and available memory*." The

---

Goodhart, "Land That Devours," 18. If we attend to the subtitle of Berrigan's Jeremiah book, *The World, the Wound of God*, it is clear where Berrigan locates the wound or gap that his midrash struggles with.

34. Wylie-Kellermann, "Taking the Book," 88–89.

35. Berrigan, *Isaiah*, 33.

36. Ibid., 12.

37. Brueggemann, *Prophetic Imagination*, x, xii, xvi. On the derivation of the type of the prophet as loner, see Wilson, *Prophecy and Society*, 58. Wilson also provides an extensive analysis of the subcommunities to which the prophets belonged.

community gathers itself through its memory and "knows that it is defined by . . . a God who as yet is unco-opted . . . by the empire." Second, "there is an available, expressed *sense of pain*."[38] Here, Brueggemann acknowledges the indispensable contribution of Abraham Heschel to our understanding of prophecy.

> The prophet does not judge the people by timeless norms but from the point of view of God. . . . He discloses a *divine pathos* not just a divine judgment. . . . This divine pathos is the key to inspired prophecy. . . . An analysis of prophetic utterances shows that the fundamental experience of the prophet is a fellowship with the feelings of God . . . which comes about through the prophet's reflection of, or participation in, the divine pathos.[39]

While Heschel's formulation reflects an earlier scholarly emphasis on the prophetic personality, Brueggemann is interested in the epistemological break that happens with grieving. "Empires," argues Brueggemann, "live by numbness," apathy in face of the human costs of war and exploitation. They create numbness because they foreclose the possibility of something radically new. Only with the onset of grief does radical criticism become possible. The true prophetic "idiom is anguish and not anger."[40]

Third, "there is an active *practice of hope*." Here the title of Brueggeman's book comes into play. It is the imagination that breaks free of the foreclosed future. Hope refuses the prevailing pretension that what is is all there can be. In hope's lyrical song (think of Berrigan's larks and nightingales) a people appropriates "the freedom of God as their own freedom."[41]

Fourth, and finally, "there is an *effective mode of discourse*." This discourse gathers memory, grief, and hope in articulating an alternative consciousness. It delegitimates the "mythic pretensions" of empire and imaginatively projects an alternative future. A people thereby regains "the linguistic capacity to confront despair."[42] Brueggemann's situating the prophets within communities of resistance and his fourfold analysis of the

38. Brueggemann, *Prophetic Imagination*, xvi, 19; italics in original.

39. Heschel, *Prophets*, 24, 26. Berrigan too is deeply indebted to Heschel, not merely as a scholar but as a prophet himself. Berrigan, Heschel, and then Lutheran minister Richard Neuhaus created Clergy and Laity Concerned about Vietman in 1965, and Berrigan became close friends with Heschel. "How blessed I was," Berrigan testifies, "that one named Abraham had stood with me, in fair weather and foul. . . . The weight of one such life . . . is of such vast import in God's sight as to restore . . . the scales of moral creation into balance once more." *Testimony*, 129–30.

40. Brueggemann, *Prophetic Imagination*, 54–55, 81, 88.

41. Ibid., xvi, 16, 65–66; italics in original.

42. Ibid., xvi, 3, 9, 77; italics in original.

prophetic task gives us a scaffolding with which to support a deeper analysis of Berrigan's wrestling with the prophets.

COMMUNITIES OF RESISTANCE AND OF HOPE

We are drawn out of the inhuman or subhuman pit, barely, by the few who hold firmly in hand a lifeline; who mercifully cast it in our direction . . . ; who in season and out of season summon us to awaken; who raise from the dead our battered humanity.[43]

In *Testimony: The Word Made Fresh*, Berrigan bears witness to those who have transformed his life: Dorothy Day, Martin Luther King Jr., Thomas Merton, Archbishop Oscar Romero, Rabbi Abraham Heschel, and Philip Berrigan, among others.[44] Each of these prophets experienced "the long loneliness," the departure from "a culture of yea-sayers," the step into a *terra incognita* where there is no sure footing. These few recognized that "peace is a verb. You make peace: You do not inherit it or hoard it. . . . Which is to say, you pay up."[45] The community of the few is a community that pays up.

Jeremiah labored for twenty-three years without completing his task. "He would perhaps say: not even begun." Then Berrigan traces a trajectory of resistance from 1968 and Catonsville through the many Plowshares actions. A trajectory longer than Jeremiah's but a "non-outcome strangely parallel to his."[46] Surrounding these actions has been a veil of silence. The media sees nothing, hears nothing, says nothing. And yet, and yet. The few who resist wear their "humanity like a Buddha, a jewel on the forehead. [Philip Berrigan] and others like him light up the national darkness. And the darkness . . . does not comprehend."[47]

43. Berrigan, *Jeremiah*, 91.

44. Although it is beyond the scope of this chapter, it would be hard to overestimate the impact that Day, Merton, and brother Philip had on Berrigan.

45. Berrigan, *Testimony*, 89, 95–96, 103.

46. Berrigan, *Jeremiah*, 105–6.

47. Berrigan, *Testimony*, 139. The Plowshares loosely knit community has sought to purify itself of what Zen Buddhists call any "gaining idea," any hankering for success, appealing to the incognito efficacy of the cross. Ibid., 214, 217–18. Others in the Catholic peace movement have challenged the repetition of similar symbolic actions as lacking what Buddhists call "skillful means." Murray Palmer and Jim O'Grady quote Catholic peace activist Tom Cornell as saying there is a time for "prophetic showdowns" and a time for "building the political institutions that will make the bomb impossible." *Disarmed and Dangerous*, 11.

From the start, Berrigan had known that resistance in the name of peace was the historical embodiment of St. John of the Cross's "Dark Night of the Soul."[48] The only change—now over a span of four decades—is that "the adamantine heart of darkness" has grown darker still. "And yet, and yet. The communities do not give up." They wane and wax; they hold together. In the midst of darkness they remain at home.[49]

By contrast, empires—all empires—are the anti-communities. They are so because through their ideologies and practices they pursue, in a phrase that Berrigan repeats frequently, "death as a social method."[50] Ironically their enslavement to death as a social method arises from aping God, chained by their delusion of omnipotence and immortality. Seeking to control time and history, the empire du jour prepares its own downfall. But with it comes the death of multitudes. Death is normalized; the citizens comatose. "Another war? It matters not at all, or little."[51] Imperial wars are total not only in their commandeering of men and women, a nation's treasure and technology. They entail "the spiritual induction of the living in the works of death; a matter of thoughtless heads nodding . . . ; a crime of silence." The common bonds of human life are sundered and history is "dismembered rather than remembered."[52]

MEMORY: THE FIRST STIPULATION

According to Moses, the truth of memory is the first stipulation. Remember, remember—where you came from, from what plight and by whose hand you were liberated.[53]

Berrigan opens his conversation in 1974 with Thich Nhat Hanh with a meditation on memory, or as he puts it, a reflection on what it means to "re-member." "It means," he suggests, "that we put broken lives together, into one body. The ability also to draw upon the future, to re-member the future, is . . . a very rich notion."[54] Empires require amnesia. Above all, the forgetting of the crimes that brought them into being. They lull us into belief:

48. See Berrigan, *Dark Night*.
49. Berrigan, *Jeremiah*, 106.
50. See, inter alia, Berrigan, *Testimony*, 221.
51. Ibid., 175–76; Berrigan, *Kings*, 41; Berrigan, *Minor Prophets*, 71.
52. Berrigan, *Minor Prophets*, 303, 361.
53. Berrigan, *No Gods but One*, 71.
54. Berrigan and Nhat Hanh, *Raft*, 1.

Thus it was, and is, and ever shall be. Even bitter memories are dangerous. Berrigan sets in contrast Ezekiel in exile, inflicted by memory, doing "harsh time." Ezekiel remembers: "I may indeed be a prisoner, a slave but I was not always such. Nor shall I always be such. *There was a before; there will be an after*."[55] In memory, the possibility of something new, an alternative future is born.

For those who dwell in the belly of the Beast, to remember would be to free ourselves from the rites of domination, from reenacting "the ancient same criminal drama."[56] But such remembering is costly. We would remember that we are not gods, or even "would-be godlings." We would need to acknowledge our criminal past and present. Paradoxically, to remember also would be to forego "the attempt to seize the times, as though the future were in your hands, or the past, or for that matter, the present."[57] All those plans for a "new world order," issuing as they do from a will to power, would need to be relinquished.[58] In short, at the collective level, a new kind of consciousness of history, born of the purging of delusive visions, would need to be enacted.

THE BITTER LITANY OF GRIEF

Yahweh: *Eat the scroll*

Me: *Eat a scroll? I hear cries of grief, lamentations. Cries, whose groans?*

Yahweh: *Anyone's, anywhere in the world. Bosnia, Somalia, Northern Ireland, Haiti.*

Myself: *Your own?*

Yahweh: *My own tears.*

Me: *Because no one hears?*

Yahweh: *Because no one hears.*

Me: *Can I be of help?*

Yahweh: *Let this be said: Bosnia, Somalia, those who die, the innocents—they need not die; they should not. Abominable! My will undone!*

55. Berrigan, *Ezekiel*, 62, 64, 82–83; italics added.
56. Berrigan, *Jeremiah*, 89.
57. Berrigan, *Isaiah*, 117–18; Berrigan, *Ezekiel*, 84.
58. Berrigan, *Minor Prophets*, 227.

Me:	*If only I could turn your weeping to—joy.*
Yahweh:	*Eat the scroll.*
Me:	*Sweet on the tongue, bitter in the guts! I read: "Love your enemies."*
Yahweh:	*If only. If only . . .*[59]

Thus, Berrigan's riff on the commission of Ezekiel (2:8—3:3). Midrash becomes something other, something more than commentary. Berrigan, the rabbi, enters into the grief of the prophet, swallows it whole. Like Ezekiel, he risks becoming simply a madman shaking his fist. At what? At everything and everybody. Brueggemann may insist that anguish, not anger, is the hallmark of the prophet. Berrigan's not so sure. "Can one speak of true religion," he asks, "as evacuated of all anger?"[60] In *Jeremiah: The World, the Wound of God*, grief and anger interpenetrate. "So much suffering needlessly, maliciously, blindly imposed," Berrigan grieves, himself wounded.

The grief of the prophets echoes through the ages—from Isaiah, Jeremiah, and Ezekiel to Job and Jesus. Grief is "an old discipline of the Word." Not to be taken up lightly nor without scarring.[61] But Jeremiah's Yahweh not only grieves; he burns with anger. "Reminded of the divine anger," Berrigan acknowledges, "one is strangely heartened." The positive side of anger is the energy that it brings to resistance: quoting Latin American theologian Ivonne Gebara, Berrigan says, "The most important thing Christianity has given me is my inability to conform to the injustice and pain of those who suffer."[62]

"But anger," Berrigan concludes, "is not God's name." Grief, Berrigan says, transforms the anger in Yahweh and in ourselves. Paradoxically it restores "emotional sanity." On the other hand, we, the powerful who act under an aura of assumed innocence while leaving a trail of blood and waste, do not know how to grieve. The inability to acknowledge our complicity in evil blocks access to the springs of sorrow. We have become "moral zombies." And Yahweh weeps.[63]

59. Berrigan, *Ezekiel*, 13.

60. Ibid., 10, 17, 19–20, 28.

61. Berrigan, *Jeremiah*, 20, 77, 79; Berrigan, *Minor Prophets*, 90.

62. Berrigan, *Jeremiah*, 20–21.

63. Berrigan, *Minor Prophets*, 97–98, 255, 317; Berrigan, *Ezekiel*, 81; Berrigan, *Isaiah*, 33.

AND YET—HOPE

It is only for the sake of those without hope that hope is given us.[64]

"And yet . . . and yet." Surely, this phrase, evocatively simple, recurs more frequently than any other in Berrigan's lexicon.[65] It appears, however, only at the nadir, at the eclipse of reasonable expectations. At times, the times may drive us to fury, most frequently they numb us—like a constant drizzle on a smouldering camp fire. Plowshares are beaten into swords. War after endless war. *Not* plowshares into swords, Berrigan insists. "It is you—whom the times have beaten . . . into the form of death. . . . You taste the death before death which we name despair."[66]

Precisely in such a time "the necessary must somehow be joined to the impossible. Something new, something beyond all effort and imagining must come to be." We are meant to live covenanted with some other God than the Bomb. And yet we are not to expect miracles, except the resurrection of hope itself, an end to the "nuclear winter in the soul." Disarm, take care of the widow, the orphan, and the poor. "It cannot be done and it must be done."[67] Do it.

Hope is more than promise and command. It is, Berrigan insists, poetry.[68] Nowhere is this more apparent than in his inspired translation of Ezekiel's vision (ch. 37) of the dry bones, "the slender bones of children / skinny thigh bones of the aged." Ezekiel is thrust not only into the place where Judea's last king was overwhelmed by the Babylonian army but into all of the killing fields: Bosnia, South Africa, Iraq, Salvador. In these places of horror Ezekiel speaks God's word:

> "I weave your nerves anew.
> I build flesh,
> I stretch a living tegument;
> I breathe
> sweetly, strongly
> you shall live. . . .[69]

64. Walter Benjamin as quoted in Berrigan, *Kings*, 152.

65. Berrigan, *Isaiah*, 41, 124; Berrigan, *Ezekiel*, 127; Berrigan, *Jeremiah*, 105–6; Berrigan, *Testimony*, 227; Berrigan, *Job*, 174.

66. Berrigan, *Testimony*, 6; Berrigan, *Isaiah*, 14.

67. Berrigan, *Testimony*, 5; Berrigan, *Isaiah*, 13–14.

68. Berrigan, *Testimony*, 226.

69. Berrigan, *Ezekiel*, 111–12, 114.

More than the words, the phrases, it is the cadence that breathes hope. Then, soberly, Berrigan muses: what if we were to take the vision and live it?[70] Beyond all expectation, hope is the ground tone, the swell that keeps us keeping on through an unending dark night.

UNCONSCRIPTED DISCOURSE

War is the great exercise in practical, lethal (inevitably linguistic) atheism.[71]

Let it be confessed: At times Berrigan's attack on the delusions of empire sounds like a repetitious rant. One thinks, if not says, "Yeah, I heard you" (a sure sign that one has not), "I don't quite buy your analysis." The prophet's word is a probe, palpating the tumor. It is also a labor to create a language that has not already been conscripted into the "war effort."[72] Terms like "peace and security," "just cause," and "collateral damage" signify the debasement of language itself. Berrigan's painful midrash on biblical texts is an attempt to counter that "wartime anti-bible." Do the people turn deaf ears on the prophets? No surprise. "For we are speaking the language," Berrigan says, quoting Horst Bienek, "that will be spoken tomorrow."[73] Language, too, is a sword that must be beaten into a plowshare.

Prophets do not aspire to be theologians. Anything but. However, there is a structure to Berrigan's counter-discourse. It rests on a solid foundation: the concept of idolatry. As we have seen, empires are invariably idolatrous, aping God even to the commandeering of time. They promise everlasting life when they are simply a name written on desert sand. Idolatry takes the form of an unholy trinity. First, the empire itself, then, a god of war created as an "imperial construct" and, finally, a priesthood to mime the words of a vengeful salvation. Faced with such a trinity, the prophets declare: "God is not like that. It is you who are like that. And further: You need not be like that. And finally, a command, peremptory: Be not like that. God would have you otherwise."[74] Take note of the progression, a hallmark of prophetic discourse: a deconstruction of the imperial construct. A rendering of accounts. The intrinsic possibility of liberation. The command: Be someone

70. Ibid., xx.
71. Berrigan, *Testimony*, 57.
72. On the impact of war on language, see Hedges, *War Is a Force*, 32–34, 72.
73. Berrigan, *No Gods but One*, 58–59.
74. Ibid., 57, 114, 116.

new. Toward the unholy trinity the prophets utter an uncompromising "no." Can Egypt be reformed? Can we create a new and improved empire? The Exodus story tells of a clean break. "Not a word of reform, accommodation, gradualism." The "no" to the prevailing empire is the precondition for an eventual "yes."[75]

Egypt, Assyria, Babylonia, Rome, and on and on. Empires are clones of one another. They each exhibit the powerful logic of the fall. They rise, commit unspeakable acts, and then they fall—their crimes come home to roost. Indeed, we hear in Berrigan far more of the fall in history than of the countervailing power of grace.[76] History, viewed from the prophets' perspective, reveals an enduring paradox, an agonizing koan: "Justice . . . is by no means to be understood as the fruit of natural evolution or of this or that form of revolution. . . . The justice of God . . . is something other—an import, gift, unknown quantity. . . . And yet . . . and yet, it remains incontestable that justice is the vocation of nations, in spite of all, in spite of themselves"[77] This paradox persists and, therefore, so does the agony of the prophet. History offers a "harsh pedagogy." Having submitted themselves to it, the prophets call upon us to undergo it as well. In this process is our only hope of knowing the one, true God.

THE BODHISATTVA SPEAKS TO THE PROPHET

This is not the place for an extended critique of Berrigan's prophetic stance. We are seeking the "blessing of elders." In chapter 3, I will begin to sort out what I argue can be taken up of Berrigan's vision into a constructive social ethics inspired by both Buddhist and Christian sources. In this chapter I have sought to present in an undiluted fashion Berrigan's challenge to us all. Nevertheless, the bodhisattva may be allowed a few observations, the

75. Berrigan, *Exodus*, 20–21.

76. Berrigan, *Minor Prophets*, 55, 86; Berrigan, *Isaiah*, 45, 101–102; Berrigan, *Testimony*, 175–76. Grace appears more frequently in the books on the prophets as mercy rather than empowerment. In terms of the categories devised by H. Richard Niebuhr, Berrigan's stance is unequivocally "Christ against Culture." Cf. Niebuhr, *Christ and Culture*. Following his close friend William Stringfellow, Berrigan aligns himself with the theology of Karl Barth in seeing the Word of God in opposition to all merely human expressions. The prophetic word stands in judgment against the nations. Berrigan, *Minor Prophets*, 14, 84, 90. Institutions as well as individuals and empires experience the incursion of the fall; they fail "to attain even a minimal amount of compassion and equity." Berrigan, *Minor Prophets*, 88. We must ask, then, if the church, too—the church which in light of the clergy abuse scandal Berrigan called "toxic"—is incapable of reform? Berrigan, *Kings*, 52. And what of the Jesuit order?

77. Berrigan, *Isaiah*, 117–18.

meaning of which will become clear, I trust, in the next chapter. First, the bodhisattva might raise a question to Berrigan about the degree to which a dualistic understanding of good and evil undergirds his reflections. To be sure, Berrigan rejects the metaphor of the children of light versus the children of darkness. He speaks of the American system in the first person plural. Yet, one suspects that the Plowshares community has somehow been freed, has freed itself from the corruption of empire. They are, in classical Christian terms, *in it but not of it*. As we will soon see, for the bodhisattva all things interpenetrate, inter are. Because I am as I am, George Bush invades Iraq and Barack Obama sends more troops to Afghanistan. There is no liberation from complicity whether one is in opposition to the empire—or even in jail—or not. The lotus must—there is no other choice—bloom in a sea of mud.

This brings us to a second point. In describing the prophets, Berrigan's favorite adjective is "adamantine." He even describes Deutero-Isaiah's suffering servant as adamant.[78] The prophet is set in stone against the "here and now." The prophet's "yes" is restricted to God's future. The bodhisattva, therefore, might say to the Christian prophet, "What of your faith in the Word made flesh, your belief in the Mystical Body of Christ?"[79]

A third and final point has to do with the anger that flares, like a fire deep in a coal mine, throughout this painful meditation on the prophets. Anger, Thich Nhat Hanh suggests, arises out of suffering. Each of us carries the seeds of anger buried deep below the level of conscious awareness. If you see a child victimized, he continues, of course you get angry at those who are the cause of it. But rendering judgment only does not help. You must see the suffering in the victimizers, as well, and act with nonviolent compassion toward them in order to bring lasting healing to all parties. Anger, like love, is organic, which means that it can be transformed. Anger is an energy that, once transformed, becomes charged compassion.[80]

At some deep level, Berrigan agrees with this critique. "Anger," he says, "is not the recommended fuel for moral clarity . . . implying as it does a dearth of tenderness and trust. . . . A cold war, in fact, threatening to explode into hot."[81] But dealing with anger involves accepting the dark night of the soul. Nowhere, I believe, is this stated more clearly than in Berrigan's prose-

78. Ibid., 154.

79. For Thich Nhat Hanh's Buddhist interpretation of the Mystical Body of Christ, see *Living Buddha*, 55–59. At one point, Berrigan himself takes issue with those who are like Job's friends, for whom "the Fall, not the Incarnation stands pivotal to our history." *Job*, 286.

80. Nhat Hanh, *Anger*, 30–31, 34–35, 69, 118, 139–40.

81. Berrigan, *Testimony*, 199.

poem "Not Feeling Poetic." The very form of the poem, not quite poetry but "an edging toward, some equivalent, some near thing," reflects a dark night struggle. Violence declares war against poetry, blasts it, scatters its broken bones. Nonetheless, "prisoners, disappeared ones, madres, dismembered bones gleaming like / phosphorous in the waste lands,—(and Christ the gleaner of this holy wheat)—sing out, sing out; 'I am here, I am with you all days, we are one!' I hear this unquenchable poetry of survival," Berrigan insists. "It will decompose, into sweet compost of song even the vile prose of hell."[82] Anger composted becomes sweet song.

The three qualms that a bodhisattva might raise cluster around the image of God as a just judge. Does Berrigan's vision of God succumb to the very "small g" god whose anger mirrors our own? Fleeing judgment, Berrigan contends, we succumb to a "social numbness." Mindfulness, Berrigan would say, does not sugarcoat reality. But to those who see judgment grounded in dualism, Berrigan offers this koan: "To judge, be it insisted, is not to condemn. . . . / To be judged is to undergo God the merciful, not / God the neutral."[83]

As if to underscore this point, Berrigan treats the book of Jonah as a parable. In it prophecy subverts the moral expectations that prophets themselves have created. First, Jonah is sent not to God's chosen people but to Nineveh, the capitol of the Assyrian "evil empire." Then, after Jonah's disobedient flight is thwarted, the people of Nineveh, contrary to everything we have heard about the hearts of the mighty turned to stone, have the nerve to repent. The logic of sin/punishment is broken. To Jonah's chagrin, Yahweh means to offer the hated oppressor divine mercy. "Nineveh," Berrigan concludes, "thus stands as a surrogate for all who are declared by insiders to be outside." And Jonah who would afflict the comfortable is himself much discomfited. Yahweh, it seems, cares more for the one hundred twenty thousand infants of Nineveh, "to say nothing of the animals," than he does for conforming to prophetic expectations. "God is ultimately the tender One" whose anger is consumed by compassion, and Berrigan himself undergoes this transformation.[84]

82. Berrigan, "Not Feeling Poetic," 343–44.

83. Berrigan, *Isaiah*, 87–88.

84. Berrigan, *Minor Prophets*, 187, 205, 208–9. Jonah remains for Berrigan the prick that deflates all self-righteousness. In "The Whale's Tale," we read the story of Jonah retold from the whale's point of view. Humor swallows the prophet's incessant "blah, blah" (325–30).

THE PROPHET AS BODHISATTVA

It would be a grave mistake to think of Berrigan, the prophet, as only a prophet. That would be to miss the wit, the Irish twinkle in the eyes, the love of words, tasting them, letting them roll around in the mind's tongue. It would also be to miss the quiet labors of Berrigan the bodhisattva. In the late '70s, Berrigan, "in the usual spinning orbit of teaching, writing, and pilgrimaging to the Pentagon to throw ashes and blood at the idols" felt empty. From a friend he heard about St. Rose's Home, a hospice for mostly poor people dying of cancer, and he asked to be a volunteer. His experience was transformative. "Slowly, I sensed that an atrophied sixth or seventh sense was coming to life; a sense of recognition." What he saw—much as a blind person might trace with outstretched hands the lineaments of a face—was the church as it was meant to be, "skilled in the thousand ways of conveying love, . . . smiling and weeping, modest as befits the human condition *in extremis*."[85]

This unobtrusive ministry intensified in the mid-'80s with the onset of the AIDS epidemic. Berrigan was asked to visit with dying gay Catholics at St. Vincent's Hospital in Greenwich Village. *Sorrow Built a Bridge* is the story of the friendships that Berrigan formed with dying AIDS patients. It is, I find, the most moving of all his writings, more intimate than his own autobiography. As at St. Rose's, Berrigan takes it slowly, with what Buddhists call "a beginner's mind." He simply stands together with parents and their dying sons.

As I understand them, the myriad guises of the bodhisattvas in the Mahayana tradition represent both infinite compassion and an infinite resourcefulness in skillful means. Berrigan as bodhisattva bears decided resemblance to a Buddhist John of the Cross. The love that suffuses *Sorrow Built a Bridge* arises in a dark night. Berrigan refuses before his patients or us to play God. "He knew the only god one could mime in such circumstances was an inferior one, a ventriloquist's doll mouthing someone else's platitudes. So he kept quiet." Nor will Berrigan sugarcoat the agony of dying. "Let it be said clearly. . . . Dying isn't a light show in a tunnel, Grandma's face by Whistler, a forest of arms incanting happy homecoming. . . . None of these."[86]

Undergoing the dark night of the soul in keeping loving company with his dying friends, Berrigan realizes the truth of emptiness. Only when he has nothing to give, no pithy words of wisdom, no spiritual placebos, can he become a friend. "It all comes down to this," he suggests. "One is forbidden to breathe the air of our world, rejoice in its beauty, and all the while remain in ignorance—of despair, delusion, fear and loss. Come down. Come down.

85. "Where Death Abounded, Life," 171, 173.

86. Berrigan, *Sorrow Built a Bridge*, 5, 68.

I can only respond with hands empty and outspread." Coming down, that is to say, emptying himself of all illusions of having something to offer proportionate to what the dying are undergoing, Berrigan does what little he can. He can offer a meal, a few hours of companionship and, for those who choose it, the Eucharist. Small gifts. "And yet that 'little' sounds its penny whistle note in the darkness: an interlude, a relief."[87] Once more we hear the refrain "and yet." Is the "coming down" a Christian kenosis or a bodhisattva's empty giving? Do the terms matter? Berrigan stakes his life on this "and yet."

Certainly there is a prophetic dimension to Berrigan's engagement. Becoming friends with dying gay Catholics, Berrigan burns with scathing denunciations of a church which at that time added its religious imprimatur to the social stigmas placed upon these men. "My friend will be judged by love. Which is to say, he will not be judged but embraced. What draws us to the embrace of love is a courage akin to his. The courage to believe, church and state notwithstanding, the only judgment will be that of love."[88] It would be obscene to suggest that Berrigan has chosen his engagement to make a prophetic point. His grief and spiritual labor are palpable. My only point is that the prophet-become-bodhisattva is still a prophet.

UNDER THE BOMBS

Now, having entered his tenth decade, Berrigan labors on. The subtitle to his 2008 commentary on the the books of Kings, "The Pathology of Power," is a clear sign that burning coal has not been lowered from his lips—or pen. Berrigan's is a life sentence. But Father Berrigan breathes more than fire. In February 1968, Berrigan was in Hanoi, along with activist, and historian Howard Zinn, to arrange the release of three American prisoners. He was there while the American bombing campaign was in full operation. Along with a group of Vietnamese children, Berrigan sought refuge in a bomb shelter. Climbing down, he scooped up a toddler and, then and there, he was hit full force with the purpose of his prophetic calling:

> In my arms fathered
> in a moment's grace, the messiah
> of all my tears. I bore, reborn
>
> a Hiroshima child from hell."[89]

87. Ibid., 51, 133, 138. There is a clear contrast between this understanding of friendship and the "friends" of Job with their counterfeit wisdom. Berrigan, *Job*, 62.

88. Berrigan, *Sorrow Built a Bridge*, 11, 91–92.

89. Berrigan, "Children in the Shelter," 114–15.

In *The Trial of the Catonsville Nine*, "Children in the Shelter" is recited in the defense's closing statement to the jury. It is, in its unique fashion, an apt performance of the prophet's vision, the prophet with the heart of a bodhisattva. There is a quiet haste; the bombs have already begun to fall. But a child is swept up from Hiroshima's hell—ground zero of the Beast of the Apocalypse. Rescued. Borne. Reborn is the messiah with rice on his face. Daniel Berrigan, witness to the dry bones come back to life, Father Berrigan, holding a child in his arms.

2

THE BODHISATTVA

Called by Many True Names

As bodhisattvas . . . , we ride joyfully on the waves of birth and death, abiding fearlessly in samsara to help guide others to liberation.[1]

—Thich Nhat Hanh, *Opening the Heart of the Cosmos*

In *Being Peace*, Thich Nhat Hanh speaks of the remarkable adaptiveness of Buddhism. The Dharma in each new culture speaks in a new idiom and a new Buddha is born. "I believe," Thich Nhat Hanh continues, "that the encounter between Buddhism and the West will bring about something very exciting, very important." He then reiterates a challenge that he presented to an American friend. "Where is your bodhisattva? Show me an American bodhisattva."[2] The truth of the matter is that American (and Western) converts to Buddhism—in contrast to ethnic Buddhist communities—have generally eschewed exploring let alone adopting Asian traditions of the bodhisattva until very recently.[3] *Faces of Compassion: Classic Bodhisattva Archetypes and Their Modern Expression*, by Taigen Daniel Leighton, is a

1. Nhat Hanh, *Opening the Heart*, 36.

2. Nhat Hanh, *Being Peace*, 85–86.

3. Jeff Wilson argues that the bodhisattva Kuan-Yin, the Chinese embodiment of Avalokiteshvara, has recently become a focus of devotion within American Zen and other Buddhist traditions. Here she is venerated not so much as the bodhisattva of great compassion but as an "affirmation of female spiritual power and worth." Wilson, "Deeply Female and Universally Human," 301.

notable exception to this iconoclastic appropriation of the Mahayana tradition. Leighton builds a bridge by linking specific bodhisattva archetypes to Western contemplatives and activists, from Nelson Mandela to Martin Luther King, from Thomas Merton to Helen Keller. Explicitly presented in early Mahayana texts written in the century before the Common Era, the figure of the bodhisattva came to embody the ideal of universal liberation.

> The word *bodhisattva* comes from the Sanskrit roots *bodhi*, meaning "awakening" or "enlightenment," and *sattva*, meaning "sentient being." *Sattva* also has etymological roots that include "intention," meaning the intention to awaken, and "courage" or "heroism," referring to the resolution and strength involved in this path. Bodhisattvas are enlightening, radiant beings who exist in innumerable forms, valiantly functioning in helpful ways in the middle of the busy-ness of the world.[4]

The emphasis here is on the gerund "enlightening," for the bodhisattva is one who has overcome the dualism of self and other. He or she embodies *bodhicitta* (enlightening mind), the mind of one dedicated to seeking enlightenment for the benefit of all. Seeking the liberation of self and other is one inconceivable practice. This intention is commonly expressed in the four bodhisattva vows:

> Living beings are infinite, I vow to free them.
> Delusions are inexhaustible, I vow to cut through them.
> Dharma gates are boundless, I vow to enter them.
> The Buddha Way is unsurpassable, I vow to realize it.[5]

By choosing to interpret classic bodhisattvas as archetypes, "fundamental models of dominant psychic aspects of the enlightening being," and offering contemporary examples of these archetypal patterns, Leighton seeks to release the bodhisattva from its cultural embeddedness within Asian Buddhist religious traditions. In doing so he is only enacting a core teaching of the Mahayana tradition, namely, that real embodiments of *bodhicitta* exist in every age and place.[6]

4. Leighton, *Faces of Compassion*, 26. Leighton notes that the figure of the bodhisattva was presented in the Pali scriptures as representing the previous lives of Shakyamuni. Ibid., 46–47, 50.

5. Ibid., 32–33.

6. Ibid., 26–27, 37.

THE LIFE OF THE BODHISATTVA

Thich Nhat Hanh was born on October 11, 1926. When he was nine years old, he saw an image of a sitting Buddha in a magazine and was immediately attracted. An older brother had become a monk, and at sixteen Thich Nhat Hanh followed him and became a novice at the Tu Hieu Pagoda near Hue in central Vietnam.[7] Stories recorded in *My Master's Robe: Memories of a Novice Monk* draw an idyllic image of his new life. The young novice spent his days memorizing the rules for monastic living while tending grazing cattle. Each day with its alternating rhythms of manual labor—hauling water, grinding rice kernels—and sitting and walking meditation challenged the novice to become mindful. Even the act of closing a door without banging required mindfulness. Above all, it was the atmosphere of the monastery, "silent and at the same time energetic, solemn but also gentle," that penetrated his being.[8]

This idyllic time was not to last. In the aftermath of World War II, the French, seeking to restore their colonial grip on Vietnam, fought a war with the Viet Minh who struggled for independence between 1946 and 1954. "We had been invaded by society and the times," Thich Nhat Hanh later recalled. "The questioning of the collective consciousness of our time became the questioning of our individual consciousness." For a time the novice and his fellow monks were forced to evacuate their temple. When they returned, the temple was scarred with bullet holes. But there would be no returning to the previous idyll. The young monk saw before him a momentous task, nothing less than a thoroughgoing reform of Buddhism.

> The task of reforming Buddhism demands a revolution in the teachings and regulations of the Buddhist institutes. . . . We have no choice but to bring Buddhism back into everyday life. War has waged disaster. Separation and hatred [have] reached a high degree. There are so many agonizing cries of death, hunger, and imprisonment. How can anyone feel peace of mind by dwelling undisturbed in a monastery?[9]

After the defeat of the French in 1954, the country was partitioned in anticipation of elections, but hostilities soon broke out between the North and the South Vietnamese, and America soon waded into the quicksand of a costly war. In the midst of war, Thich Nhat Hanh continued to pursue

7. Nhat Hanh, *Cultivating Love*, 11–13.

8. Nhat Hanh, *My Master's Robe*, 14, 41. The book was originally published serially in a Vietnamese magazine between 1956 and 1959. Ibid., ix.

9. Ibid., 19–20, 77.

his dream of a reformed Buddhism, what he would later call "engaged Buddhism."[10] But he repeatedly met with rejection at the hands of the elder Buddhist monastic establishment. "We all suffered because of the situation of our country and because of the state of Buddhism," Thich Nhat Hanh recalled. "We tried to create a grassroots Buddhism that would draw on the aspirations of the people, but we weren't successful."[11] What Thich Nhat Hanh meant by a "grassroots Budddhism" is nicely captured by his encounter in late 1960 with a young woman, Cao Ngoc Phuong, who would later became Sister Chan Khong, his indispensable associate. At the time she was deeply involved in a life of service to the poor in the slums of Saigon, yet also attracted to Buddhism. However, she had been repelled by previous conversations with Buddhist monks who told her to seek enlightenment first, only after which could she help other beings. When she finally met Thich Nhat Hanh, he counseled her: "We should not be dualistic. We should just be ourselves and live our lives in the most mindful and deepest way we can." He told her that enlightenment could be achieved in the very midst of her work with the poor.[12]

Buffeted by Buddhist authorities, Thich Nhat Hanh and a few fellow monks created their own rural retreat, Phuong Boi (Fragrant Palm Leaves) monastery. Between 1957 and late 1961 his life consisted in teaching this new—he would say truly classical—form of Buddhism at various temples in and around Saigon while retreating to Phuong Boi after repeated expulsions. Meanwhile, he attracted a strong following of young people.[13] His work also attracted the attention of the South Vietnam government's security agents who suspected the small community of engaging in "clandestine activities."

Encouraged by friends who feared for his safety because of his writings in opposition to the South Vietnamese regime's prosecution of war under the leadership of Diem, Thich Nhat Hanh accepted a fellowship to study at Princeton and left for the States in autumn 1961.[14] Thich Nhat Hanh's time in the United States was anything but a reprieve from his struggles

10. Thich Nhat Hanh is credited for coining the term "engaged Buddhism." See King, *Socially Engaged Buddhism*, 4. I have gone back and forth about whether to refer to engaged Buddhism with a capitol "E" in recognition of its spread throughout the globe. I am persuaded by Sulak Sivaraksa's argument that engaged Buddhists practice Buddhism with a small "b." They engage in a struggle with others committed to peace and justice without seeking to impose their Buddhist philosophy. *Seeds of Peace*, 62–72.

11. Nhat Hanh, *Fragrant Palm Leaves*, 6.

12. Cao Ngoc Phoung later became Sister Chan Khong. *Learning Love*, 14–15, 25–26.

13. Ibid., 29; Nhat Hanh, *Fragrant Palm Leaves*, 7–9.

14. Chan Kong, *Learning Love*, 30.

for peace in Vietnam. Removed from the immediacy of his suffering fellows, Thich Nhat Hanh suffered all the more. "I became a battlefield," he said simply. Alone in a strange country, grieving on the anniversary of his mother's death, he underwent a protracted spiritual crisis between early autumn and late December of 1962.[15] The crisis appears to have been punctuated by experiences of *satori*, experiences of enlightenment. Of one of these, Thich Nhat Hanh said: "I was carefree as a grasshopper pausing on a blade of grass. Like the grasshopper, I had no thoughts of the divine." For our purposes it is important to note that the resolution of this crisis blossomed immediately into a sense of intimacy with all bodhisattvas and a sense of their everyday-down-to-earthness. "We needn't think of them as remote beings on pedestals. We can recognize their presence everyday among those we see."[16]

With the fall of the Diem regime in late 1963, one of the elder monks, Thich Tri Quang, a former opponent of Thich Nhat Hanh's proposals for an engaged Buddhism, pleaded with him to return to Vietnam, which he did in December. Shortly thereafter Thich Nhat Hanh proposed to the Buddhist hierarchy a three-point plan involving: (1) calling publicly for an end of the war, (2) creating an institute for the study of Buddhism in an atmosphere of openness, and (3) developing a training center in methods of nonviolent social change. This, however, was too much to ask of the hierarchy and only the second proposition was accepted.[17]

The next two years were a whirlwind of activity. The reluctance of the conservative hierarchy did not deter Thich Nhat Hanh. After establishing the Buddhist institute as Van Hanh University, he called upon Cao Ngoc Phoung to help him create a School of Youth for Social Service within the university, fulfilling the third point of the proposal. Before long several hundred graduates of the SYSS were working alongside peasants in self-help development efforts, in stark contrast to the American policy of herding peasants into barbed wire–surrounded "strategic hamlets." Simultaneously, in fulfillment of the first point of his proposal, he published a number of books grieving the suffering of the Vietnamese people and calling upon all sides of the conflict to make peace. The most famous of these publications, *Vietnam: Lotus in a Sea of Fire*, was denounced by the Saigon regime as "communist propaganda."[18]

15. Nhat Hanh, *Fragrant Palm Leaves*, 93. See esp. 83–109.

16. Ibid., 83, 112.

17. Chan Kong, *Learning Love*, 47–49.

18. Ibid., 50–54, 72; Nhat Hanh, *Fragrant Palm Leaves*, 150, 185–87, 199.

Perhaps the innovation that was most significant for the decades to come was the ordination in early 1966 of six individuals, including Cao Ngoc Phuong, as members of a new order that would include both monastics and lay persons, the Tiep Hien Order which was dedicated to engaging Buddhism with the world's suffering.[19] In later writings Thich Nhat Hanh explained:

> "Tiep" means "to be in touch." . . . So, first of all, "in touch" means in touch with oneself in order to find out the source of wisdom, understanding and compassion in each of us, . . . the second part of "tiep" is "to continue. . . . It means that the career of understanding and compassion started by Buddhas and bodhisattvas should be continued. . . . "Hien" means "the present time." . . . [It] also means "to make real, to manifest, realization." Love and understanding are not only concepts and words. They must be real things, realized in oneself and society.[20]

In the spring of 1966, while the bombs rained on Vietnamese villages, the Fellowship of Reconciliation, a consortium of religiously based peace organizations, invited Thich Nhat Hanh to take part in a lecture tour in the United States. Believing that the war would end only when Americans saw the endless suffering that their government's prosecution of the war caused, Thich Nhat Hanh left Vietnam with a five-point peace proposal in hand. The decision proved to be momentous. He was denounced as a traitor by the South and at the war's end would not be allowed by the victorious North Vietnamese regime to return to his homeland for almost forty years.[21]

In exile, Thich Nhat Hanh threw himself into working for peace. *Vietnam: Lotus in a Sea of Fire* was translated into English and was crucial in grounding the religiously committed wing of the American peace movement. Other factions within the movement, however, excoriated him for not siding with the North Vietnamese. In 1969, Thich Nhat Hanh was named chair of the newly formed Vietnamese Buddhist Peace Delegation to the Paris Peace Accords by the Vietnamese Buddhist hierarchy. What followed were several years of intense activity with Cao Ngoc Phoung as his assistant. Following the takeover of the South in April, 1975, the North Vietnamese regime shut down the SYSS and seized its property. The regime painted

19. Chan Khong, *Learning Love*, 77.

20. Nhat Hanh, *Being Peace*, 87–88. In the West, the Tiep Hien Order became the Order of Interbeing.

21. Thich Nhat Hanh finally returned to Vietnam in January 2005. Chan Kong, *Learning Love*, 274.

Thich Nhat Hanh and Cao Ngoc Phoung as CIA agents. Return to Vietnam became impossible.[22]

The next few years were a time of spiritual searching as Thich Nhat Hanh and a small group of followers left for a farm southeast of Paris. The answer to the searching would come only by remaining calm in the midst of turbulence. Turbulence came in the form of thousands of Vietnamese "boat people" caught on the high seas in leaky boats or languishing in refugee camps across Southeast Asia. Thich Nhat Hanh and, especially, Cao Ngoc Phoung tried to organize rescue efforts, but their direct action methods—pressuring Western governments to enlarge their visa quotas and hiring a ship to rescue the boat people—ran afoul of the UN High Commission on Refugees, and support for their efforts by religious groups was withdrawn.[23]

In October 1982, the small community moved to southern France to what became Plum Village. There a core sangha of monks, nuns, and lay people began to flourish. Also in 1982, Thich Nhat Hanh began to offer retreats worldwide.[24] "Sangha building," he would say later, "is what we do. It is the practice." True sanghas, he insisted, cannot be a place to hide but a place where we collect and transform the world's sufferings. Likewise, the sanghas that Thich Nhat Hanh envisioned needed to be built at every level from the intimate to the international, welding groups together across the fault lines of their conflicts.[25] Maitreya, the Buddha of the future, he often said, would take the body of a community, not of an individual. Practicing together, we bring Maitreya to life. "All of us," he insisted, "have the duty to bring that Buddha into being, not only for our sake but for the sake of our children and the planet Earth."[26] For the past three decades, Thich Nhat Hanh has indefatigably engaged in the practice of building sanghas. Through his retreats and many writings his message has spread across the globe.

THE BODHISATTVA'S COMMENTARY ON THE BODHISATTVAS

While Leighton gives a detailed analysis of classic bodhisattvas, Thich Nhat Hanh follows a different strategy. He does not give the kind of extended

22. Ibid., 126–29, 134–35, 151–53, 165–66.

23. Ibid., 169, 173, 180–93.

24. Ibid., 216, 230–32, 242.

25. Nhat Hanh, "Go as a Sangha," 19, 46; Nhat Hanh, "Spirituality in the Twenty-First Century," 16.

26. Nhat Hanh, "Go as a Sangha," 17.

treatment that Berrigan gives to the prophets. With the exception of *Opening the Heart of the Cosmos*, his commentary on the Lotus Sutra, Thich Nhat Hanh makes only passing references to classic bodhisattvas while, nevertheless, encouraging his followers to take the bodhisattva path. Numerous books by Thich Nhat Hanh deal with the classical Buddhist corpus and more specifically with Mahayana teachings. In all of these commentaries Thich Nhat Hanh has, with a remarkably sure hand, cast the Dharma in a new idiom. Whereas Berrigan's challenge was to breathe new life into familiar texts, Thich Nhat Hanh's was to make accessible the strange language and imagery of the Mahayana tradition. What this means for our analysis is that we must distill the bodhisattva, primarily *as a form (or family of forms) of spiritual practice*, from writings which embody it without necessarily naming it as such.

The exception, as I mentioned, is *Opening the Heart of the Cosmos*. The heart of this commentary treats chapter 25 of the *Lotus Sutra*, which focuses on Avalokiteshvara as "the manifestation of the universal gate." Avalokiteshvara is manifest, sometimes as male, sometimes as female, all over East Asia. To reflect on him/her is, indeed, to meditate on the heart of the Mahayana tradition. How Thich Nhat Hanh proceeds with this chapter conveys his method. As with Berrigan, he works closely with the flow of the narrative. In chapter 25, a follower of the Buddha asks the meaning of the name Avalokiteshvara, "Observer of the Sounds of the World." He/she, the Buddha says, "responds well to all places and in all directions." This prompts Thich Nhat Hanh to suggest that Avalokiteshvara "can manifest as a businessman, as a politician, as a child, as a dragon, as a horse, as a flower—in whatever form is most appropriate to respond to the needs of the supplicant." Thich Nhat Hanh draws us closer by translating two Vietnamese names for Avalokiteshvara. Quan Tu Tai, we are told, combines "looking deeply" with freedom. "Thanks to the practice of stopping and looking deeply you attain freedom from suffering." Quan The Am means "to hear the cries of the world."[27] Liberation and compassion are fused in these two names.

Looking deeply into the meaning and efficacy of Avalokiteshvara, Thich Nhat Hanh finds a stanza in the Lotus Sutra that is both a word of hope and a moral challenge to our situation. "Even if someone whose thoughts are malicious / Should push one into a great pit of fire, / By virtue of the constant mindfulness of Sound-Observer / The pit of fire would turn into a pool."[28] "The word 'fire' in this verse," Thich Nhat Hanh comments, "represents anger. . . . Sometimes an entire country can be plunged into a pit

27. Nhat Hanh, *Opening the Heart*, 121–23

28. Ibid., 126.

of fire. The September 11 [2001] attacks in New York and Washington, D.C. triggered a huge sea of anger, despair and fear."[29] Some Americans remained mindful and compassionate, cooling the fire, but in the realm of politics the fire raged. The rhetoric of retaliation fanned the flames. But violent reactions compound the injustice. "When . . . you are about to fall into a pit of fire, if you know how to practice mindfulness of compassion, . . . then you will be able to stop, calm yourself, and look more deeply and clearly into the situation . . . and you will be able to find a better way to respond."[30]

Here we see the firmness of Thich Nhat Hanh's injunction—Stop!—tempered by the offering of a practice, a step-by-step method. Suffering, despair, and anger are very real, as is the urge to retaliate, but "we can turn the ocean of fire into a cool lake by practicing the mindfulness of love and invoking the messenger of love, Avalokiteshvara."[31]

THE BODHISATTVA IN HELL

Kshitigarbha, Earth Storehouse or Earth-Womb bodhisattva, known in Japan as Jizo, can often be found in hell realms seeking to liberate those who are trapped there. In some sutras there are hundreds even hundreds of thousands of hells clustered together. But hell is also a state of being that we create for ourselves—and for others—by our actions.[32] In some stories, Jizo is the daughter of a mother who, because she has flaunted her sins and ridiculed Buddhist practice, ends up in hell. Through concentrated effort the daughter not only gains her mother's liberation but that of all beings currently in hell. In his commentary on the Lotus Sutra, Thich Nhat Hanh encourages us to become the hands and arms of Kshitigarbha. Such a bodhisattva "vows to go to the darkest places of the universe . . . where there is no freedom, no democracy, no compassion or human dignity, where there is oppression, injustice, social inequality, and war. Hell is the place where Earth-Store wants to go." But we don't need to go to a foreign country to touch such deep suffering. Hell is all around us.[33]

Just as the war in Vietnam was *the* turning point in Daniel Berrigan's life, it became also a literal point of no return for Thich Nhat Hanh. Only this war had been going on with hardly a break since the end of World War II. Writing in *Vietnam: Lotus in a Sea of Fire*, Thich Nhat Hanh spoke

29. Ibid., 126–27.

30. Ibid., 127.

31. Ibid., 126–27.

32. Leighton, *Faces of Compassion*, 212–13, 215–16, 218.

33. Nhat Hanh, *Opening the Heart*, 149–50.

out against those who labeled monks who immolated themselves as aberrant militants. "In a river current" he argued, "it is not the water in front that pulls the river along, but the water in the rear that acts as the driving force. . . . Objective conditions in Vietnamese society have compelled the Buddhist religion to engage itself in the life of the nation." It was their desire to move the hearts of all sides of the conflict, to focus attention of the whole world on the suffering of the Vietnamese people that led the monks to burn themselves.[34] What we now call "engaged Buddhism" was born in this sea of fire.

Not surprisingly, the deepest record of Thich Nhat Hanh's experience during these years is not the chronicle of his leadership of the Buddhist peace movement but the poetry that he wrote during the most intense years of the conflict. Thich Nhat Hanh—in a poem read at a peace rally with Daniel Berrigan in New York in 1967—gives us fair warning:

> Don't listen to the poet.
> In his morning coffee, there is a teardrop.
>
> Don't listen to me
> Please don't.
> In my morning coffee, there is a drop of blood.[35]

In "Our Green Garden," "Fires spring up at all ten points of the universe / a furious acrid wind sweeps them toward us from all sides." Yet this is not the nadir, the real pit of suffering. That occurs when the poet calls out to his brother, calls him to be aware of their mother's heart as it "shrivels and / fades like a dying flower." Once more he calls to his brother:

> Dearest brother, I know it is *you* who will shoot me tonight,
> piercing our mother's heart with a wound that can never heal.[36]

The poet-bodhisattva becomes a prophet in "Condemnation," a poem that aroused the peace movement in Vietnam and in America:

> Listen to this:
> yesterday six Vietcong came through my village,
> and because of this, the village was bombed.
> Every soul was killed.
> . . .

34. Nhat Hanh, *Lotus in a Sea of Fire*, 3, 106–8.
35. Nhat Hanh, "Mudra," 8.
36. Nhat Hanh, "Our Green Gardens," 6.

Here in the presence of the undisturbed stars,
in the invisible presence of all people still alive on Earth,
let me raise my voice to denounce this dreadful war.
. . .
I am like the bird who dies for the sake of its mate,
dripping blood from its broken beak and crying out,
"Beware! Turn around and face your real enemies—
ambition, violence, hatred, and greed."

Humans are not our enemies—even those called "Vietcong."
If we kill our brothers and sisters, what will we have left?
With whom then shall we live?[37]

Grieving, the poet gives voice to the full catastrophe of war in precise detail. The child with dysentery and no medicine. The husband/father staring empty eyed into space having lost his whole family. The white-haired elder bowing in gratitude to a mere boy who has given him a bit of rice. There are, however, moments when tear drops dampen the flames. Above all, he salutes the work of his students, from the School of Youth for Social Service which he founded to care for the victims of the war.

Under palm-leaf hats,
brown-clothed and barefoot,
are they not Quan-Yin [Avalokiteshvara] in all her glory,
her charity, her fearlessness?[38]

Many young men and women who were part of Thich Nhat Hanh's School of Youth for Social Service became the lightning rods of murderous violence. It was the murders of these students which most deeply crushed his heart. In one incident, five students were dragged from their beds just after midnight on July 5, 1967, and taken to a riverside where four were murdered but one escaped death. Struggling with his pain, Thich Nhat Hanh created "The Path of Return Continues the Journey," a poem-play in honor of these bodhisattvas.

Thich Nhat Hanh tells the story from the point of view of the newly dead—four young men who have been picked up in a boat by a Buddhist nun who had recently immolated herself for peace. Opening the play, Thich Nhat Hanh expresses all of our apprehensions about death: "Are the other shore and this shore one or two? Is there a river that separates the two sides, a river that no boat can cross?" He then replies: "Please come over to my boat. I will show you that there is a river, but there is no separation." Rowing

37. Nhat Hanh, "Condemnation," 37.

38. Nhat Hanh, "Experience," 10–13.

gently on that current, the dead are not as the living—they float free of the anger and desire for revenge that entangle us. Neither are they separate, cut off from the living. They are present like the afterlife of burnt charcoal; only no relentless entropy impedes the infinite chain reactions sparked by the heat of their lives. "Nothing can be lost; yet at the same time nothing . . . can keep its nature intact."[39]

At the end of his praise-poem "Song of Myself," Walt Whitman says of his death, "I bequeath myself to the dirt to grow from the grass I love. / If you want me again look for me under your boot-soles. / You will hardly know who I am or what I mean, / but I shall be good health to you nevertheless, / And filter and fibre your blood."[40] The same holds true of the youth in this play but with one crucial difference: love has overcome not only the seeming separation of death but the karmic reality of murder.

Murder, the wanton violence of war, it seems, is really a case of mistaken identity. Feared and despised by both sides of the conflict, the Youth for Social Service had become a screen on which the two sides projected their common ignorance. As one of the dead students puts it:

> "Youth for Social Service" is just a label that they pasted on the objects of their hatred or fear, an object that exists only in their perception. It has nothing to do with us as persons. They shot only at the object of their fear and hatred, but because they had pasted the label of this object on us, they ended up shooting us, and we died by mistake. They killed us because they truly did not know who we were.[41]

Faced with such ignorance, one of the dead young men exclaims, "The world of the living is shrouded in fog. All I feel now is compassion for the destiny of mankind. It is like walking in a moonless, starless night."[42] In his foreword to the play, Daniel Berrigan suggests that something authentically Buddhist in Thich Nhat Hanh's portrayal of the serenely dead utterly eludes him—and by implication all or most of us. We mistake serenity in the face of death for stoicism. It is the inwardness not the death of Thich Nhat Hanh's characters that escapes us.[43] Thich Nhat Hanh puts it more simply, "Love enables us to see things that those who are without love cannot see."[44] It is love that enables us to see these newly dead as genuine bodhisattvas.

39. Nhat Hanh, "Path of Return," 10, 26.
40. Whitman, "Song of Myself," 68.
41. Nhat Hanh, "Path of Return," 30.
42. Ibid., 32.
43. Berrigan, foreword to *Love in Action*, 7.
44. Nhat Hanh, "Path of Return," 10.

While Thich Nhat Hanh's brave dead exhibit only compassion, there can be no sugarcoating of the karmic effects of violence. In "Those That Have Not Exploded," Thich Nhat Hanh refers to a grenade attack on the School of Youth for Social Service that killed two students and wounded others. The poet confesses his inability to understand those who hurled the grenades at his young followers. Their crimes? Helping villagers, teaching children, working in rice paddies. While death and sorrow are accepted, the poet calls attention to the sky, which has been "ripped apart," and then he announces in prophetic tones: "There are more grenades / caught in the heart of life. / Do you hear me? / There are more that are yet to burst."[45] This cry is urgent, an appeal to defuse the bombs and untangle the karmic knot.

Passion and compassion strive mightily with one another in these poems, reflecting Thich Nhat Hanh's own heart. Jim Forest tells a story of a meeting in St. Louis in 1968 when Thich Nhat Hanh was in the United States appealing to Americans with his message of peace and reconciliation. The meeting at a Christian church was plunged into turmoil when one man stood up and spoke "with searing scorn of the 'supposed compassion' of 'this Mr. Hanh.' 'If you care so much about your people, Mr. Hanh, why are you here . . . ? Why don't you spend your time with them?'" Thich Nhat Hanh quietly responded: "Many of the roots of the war are here, in your country. To help the people who are to be bombed, to try to protect them from suffering, I have to come here." "In the man's fury," comments Forest, "we had experienced our own furies; we had seen the world as through a bomb bay."[46] But the story doesn't end there. Shortly thereafter, Thich Nhat Hanh left the room and Forest, sensing something wrong, followed him outside into the crisp, cool air. Thich Nhat Hanh was gasping for breath like someone who had just surfaced from deep under water. Forest saw, and we see, not the stereotype of a Buddha sitting in sublime indifference but a human being whose peaceful and compassionate speech grew (and grows) from passion transformed.

The passion and compassion of Thich Nhat Hanh the poet-bodhisattva is transformed by hard, continuous practice. Forest learned a lesson about the astonishing power of breathing. "It is like a mystery novelist's idea of hiding the diamonds in the goldfish bowl: too obvious to notice." While some may find the obvious to be obviously absurd, Forest concluded that "until there is a more meditative dimension in the peace movement, our

45. Nhat Hanh, "Those That Have Not Exploded," 22–23.

46. Forrest, "Thich Nhat Hanh's Eyes of Compassion," 102–3.

perception of reality (and thus our ability to help occasion understanding and transformation) will be terribly crippled."[47]

COMMUNITY OF MINDFULNESS AND COMPASSION

Community building is our true practice.[48]

Dwelling in one of the many hells that we create is one indicator of the lengths that a bodhisattva is willing to go to fulfill her vow to liberate all sentient beings. But we should not misread this commitment as a form of sacrificial altruism. Rather, bodhisattvas dwell in all places because they are inextricably interconnected with all beings. They seek to liberate from within a community of sufferers coextensive with the cosmos.

In 1965, Thich Nhat Hanh composed "Recommendation," a poem encouraging the young men and women of the School of Youth for Social Service to remain compassionate in the face of violence: "Even as they / strike you down / . . . remember: / man is not our enemy." He ends the poem in a stanza that foreshadowed the long exile that would soon commence.

> Alone again,
> I will go on with bent head,
> knowing that love has become eternal.[49]

After the hard labor of leading the Buddhist Peace delegation to the Paris Peace talks and after a concerted effort in late 1976 and early 1977 to assist the Vietnamese "boat people," Thich Nhat Hanh and a few followers struggled to find their way in exile.[50] The practice that began during this retreat and during the decades that followed the sangha's move to Plum Village in southern France in 1982 was simply creating on a microcosmic level what needs to happen on the macrocosmic level. "We suffered tremendously during the twentieth century," Thich Nhat Hanh says looking backward: "Individualism prevailed. Families were broken up, society was deeply divided. That is why . . . the twenty-first century . . . should be built by

47. Ibid., 102–4, 106–7.

48. Nhat Hanh, *Calming Mind*, 85.

49. Nhat Hanh, "Recommendation," 18–19.

50. King, *Merton and Thich Nhat Hanh*, 90–96. Thich Nhat Hanh has written that when he first realized that he could not return home, "I was like a cell removed from its body. The sangha is like a body, and each member is just a cell of the body. But I didn't dry up and die as a cell, because I brought the whole sangha in my heart . . . and right away I began to build a little sangha in the West." *Power*, 171.

the spirit of togetherness, where . . . we do everything together. When you live in a community, you learn how to see the Sangha body, the *Sanghakaya* as your own body." Individualism, then, is the experience of alienation, alienation that Thich Nhat Hanh and his small community of exiles had to overcome in order to be of help to others. "The practice is, therefore, to grow some roots. The Sangha is not a place to hide in order to avoid your responsibilities. The Sangha is a place to practice for the transformation and healing of self and society."[51]

This new community in many ways reflected the one that Thich Nhat Hanh and others built in the 1950s at Phuong Bai. It would be inclusive—monks, nuns, laymen and women—and not isolated from but responsive to the needs of the surrounding society. Speaking with Daniel Berrigan in the mid-'70s, Thich Nhat Hanh agreed that such a community would also have to be a community of resistance but now, resistance would need to be construed more broadly as resistance "against all kinds of things that are like war. Because living in modern society," he continued, "one feels that he cannot easily retain integrity, wholeness. . . . So perhaps, first of all, resistance means opposition to being invaded, occupied, assaulted and destroyed by the system."[52]

The community that Thich Nhat Hanh and his followers established became known as "The Order of Interbeing." It is the continuation of the Tiep Hien Order that he had founded in Vietnam during the war to be the embodiment of engaged Buddhism. Thich Nhat Hanh describes the neologism, "interbeing," in his classic work, *Being Peace*, "It is a compound term which means 'mutual' and 'to be.' . . . I am, therefore, you are. You are, therefore I am."[53] In this simple term, Thich Nhat Hanh conveys the Buddhist concept of dependent co-arising (*pratitya samutpada* in Sanskrit). As numerous classic Buddhist texts put it: "This is, because that is. This is not, because that is not. This comes to be, because that comes to be. This ceases to be, because that ceases to be."[54] What this means is that all reality is, in Buddhist terms, a result of causes and conditions or, to put it more positively, all being is radically relational and empty of any independent substance. "In Buddhism," Thich Nhat Hanh states bluntly, "there is no such thing as an individual."[55]

51. Nhat Hanh, "Go as a Sangha," 11, 20.
52. Berrigan and Nhat Hanh, *Raft*, 127, 129.
53. Nhat Hanh, *Being Peace*, 88.
54. Nhat Hanh, *Heart of the Buddha's Teachings*, 221.
55. Nhat Hanh, *Being Peace*, 42, 52–53.

The deeply positive meaning of this concept of interbeing is revealed in the image of Indra's Net from the Chinese school known as HuaYen.[56] Indra's Net is an infinite cosmic net, each node of which contains a jewel with infinite facets that reflect all of the other jewels. We *are* such a node. Commenting upon the image of light in Chapter 21 of the Lotus Sutra, Thich Nhat Hanh conveys the deep spiritual meaning of Indra's Net.

> The world of [Indra's Net] is a world of light. The Buddha is light; beams of light stream out from each pore of his body . . . and with that light the Tathagata is able to illuminate all the world-spheres. . . . When we live in mindfulness, it is as if there are rays of light coming from the pores of our body that touch all those around us. . . . In Sangha life, if even one person has mindfulness, the light of that mindfulness benefits the entire community. One person gives rise to mindfulness, and then the light of that mindfulness touches another person . . . and so on until every person, every jewel in the net, is shining with the light of mindfulness.[57]

If Indra's Net epitomizes genuine community, then the anti-community is one, as we can gather from the need for communities of resistance, that disperses, separating one being from another. A society given over to mindless consumption is one that both prevents us from coming home to ourselves and leads us by the nose of our endless cravings. Far worse, however, is the gated nation that walls itself off from others' suffering. Despite the surfeit of information that gluts our minds, we fail to hear the cries of a suffering world. "I hope you will find some way to nourish the awareness of the existence of suffering in the world . . . ," Thich Nhat Hanh says. "If we . . . are moved by that suffering, we may come forward to help the people who are suffering, and our own suffering may just vanish."[58]

THE MIRACLE OF MINDFULNESS

Mindfulness is at the base of all Buddhist practice. . . . The ancient Zen masters used to say, "If we live in forgetfulness, we die in a dream."[59]

56. For an introduction to HuaYen Buddhism, see Cleary, *Entry into the Inconceivable*.

57. Nhat Hanh, *Opening the Heart*, 90–92.

58. Nhat Hanh, *Being Peace*, 93–94.

59. Nhat Hanh, *Zen Keys*, 26.

In the previous chapter, focusing on Berrigan's readings of the Hebrew prophets, I followed Walter Brueggemann's suggestion that there are four traits that characterized prophetic communities: an "available memory," a "sense of pain," a "practice of hope," and a "mode of discourse." Here I will parallel this treatment by viewing Thich Nhat Hanh's understanding of the practice of the bodhisattva but focusing on: (1) mindfulness, (2) composting our feelings and cultivating the mind of love, (3) the practice of touching the ultimate in the present moment, and (4) the bodhisattva's mode of discourse.

As we saw earlier, Daniel Berrigan opened his conversations with Thich Nhat Hanh published in *The Raft Is Not the Shore* with a reflection on memory. Thich Nhat Hanh's response focused on the meaning of the French word *recueillement*. This word, he says, captures "the attitude of someone trying to be himself, not to be dispersed, one member of the body here, another there. One tries to recover . . . to become whole again. And I think that is the beginning of awakening."[60] This leads Thich Nhat Hanh to a remarkable interpretation of the Eucharist. Jesus' disciples had shared his daily life but had never really seen him. When Jesus shared bread and wine at the Last Supper, saying, "This is my body; this is my blood," he was using drastic means to wake them up. "We eat a lot, we drink a lot; but what do we eat?" asks Thich Nhat Hanh. "We eat phantoms; we drink ghosts. We don't eat real bread—reality."[61] Elsewhere, he likens the Eucharist to mindfully eating a carrot. Before putting it into our mouth we say the word "carrot." "As you chew the piece of carrot, you know that you are chewing your carrot and not your project, your sorrow, your anger, the past, or the future." Looking deeply you see sunshine, clouds, the whole cosmos; in other words, you see the true nature of the carrot. Chewing mindfully, you receive "the body of the cosmos" as miraculously as Christians receive the Eucharist.[62]

In teaching lay persons and monastics around the globe, Thich Nhat Hanh is simply passing on the very basic lessons that he was taught as a young novice. As I mentioned earlier, the novice monk had been given a slim book, "The Essential Discipline for Daily Use," and told to memorize it. The book contained a series of *gatha* (mental "post-it notes," as it were) designed to summon the young monks to mindfulness in all of their daily actions, beginning with their waking breath: "Just awakened, I hope that every person will attain great awareness and see in complete clarity."[63] As

60. Berrigan and Nhat Hanh, *Raft*, 2.

61. Ibid., 3.

62. Nhat Hanh, *Power*, 197.

63. Nhat Hanh, *Miracle of Mindfulness*, 6–7.

this *gatha* makes clear, mindful action is designed not only to recall the dispersed self but also to benefit all beings. Just as the one who is committed to the practice of mindfulness brings everyone and everything to the meditation cushion, so also does the practice flow out of the meditation hall and into everyday life.[64]

This is quite a leap, we may well say. There does appear to be some "miracle" involved here. But, Thich Nhat Hanh suggests, it is a very down-to-earth miracle.[65] What sort of mindfulness of the present moment can work this sort of miracle? Presume for a moment that our everyday monkey mind—swinging constantly from thought to thought—has come, for the moment, to rest. In this moment the distinction of subject and object of mind evaporates.[66] Stopping, coming to rest is the first step; looking deeply is the second. Looking deeply reveals that, as Thich Nhat Hanh frequently says, each of us is made up of non-self elements. Alternatively stated, we "inter-are" with all other beings. Looking deeply into the "suchness" of each reality, I see the whole cosmos. "Whenever I touch a flower I touch the sun and yet I don't get burned. When I touch the flower, I touch a cloud without flying to the sky." The same holds true for becoming mindful of our own self. "Look more deeply, and you will see yourself as multitudes, penetrating everywhere, interbeing with everyone and everything."[67] To be empty, Thich Nhat Hanh insists, "means to be alive, to breathe in and to breathe out. . . . Emptiness is impermanence, it is change." Like a wave that constantly transforms itself but knows that it is no other than water, we touch the reality of "no birth and no death."[68]

While grounding mindfulness in the ordinariness of breath practice, Thich Nhat Hanh, nonetheless opens us up to a vision of ultimacy as the *Dharmakaya*, the cosmic body of the living Dharma. We saw earlier that ultimate reality is conceived of as "Indra's Net," and countless Buddhas and bodhisattvas emanate light, suffusing the Net. "Allow yourself to be transformed by light," Thich Nhat Hanh concludes. "*Mindfulness is light. . . .* When you do, you will become a bodhisattva emanating light also."[69]

64. Nhat Hanh, *Being Peace*, 52.

65. Thich Nhat Hanh has repeatedly said that the real miracle is not to walk on water but to walk (mindfully) on the earth. See, inter alia, *Miracle of Mindfulness*, 12.

66. Ibid., 41–42.

67. Nhat Hanh, *Cultivating Love*, 89.

68. Nhat Hanh, *Heart of Understanding*, 17, 27.

69. Nhat Hanh, *Cultivating Love*, 84–85, 87; italics added.

COMPOSTING OUR FEELINGS, CULTIVATING THE MIND OF LOVE

You can help your country go home to herself, recognize her pain, anger, sorrow and fear, and get some relief. This is the work of a bodhisattva.[70]

While the prophet expresses God's grief, the bodhisattva replies that "suffering is not enough."[71] A strange reply, indeed, given the Buddhist acceptance of the First Noble Truth that life is suffering (*dukkha*). Yet, on second thought, this affirmation is not so strange. We are not meant to remain trapped in dukkha but to live out the meaning of the Second Noble Truth (unveiling the cause of dukkha), the Third Noble Truth (recognizing our capacity to free ourselves from dukkha), and the Fourth Noble Truth (following the path of liberation).[72] In chapter 1 we saw the bodhisattva suggest that the prophet ought to "compost" his anger. It is above all through showing us how to compassionately transform our feelings—composting cravings and our hatreds and cultivating the mind of love—that the bodhisattva's practice fully flowers.

As I mentioned at the beginning of this chapter, each of us enters the path of the bodhisattva by generating *bodhicitta*, that is "the aspiration to attain enlightenment not for one's own liberation only but in order to help all other beings to liberation."[73] To help us understand *bodhicitta*, Thich Nhat Hanh tells us, in *Cultivating the Mind of Love*, the story of his falling in love as a young monk with a young nun. Meeting by chance at a temple, both persons experienced a strong wave of attraction but both also sensed

70. Nhat Hanh, *Calming Mind*, 14.

71. Nhat Hanh, *Being Peace*, 13.

72. Dukkha is usually translated into English as suffering, but numerous commentators point out that the term is better translated as unsatisfactoriness or dis-ease. Life is out of kilter or, as David Loy puts it, we trap ourselves into a perpetual sense of lack, something always seems not quite right and that something is our lack of a core permanent self. Dukkha arises from the three poisons: craving or greed, aversion or hatred, delusion or ignorance. Of the three poisons, ignorance, the delusion that I am a separate self when I am empty of any substantial reality that sets me apart from all others, is most fundamental. Frequently medical metaphors are used to describe the Four Noble truths: That we all experience dukkha or dis-ease is the First Noble Truth. Identifying the roots of dukkha (the diagnosis) is the Second. The Third Noble Truth affirms our innate capacity to overcome dukkha (prognosis) and the Fourth offers a complex set of practices (the Eightfold Path—the prescription) to overcome it. See, inter alia, Loy, *Money, Sex, War, Karma*, 15–23.

73. Nhat Hanh, *Opening the Heart*, 203n7.

each other's deep reservoir of commitment to the monastic life. By mutual consent and the support of their *sanghas*, first love was transformed into compassionate empowerment of each one's vocation, each one's *bodhicitta*. "*Bodhicitta* is a source of power within you," Thich Nhat Hanh reflects. "The best thing you can do for others is to help them touch the *bodhicitta* in themselves. The seed of *bodhicitta* is there; it is a matter of watering that seed and bringing it to life."[74]

What is true of pleasant feelings is also true of feelings of anger or other "negative" emotions. We saw earlier Thich Nhat Hanh struggling to calm himself after he was verbally attacked by an irate American citizen while he was pleading for peace in Vietnam. Thich Nhat Hanh speaks frankly of the anger that arose in him when he witnessed the wanton destruction of human life and the natural environment during that war. He practiced stopping and not responding until he could create peace within himself.[75] Composting anger is a challenging and delicate form of practice. Suffused by anger we are like a muddy pond. When we let the mud settle our inherent, clear Buddha Nature appears. The emphasis is on our own power to transform wild and aberrant emotions. Mindfulness, like the light of the sun, may not appear to be doing much but under its influence something akin to photosynthesis takes place within us, producing new life.[76]

Earlier in the chapter we looked at Thich Nhat Hanh's response to the most recent and seemingly overwhelming collective challenge to such a practice, namely, the events of September 11, 2001, and the reaction of the entire American country that they provoked. In *Calming the Fearful Mind: A Zen Response to Terrorism*, Thich Nhat Hanh's elaborated that response. The first step, then and now, is to stop and address one's own anger. "When our house is on fire," he insists, "we must first put out the fire before investigating its cause."[77]

The second step, then, is to look deeply. When we do so, we become aware of the karmic web that entangles us. We see the multitude of causes and conditions that caught fire on September 11. The anger that we express in retaliatory violence mirrors the anger and violence of the terrorist. The violence spirals into the future but it also has deep roots in the past. "Our children will say, 'You killed my grandfather, now I have to kill you.'" To break the spiral we must look beneath the hatred directed toward us. We

74. Nhat Hanh, *Cultivating Love*, 112. See also 11–36.

75. Nhat Hanh, *Calming Mind*, 11, 105.

76. Nhat Hanh, *Being Peace*, 46–47; Nhat Hanh, *Transformation and Healing*, 72–73.

77. Nhat Hanh, *Calming Mind*, 11, 108.

think that it is we alone who suffer but the terrorist too suffers. Some injustice gives rise to hatred; some wrong perception projects the source of suffering solely on us. Putting terrorists in prison while their hatred burns may well be necessary, Thich Nhat Hanh agrees, but it does not undo the karmic entanglement. "An act of cruelty is born of many conditions coming together," Thich Nhat Hanh continues, "not by any separate, individual actor. . . . All of us are responsible. . . . No one can say they are not responsible for the [war in the aftermath of 9/11], even if we oppose our country's actions. . . . Maybe we have not done enough."[78]

The dualistic mind focuses on what *they* did, whether the "they" is the 9/11 terrorists or the American military. Looking deeply, we see people who suffer as we do. Such understanding gives birth to compassion which, alone, can undo the karmic entanglement. This is the third step. We must take Jesus' saying to heart: "Forgive them for they know not what they do." Compassion is not naïve or stupid, Thich Nhat Hanh argues. We must recognize that our retaliatory violence is blind; it has only entangled us further—as we once were in Vietnam. Only when compassion born of understanding emerges can we begin to see the possibility of political solutions which deescalate the violence.[79]

THE PRACTICE OF TOUCHING THE ULTIMATE IN THE PRESENT MOMENT

If while washing dishes, we think only of the cup of tea that awaits us, thus hurrying to get the dishes out of the way as if they were a nuisance, then . . . we are not alive during the time we are washing the dishes. In fact, we are completely incapable of realizing the miracle of life while standing at the sink. . . . Thus we are sucked away into the future—and we are incapable of actually living one minute of life.[80]

Thich Nhat Hanh's comment on washing dishes comes in *The Miracle of Mindfulness*, after he tells the story of washing the dishes of one hundred monks as a novice in Vietnam using ashes and coconut bark, and after he challenges visiting American peace activist Jim Forest not to wash dishes to get them out of the way but just to wash dishes. The story and its lesson echo

78. Ibid., 37, 42–43, 58, 93.

79. Ibid., 30, 33, 38–39, 109.

80. Nhat Hanh, *Miracle of Mindfulness*, 4–5.

a famous Zen koan in which a young monk, having traveled far to study under a famous master, introduces himself expecting some sort of profound direction. The master, instead, asks the monk if he has eaten breakfast. "Yes," the monk replies. "Then wash your bowl," the master insists.[81] Expecting some deep spiritual insight, the young monk is confounded when he is turned to the present moment with its prosaic demand. The prosaic, we might say, is the Dharma.

If the prophet is motivated by a sacred discontent with the faithless present and sustained by hope, the bodhisattva recognizes that despite the clouds that shroud it, the sun *is* shining. It is a matter of seeing what is truly present behind the veil of ignorance. As the seventeenth-century Japanese Zen master Hakuin puts it, "This very body is the body of the Buddha. This land is the Pure Land."[82] Speaking more colloquially, Thich Nhat Hanh frequently says, "The Kingdom of God is now or never." There is an urgency to this expression which is akin to that of the prophet, but it is not the demand to break the hold of an oppressive present but the encouragement to penetrate the shrouded present.[83] Wherever we are, we stand on a threshold. We have only to walk through the open door.

Touching the ultimate dimension and living mindfully in the historical dimension are not two. It is interesting that his most sustained treatment of this idea comes in *Living Buddha, Living Christ*, a book which examines the interpenetration of Buddhism and Christianity.[84] Throughout this work, Thich Nhat Hanh speaks of the utter availability of the kingdom of God. "We do not have to die to arrive at the gates of heaven. In fact, we have to be truly alive. The practice is to touch life deeply so that the Kingdom of God becomes a reality."[85]

At its deepest level, *Living Buddha, Living Christ* is a fusion, a transfusion of mystical horizons. The radical availability of the kingdom is undergirded by a strong theology of the Holy Spirit.[86] The Spirit is God-within-us,

81. Cleary, *No Barrier*, 39.

82. "Zen Master Hakuin's Chant," 182–83.

83. Nhat Hanh, *Being Peace*, 113.

84. Nhat Hanh, *Living Buddha*, 11, 197. Each of these traditions inter-are in the sense that Buddhism is made of non-Buddhist elements and Christianity is made of non-Christian elements. Thich Nhat Hanh's approach to Christianity and to interreligious dialogue does not easily fit with any of the three current labels (exclusivist, inclusivist, pluralist) used to characterize approaches to other religions. As I have indicated, the clue to Thich Nhat Hanh's approach lies within his concept of "interbeing."

85. Ibid., 38.

86. More precisely stated, Thich Nhat Hanh believes that it is "safer to approach through the Holy Spirit than through the door of theology." Ibid., 151.

hich Nhat Hanh identifies with the mustard seed of Jesus' parable. ed—which a Buddhist will call Buddha Nature—is buried in the soil consciousness. Mindful practice waters it. If the kingdom of God is radically available, it is also experienced as a radical openness to all that is. "When St. Francis looked deeply at an almond tree in winter and asked it to speak to him of God," Thich Nhat Hanh says, "the tree was instantly covered with blossoms."[87] Openness to the "suchness" of reality is also radical openness to all time. "When we touch one thing with deep awareness, we touch everything. Focusing on the present moment, we realize that the present is made of the past and is creating the future. When we drink a cup of tea very deeply, we touch the whole of time."[88] Francis, seeing the blossoms, is aware of the suchness of the almond tree, but simultaneously he is, in the tradition of Christian contemplation, resting in God.

Developing the Buddhist understanding of Buddha Nature (*tathagatagarbha* or womb of the Buddha), Thich Nhat Hanh says that "we are all mothers of the Buddha," linking that image with that of Mary, as Mother of God. He sees both images as representing our capacity to give birth to compassion. Otherwise put, we make manifest the *Dharmakaya* or the cosmic body of the Buddha and the mystical Body of Christ. "Your body is the Body of Christ," he insists, but with a distinctively Buddhist twist to its meaning.[89]

In *Living Buddha Living Christ*, Thich Nhat Hanh's method is to tack back and forth between Buddhist and Christian streams of thought. Ultimately we are driven by the same inconceivable wind. So, the Eucharist that resurrects us to touch the kingdom "is a strong bell of mindfulness." But mindfully eating our daily bread also enables us to touch the kingdom. "Each of us has the capacity of transforming many living beings if we know how to cultivate the seed of enlightenment within ourselves." Jesus too calls us to be the light of the world, and the salt of the earth. For a Buddhist, Thich Nhat Hanh insists, this entails mindful practice. "[Jesus'] teaching was clear and strong. If the church practices well the teachings of Jesus, the

87. Ibid., 43, 152–55.

88. Ibid., 153.

89. Ibid., 40–41, 56–58, 123, 126. The idea that all living beings have a Buddha Nature (*Tathagatagarbha*—Buddha womb or Buddha embryo) or, more precisely, that all living beings *are* Buddha was fully developed in the Chinese schools of Buddhism. This teaching can be read as a radicalization of the Third Noble Truth which affirms our capacity to awaken, to liberate ourselves from dukkha. Because we *are* Buddha, we do not need to gain anything. We only need to manifest what we truly are. So, Buddhism rejects any dualistic projection of an ideal self over against our "real" self. On the development of this concept and practice, see King, *Buddha Nature*.

Trinity will always be present and the church will have the healing power to transform all it touches."[90]

DISCOURSE: FINGERS POINTING TO THE MOON

> *If you look closely at the figure of the thousand-armed bodhisattva, you will see that in the palm of each hand is an eye. The eye symbolizes the presence of understanding, wisdom, prajña. We need both compassion and wisdom to progress on the path. . . . Avalokiteshvara has so many arms because love needs to express itself in many different forms. . . . That is why every arm is holding a different instrument and in every hand is the eye of wisdom.*[91]

The implication of recognizing that not only is the self empty but our ideas are empty, that is, impermanent and by no means absolute, is that Thich Nhat Hanh can take radical freedom in adapting Buddhist teachings to Western minds. After all, the teachings are, as is often said by Zen teachers, but skillful means, fingers pointing to the moon, not the moon itself. the Lotus Sutra with its fantastic pantheon of bodhisattvas is itself only a skillful means of liberation, "The dramatic language and images are the literary equivalent of a statue of the Buddha seated on a lotus throne."[92] Buddhas themselves use the teachings to create "Dharma doors," which they enter at will beckoning us to follow. Each of these Dharma doors—said to number eight-four thousand—opens us up to the reality of our own innate Buddha Nature. We need, Thich Nhat Hanh says, to look past the fantastic images, like that of many-armed Avalokiteshvara, to understand the message of texts like the Lotus Sutra. Looking past is probably not the right metaphor; *looking through* is more apt.

As *upaya* or skillful means, the discourse of the bodhisattva is tailored to the needs of each student.[93] The teacher becomes a "transformation body," an instrument for the liberation of sentient beings. Each of his books is a transformation body, Thich Nhat Hanh says, through which he even crosses the walls of prisons, and the political barriers that kept him in exile for decades from his native land. "Each of us has many transformation

90. Ibid., 30–31, 70, 146.
91. Nhat Hanh, *Opening the Heart*, 132–33.
92. Ibid., 3–4.
93. Nhat Hanh, *Zen Keys*, 51–52.

bodies, and that is why it is so important to recognize our transformation bodies. . . . Just like Avalokiteshvara, we manifest ourselves in . . . many forms, in order to help as many people as possible."[94]

In the previous chapter, I discussed three aspects of the discourse of the prophet: (a) the critique of idolatry, (b) the unequivocal "no" that precedes any proclamation of liberation, and (c) the paradox or koan of justice as a transcendent imperative, both impossible of attainment yet categorically demanded. Here I would like to underline three corresponding traits of the discourse of the bodhisattva: (a) not clinging to any ideology, (b) the dialectics of *prajnaparamita*, and (c) the koan of commonplace actions.

In the first three of the Fourteen Mindfulness Trainings of the Order of Interbeing, Thich Nhat Hanh presents a cluster of practices that addresses the perils of all ideological discourse. Commenting on the Zen aphorism "If you meet the Buddha, kill the Buddha," Thich Nhat Hanh insists that "truth is not a concept. If we cling to our concepts, we lose reality. . . . To kill the Buddha is the only way to see the Buddha."[95] What the Eightfold Noble Path refers to as right views is crystallized in this aphorism, and is a condition for right speech. In the opening sentence of the First Mindfulness Training, Thich Nhat Hanh says: "Aware of the suffering created by fanaticism and intolerance, I am determined not to be idolatrous about or bound to any doctrine, theory or ideology even Buddhist ones." Quickly Thich Nhat Hanh establishes the connection between ideological rigidity and murder. "We usually think that killing occurs in the domain of the body, but a fanatical mind can cause the killing of not just one, but millions of human beings."[96]

The Second Mindfulness Training emphasizes nonattachment to views, as well, but here the focus is not on preventing ideologically justified murder but, more positively, on opening oneself to the ideas and insights of others. We cultivate the mind of "nondiscriminative understanding," which sees all realities in their interdependent coarising. Then the Third Training focuses on *how* we convey our ideas to others. It calls us to avoid all coercive ways of imposing our ideas on others, whether through propaganda, indoctrination, intimidation, or seduction.[97] In such comments we see something similar to Berrigan's critique of the sacriligeous character of imperial pretensions, their aping God. But rather than the prophet's categorical "no," the three mindfulness trainings suggest an ongoing process. The second of the Bodhisattva vows reads, "Delusions are endless, I vow to cut through them

94. Nhat Hanh, *Opening the Heart*, 134.

95. Nhat Hanh, *Keys*, 52–54.

96. Nhat Hanh, *Interbeing*, 23, 25.

97. Ibid., 26–29.

all." To train oneself takes patience, undoing knots of self-deception one at a time.

The bodhisattva's discourse, reflecting a nondiscriminatory mind, is self-emptying. In other words, the bodhisattva practices the "dialectics of prajñaparamita," or the dialectics of perfect understanding. These dialectics are designed to combat the endless delusions which arise with our discriminating mind. They are often conveyed in the paradoxical language of this classical Zen Buddhist aphorism: "Before I began to practice, mountains were mountains and rivers were rivers. After I began to practice, mountains were no longer mountains and rivers were no longer rivers. Now, I have practiced for some time, and mountains are again mountains and rivers are again rivers."[98] Paradoxical discourse confounds the discriminating mind, especially the mind that would discriminate between the sacred and the profane, as in the saying of the Zen master who confessed that every time that he uttered the word "Buddha," he had to go to the river to wash out his mouth three times.[99] To truly understand such sayings we must realize that they are more to be understood in a moral than in an epistemological sense. We work on ourselves first of all by not claiming any status that separates ourselves from others; we recognize the ways in which we inter-are with those whose actions we condemn. Quoting the Diamond Sutra, Thich Nhat Hanh can say, "A bodhisattva is not a bodhisattva, that is why he is truly a bodhisattva."[100]

The third trait of prophetic discourse was that it forms a kind of koan—the recognition that justice ultimately is God's gift and yet it is demanded of us both individually and collectively. Thich Nhat Hanh, the Zen master, reminds us that koans are not puzzles to be solved. We respond not with our minds but with our lives. As we have seen, the koans that the bodhisattva offers point us toward the most commonplace actions—drinking a cup of tea, taking a walk with a child, breathing mindfully—and then he tells us: "These things are very important. They can change our civilization."[101] It all sounds so very appealing. But, of course, deep down we don't believe it. We mouth the words. We put on the appearance of being good, of acting well, so others will think well of us. We fall far short—as one of the Plum village chants puts it—of taking refuge in the Buddha-in-myself, of believing that my actions, too, ripple across Indra's Net transforming and healing. But then Thich Nhat Hanh replies: "Faith is having a path that leads you to

98. Nhat Hanh, *Cultivating Love*, 77.

99. Ibid.

100. Ibid., 75.

101. Nhat Hanh, *Being Peace*, 113, 118.

freedom, liberation. . . . If you have a path to go on, you have power."[102] An answer which is a non-answer, a koan. Just practice. Just pour the tea with your full attention, not as a project to attain buddhahood. There is nothing to attain. You are Buddha. Just pour the tea.

THE BODHISATTVA AS PROPHET

It is possible to miss the firm backbone that supports the Dharma as Thich Nhat Hanh communicates it to us. The words fall so sweetly on our ears. The teaching of interdependence is a case in point. "If you are a poet, you will see clearly that there is a cloud floating in this sheet of paper. Without a cloud, there will be no rain; without rain, the trees cannot grow, and without trees we cannot make paper. . . . So we can say that the cloud and the paper *inter-are.*" After explaining how the sunshine, the logger, and the farmer whose crops feed the logger are also present in this paper when we look deeply, Thich Nhat Hanh concludes, "The fact is that this sheet of paper is made up only of 'non paper elements.'" Even the awareness that the self is also made up of "non self elements" tastes sweet when we are told that to be empty, to be devoid of a separate, independent existence is to be open to all that is.[103] But mentally I assume that I will get to pick and choose which non-self elements to include and which to exclude in constituting my self.

Likewise, I resonate to the beauty of Thich Nhat Hanh's translation of the saying from the Avatamsaka Sutra: "All times penetrate one time. One time penetrates all times, past present, future."[104] But then I remember that he has not forgotten, never forgotten his brother monk who immolated himself in the midst of a cruel war.

> I hear you now.
> The storm screams with your cries.
> Hearing you,
> each cell in me, O my brother,
> brims with tears.
>
> I still hear you,
> your appeal from heaven or hell,
> and I turn to you
> wherever you are.[105]

102. Nhat Hanh, *Power*, 15, 43–44, 101.
103. Nhat Hanh, *Heart of Understanding*, 3–4. Ibid., 10, 16–17.
104. Nhat Hanh, "Sun My Heart," 137.
105. Nhat Hanh, "Fire That Consumes My Brother," 48.

Like Berrigan's life, my life, too, has been marked by endless wars. The storm screams with so many cries. But opposition to the empire's wars carries its own perils. The rituals of protest, no less than the liturgies of death that they resist, all too quickly become rigid. Voices become louder, strident and divisive. The rhetoric of resistance soon enough creates its own fixed universe of good and evil. Against this rigor mortis of those who assume a prophet's mantle, Thich Nhat Hanh offers a different model of social engagement. Above all, it appears in what has become his signature poem, "Please Call Me by My True Names." Thich Nhat Hanh has recited it on many occasions before different audiences. I find it instructive, however, that I first discovered the poem in the context of a series of guided meditations given to peace activists.[106] Like the parables of Jesus, Thich Nhat Hanh's poem seems particularly attuned to a pathology of religiously engaged persons, the hankering to be seen (revered?) as children of light. The poem's rhythm is set by the opening stanzas. "Don't say that I will depart tomorrow. . . . / Look deeply: every second I am arriving / to be a bud on a spring branch." Dependent co-arising and co-ceasing appear as the sweet eternity of Nature, about as far from the clangor of war and violence as one can imagine. Even when I recite that "I am" the bird who swallows the mayfly or the snake who consumes the frog, I can affirm the rhythms of Nature as my own. "The rhythm of my heart is the birth and death / of all that is alive." But in three swift stanzas, Thich Nhat Hanh plunges us into a heart of darkness. Reciting, no, chanting the poem, I find myself confessing that I am the arms merchant whose dark deals starve a child in Uganda. I am the bureaucrat processing the orders of a repressive regime, as well as the inmate of its death camp. And at the very heart of the poem I find myself chanting:

> I am the twelve-year-old girl,
> refugee on a small boat,
> who throws herself into the ocean
> after being raped by a sea pirate.
> And I am the pirate,
> my heart not yet capable
> of seeing and loving.[107]

Too sweet? I suggest that for those who see themselves as seekers of peace and justice the teaching of the interdependent co-arising of evil is the hardest of all truths to swallow. Elsewhere, I put the spiritual dilemma that confronts us in this poem in this way:

106. Nhat Hanh, *Being Peace*, 66–68.
107. Nhat Hanh, "Please Call Me," 72.

> Can I integrate this concrete horror with the rhythms of my heart . . . ? Can I say "I am that" without choking and drowning myself . . . ? To become aware that I dependently co-arise with all beings is to destroy any ready identification with the victim (read: solidarity with the oppressed) that cleanses me of my complicity with her rapist. I can speak in ethical abstractness of degrees of moral complicity and responsibility or I can take a stand in righteous anger against oppressors but in either case what I can be absolutely sure of is this: If I remain as I am with my lifestyle and patterns of consumption, new generations of sea pirates will follow old. "Please call me by my true names, / so I can wake up . . . ." the poem ends. Only an awareness capable of integrating the full horror of the web of violence etched on the face of the world can ground responsible action—"and so the door of my heart can be left open, 'the door of compassion.'" I transmute the horror of self-knowledge, of knowing my true names, by going through that door.[108]

Earlier we looked at the narrative of Kshitigarbha's willingness to descend into many hells in order to rescue other living beings. This poem has taught me how to understand those narratives afresh. To live compassionately in hell is to live serenely without moral self-insulation, to act without traces of self-justification, and to resist evil without ritually expressing the need to separate oneself from sea pirates. I suggest that this awareness is an absolutely necessary Buddhist element in any authentic prophetic consciousness. Prophets, too, must be made up of non-prophet elements.[109]

THE BODHISATTVA FROM THE DEPTHS OF THE OCEAN

Thich Nhat Hanh has written a number of short stories. They are told as simple tales for children with hidden depths that entrance adults, as well. The "real" and the fantastic flow seamlessly together. In "A Lone Pink Fish," we hear the painful story of the Vietnamese boat people, of their perilous journeys across the unforgiving sea, of the pirates who rob and rape them, of the authorities in Malaysia, Singapore, and Thailand who force the refugees to return to the sea, and of the few who venture out in crafts disguised

108. Strain, "Sapiential Eschatology," 120.

109. Rita Gross discusses Buddhists assuming a prophetic voice in *Soaring and Settling*, 13–18.

as fishing boats to rescue the refugees.[110] In this story, Thich Nhat Hanh returns to the horrifying story told in "Please Call Me by My True Names." A girl of ten is kicked overboard by pirates but finds herself transformed into a pink fish. While searching in vain for her own mother, she is able to carry drowning refugees to shore and guide leaky boats safely past pirates and police.

Able to transform from fish to girl and back, the girl known as Hong teaches one such rescued young woman, Dao, how to chant the Heart Sutra, Avalokiteshvara's fearless teaching of no birth and no death, to ease her pain at the unspeakable cruelty of the world. When Dao marvels at Hong's tale of wondrous transformation, Hong teaches Dao to see the preciousness of everyday things, the taste of guava fruit, holding hands with her lover. The radical identification with suffering, with victims and victimizers, is transformed into equanimity and compassion as Dao herself begins to recite the Heart Sutra. "She smiled when she realized she was imitating Hong's voice. She did not understand the meaning of the sutra's words, but their sounds were joyous and comforting. . . . It seemed to her that if she repeated this a thousand times, she might understand the deep meaning of the sutra."[111] Dao is set on her way, admonished by Hong to care for others in the refugee camp, while Hong herself returns to the depths of the ocean. Just so, the bodhisattva's light illuminates the cosmos, leaping from node to node across the whole of Indra's Net. The bodhisattva too is a bearer of good news and we have ears that can hear:

> Listen . . . !
> Leave behind the world of sorrow
> and preoccupation
> and get free.
> The latest good news
> is that you can do it.[112]

110. Nhat Hanh, "Lone Pink Fish," 57–105. The story reflects the actual heroic efforts of Thich Nhat Hanh's associate Sister Chan Khong in attempting to rescue Vietnamese "boat people." See her *Learning Love*, 180–93.

111. Nhat Hanh, "Lone Pink Fish," 101.

112. Nhat Hanh, "Good News," 169.

Part II

THE SOCIAL ETHICS OF THE PROPHET AND THE BODHISATTVA

Three Approaches

3

VISION AND VIRTUE IN THE ETHICS OF THE PROPHET AND THE BODHISATTVA

I OPEN THIS CHAPTER, the first of three that locate the writings and lives of Daniel Berrigan and Thich Nhat Hanh within more formal ethical frameworks, with two narratives whose imaginative reach outlines two different but complementary approaches to the moral life. Mrs. Curren, the protagonist of *Age of Iron*, Nobel laureate J. M. Coetzee's searing indictment of apartheid South Africa, is dying of cancer. But more than life is being stripped from her. A retired, liberal professor, she is plunged into the full horror and violence of the apartheid system; she is made to confront the depths of her complicity. At a crucial point in the novel she confronts the glaring face—bunched and closed—of a woman in a passing car. "A thickening of the membrane between the world and the self inside," she reflects.

> A thickening become thickness. Evolution but evolution backward. Fish from the primitive depths . . . grew patches of skin sensitive to the fingerings of light, patches that in time became eyes. Now, in South Africa, I see eyes clouding over again, scales thickening on them, as the land of explorers, the colonists prepare to return to the deep.[1]

I call Mrs. Curren's experience "moral devolution," the eclipse of the moral life. "How do I know," she concludes, "that the scales are not thickening

1. Coetzee, *Age of Iron*, 127.

over my own eyes?"[2] Indeed. How do any of us know? My hypothesis in this chapter is that it is the prophet, as she may arise in any tradition, who performs laser surgery on the thickening scales. Our eyes, our moral sensitivity, must be peeled back.

The second narrative comes from Native American writer Leslie Marmon Silko. *Ceremony* is her richly detailed story of the healing of Tayo, a Laguna World War II veteran. Tayo is suffering from what my colleague John Dominic Crossan calls a "sociosomatic" illness in which the individual's sickness mirrors a collective derangement.[3] Tayo is visited by a Laguna holy man, Old Ku'oosh, who offers this diagnosis: "But you know, grandson, this world is fragile." And the narrator comments: "The word he chose to express 'fragile' was filled with the intricacies of a continuing process, and with the strength inherent in spider webs woven across paths through sand hills where early in the morning the sun becomes entangled in each filament of the web."[4] Tayo's healing, Old Ku'oosh concludes, is important "not only for your sake, but for this fragile world." Tayo, however, whose moral journey has barely begun, at this stage sees only how one person's action can tear the fragile web.[5]

Repairing the fragile web and, just as importantly, weaving new connections requires a different orientation to the moral life than performing laser surgery. My hypothesis here will be that the bodhisattva tradition, especially as mediated by what we saw earlier in the image of Indra's Net and as elaborated in the Avatamsaka Sutra, is geared toward web repair. To revert to Coetzee's image, the bodhisattva is one who patiently evolves new forms of moral perception, new eyes of compassion by tracing our interconnections.

It is most appropriate that we begin this chapter with these two stories with their arresting imagery. Both Daniel Berrigan and Thich Nhat Hanh envision ethics through a poetic lens. Each lays out the moral landscape through what Mark Johnson calls "multiple metaphoric mappings." Rather than dictating a set of moral propositions, each sees the larger task of ethics as "the cultivation of the moral imagination."[6] Imagination, in turn, discloses a path, a way of being a moral agent. This is not to say that Berrigan and Thich Nhat Hanh do not provide moral guidelines; it is rather to say that wrestling with the Hebrew Bible's prophetic narratives in Berrigan's case and

2. Ibid.
3. Crossan, *God and Empire*, 19–21.
4. Silko, *Ceremony*, 35–36.
5. Ibid., 38.
6. Johnson, *Moral Imagination*, xii, 2.

transforming the Buddhist Dharma into compelling extended metaphors and stories in Thich Nhat Hanh's case are the sites in which moral guidelines emerge.

Peter Ronald Gathje points out that Berrigan's lack of a systematic development of his ethics has meant that he has been largely ignored by academic ethicists. Gathje seeks to remedy this situation by treating Berrigan's ethics as a species of virtue ethics.[7] But this is a very different type of virtue ethics than Aristotle's in which seeds are nurtured so that they reach their inner telos. Gathje, instead, compares Berrigan with the work of Stanley Hauerwas. While the two are similar in terms of seeing the Christian community as a community of resistance sustaining a way of life alternative to the dominant culture, Gathje argues that Berrigan holds out the possibility that the church can also be a force for transforming culture.[8] To understand that transforming role, we will have to discuss the sacramental power of the acts of resistance that Daniel and Philip Berrigan performed. Wrestling with the prophets became an extension of these performances. Reimagining the moral landscape of the prophets' own performances, Berrigan confronts the reader with the need to act.

> What then of us, living as we do in a contemporary Babylon . . . ? Can a community of conscience offer a measure of hope and light, when the public light is all but quenched, and the law of war and weaponry bears down hard . . . ? Symbolic, nonviolent acts of resistance are in order. Our instructor in these is Jeremiah himself—bearing the yoke, breaking the jar, witnessing the vision of the basket of figs, the signs of drought, the vine devoid of grapes. Each of these bespeaks a nonviolent effort of conscience. . . . They challenge the tyranny implicit in "things as they are."[9]

Similarly, I will argue in this chapter that Thich Nhat Hanh offers a distinctive form of virtue ethics. This argument is consistent with that of Damien Keown, who argues persuasively that Buddhist ethics most closely resembles Aristotelian ethics with its cultivation of the self to reach an inner perfection. Buddhism shares with Aristotle this commitment to further an innate human potential. "But the virtues are not simply instrumental means to an end which transcends them," Keown insists. "What is distinctive about

7. Gathje, "Cost of Virtue," 6.

8. Ibid., 8–10, 14, 16. Gathje argues persuasively that the Berrigans' commitment to the Mystical Body of Christ, as articulated in an incarnational theology, kept them from a wholly sectarian ethics. Ibid., 139–40.

9. Berrigan, *Jeremiah*, 133–34.

the virtues is that they participate in and *constitute* the end." The Buddha exemplified this life of virtue both *before and after* his experience of enlightenment. This life of practice is conveyed in the Third and Fourth Noble Truths, i.e., the core of Buddhist soteriology: There is a path and you have the ability to walk it.[10] Thich Nhat Hanh follows the Zen tradition in seeing that simply walking the path is already reaching the goal. Practice and realization, as the thirteenth-century Japanese Zen master Dogen taught, are one.[11] The Buddhist precepts in Thich Nhat Hanh's rendering become "mindfulness trainings." Where Berrigan focuses on sacramental performances, Thich Nhat Hanh counsels practice. Mindful breathing, walking, drinking tea, such simple practices can transform our civilization.[12]

DANIEL BERRIGAN: OVERCOMING DEATH AS A SOCIAL METHOD

Berrigan's prophetic imagination is expressed in the *form* of his writings on the prophets. Chapter 1 described Berrigan's twenty-five-years-long wrestling match. "Lacerating, relentless and intemperate," each prophet lays hold of us as he "strives for a divine . . . breakthrough in the human tribe."[13] Recall Abraham Heschel's argument that the prophet is a person attuned to God's *pathos*. Like a tuning fork, the prophet vibrates, undergoes God's suffering. Here we suggest that Berrigan's careful tracing of the prophetic narratives undergoes the same suffering and we, in turn, must grapple with this claim upon us of God's pathos. The message could not be clearer: Like Jacob, no one who wrestles emerges unscathed. Wrestling is an apt metaphor for coming to terms with the cost of virtue. The chain of wrestlers—the prophets with God, Berrigan with the prophets and we with Berrigan—is a metaphor for the process we call "tradition" in which a life of virtue finds its context and meaning.

There is an even more disturbing image of what is going on in Berrigan's purgatorial wrestling. Chapter 1 viewed Berrigan's poetic rendering of Yahweh's command to Ezekiel to eat the scroll before going to speak to the people (Ezekiel 3:1–3). The command is repeated in the book of Revelation 10:10, and Berrigan, again, sees there a paradigm of the prophet's pathos from which the moral imagination emerges. In "A Chancy Encounter with an Angel," he invents a dramatic interchange between "Myself" and

10. Keown, *Buddhist Ethics*, 2, 193–94.

11. Dogen, "Guidelines for the Study of the Way," 131–43.

12. See, inter alia, Nhat Hanh, *Peace Is Every Step*, 33, 47.

13. Berrigan, *Jeremiah*, xi.

an "Angel" over the insane demand. "Myself" recoils at the image of a mad man cowering in a corner chewing on parchment, but "Angel" is adamant: Devouring God's word might be an emetic, purging you of an endemic poison.[14] If prophets are driven sane by this taste of madness, the denizens of empires are oblivious to the poison in their system. Inured to endless warfare, blind to the global reach of exploitation, only the perpetrators fail to see that they have blood on their hands.[15] So, moral awareness is not a quiet awakening from sleep. Laser surgery on thickening membranes is required. The prophets'—and Berrigan's—contribution to ethics is, first, an electric shock, a lacerating word—"no." "Everything begins with that no . . . ," Berrigan insists, "a suffering and prophetic word."[16]

But no to what? As we saw in chapter 1, the most consistent refrain, repeated throughout the full breadth of Berrigan's writings is no to "death as a social method." In *No Bars to Manhood*, published shortly after Catonsville while the war in Vietnam was still in full flood, Berrigan elaborates this cryptic phrase. It is the choice of bloodletting, destruction and division as the preferred method of social change. It is the orientation of huge sectors of our economy to the preparation for killing. It is the wanton napalming of nature. Death invades our consciousness. Public speech under the aegis of death becomes religious mystification. Death as a social method is "the extinction of . . . the power of imaging alternatives to death itself."[17] This last is crucial; imperial numbness anesthetizes the prophetic imagination whose primary task is, in Brueggemann's words, "to nurture, nourish and evoke a consciousness and perception alternative to the consciousness and perception of the dominant culture around us."[18] Roped together as we are on this treacherous glacier—death's ubiquitous slippery slope—at least one must ram an ice pick home if we are not to slide into the abyss. The prophetic no is that ice pick. No moral ascension is possible without a repeated, uncompromising no.

That no strikes hard against the very mainspring of modern political life rooted as it is in revolution giving birth to the nation state. "Modern revolutions, like all revolutions, start out affirming liberty; they consummate their efforts in tyranny. Pleading for a more abundant life, they ended under a single sign; hecatombs of political victims. Murder becomes the privileged means of pursuing a relentlessly receding utopian end and, in

14. Berrigan, *Testimony*, 195–96.

15. Berrigan, *Isaiah*, 33; Berrigan, *Eziekiel*, 60.

16. Berrigan, *Dark Night of Resistance*, 2.

17. Berrigan, *No Bars to Manhood*, 60–67.

18. Brueggemann, *Prophetic Imagination*, 3; see Berrigan, *Isaiah*, 87.

this process, revolution becomes "merely the retooling of the old murderous machinery."[19] Like Camus's rebel, we must say no to this method of social change in all of its manifestations.

As if to twist the multiple coils of evil into one Gordian knot, Berrigan, well into his eighties, tackled the two books of Kings. His subtitle, "The Pathology of Power," tells the tale. He puzzles over how such unremitting accounts of "mayhem, slaughter, betrayal and bravado" could be thought to be divinely inspired. He concludes that these books offer "a harsh, even shaming pedagogy. . . . We must come to know the worst of our ancestry—as well as the worst that lurks in ourselves." We must learn the truth about the systems that harbor power's deadly virus. Even the god, especially the god of *Kings*, must be unmasked as a projection, the mirror image of the kings themselves. Or, as Berrigan puts it most damningly, "a ventriloquist's dummy."[20] The prophetic no is ultimately focused on this idolatrous pretension of power. The business of empires and the business of idolatry are one and the same. Aping the God of life, the kings and their gods make of the world a killing field. Death as a social method is the work of idolatry.[21] The lesson of the books of Kings: Read them and weep.

It is tempting to think of moral perception as an awareness that can be switched on at will. Coetzee's parable of moral devolution suggests otherwise. The scales might thicken over our eyes imperceptibly and we might lose all memory of what it meant to see the world through a moral lens. Those of us who live within a mighty empire must assume that laser surgery is an immediate necessity. The fog of endless wars, the moral blur, is a function of our own cataracts. The prophetic no unmasks as counterfeit any ethics that does not take seriously the way in which the kings, with the blessing of their gods, are given over to death as a social method. The two prime candidates for such an ethics of resignation are the just war theory and what Berrigan labels as an "interim ethics." In his mind the theory of a just war is always an exercise in casuistry that serves only to vindicate the sword.[22] Just war thinking overturns the "plain sense" of the Bible and offers us instead the Bible as a "military manual." It justifies war as "practical atheism."[23] Gathje points out that the rule-guided propositions of the just war theory ignore the formation of a moral character in attunement with Christian narratives. Berrigan pushes further in suggesting that the theory

19. Berrigan, *No Bars to Manhood*, 131.

20. Berrigan, *Kings*, 1–2, 4, 93.

21. Berrigan, *Isaiah*, 125–26.

22. Ibid., 13.

23. Berrigan, *Testimony*, 57.

ignores how militarism creates "a nuclear winter in our souls."[24] In a more comprehensive vein, Berrigan challenges an "interim ethics" that argues that Jesus' teaching on war and peace were intended for the reign of God which is not yet. In the meantime, another ethics must prevail, an ethics that resigns itself to war until the end of time. The Christian is called only to play out a "bad deal of cards." The end result: The Sermon on the Mount has been "nuked."[25]

Along with the no to this interim ethic and the traditional just war ethics, there is a no directed to liberal theology and the ethics of reform. The latter Berrigan describes as "useless chatter." Something more profound is required, a bending of the "instruments of death and the structures of injustice into a new form."[26] By contrast, Berrigan points to Isaiah, for whom ethics arises out of a vision of hope. Vision and command are conjoined. This is not deontological ethics, the fruit of practical reason. The vision overturns expectations. For Berrigan and the Plowshares Movement, the link to Isaiah and thence to God is through a commanding text, "a word that sets the human in motion."[27] But this command delivers us from resignation, moral numbness and despair. "Arise and walk."[28]

In contrast to both just war theory and any interim ethics, Berrigan offers an "Ethic of Resurrection." His essay by that title is as close as Berrigan comes to a formal presentation of his ethical framework and the guiding principles derived from it. They include:

- The operative principle is that the "Realm of God" transcends all political systems.
- The gospel is utterly incompatible with all forms of warfare.
- There can be no just war. "We are done with that theory forever."
- No praxis can be called Christian which avoids suffering.There must be no complicity with secular power through acknowledging the legitimacy of laws that protect "the realm of death."
- The Christian is called to be a martyr, i.e., a "witness of the resurrection." "We practice resurrection."[29]

Speaking of Thomas Merton and Dorothy Day, as well as the Berrigan brothers, Lisa Sowle Cahill observes that the tendency to see Catholic pacifists as

24. Gathje, "Cost of Virtue," 252–53; Berrigan, *Testimony*, 7.

25. Berrigan, *Testimony*, 86–87.

26. Ibid., 16.

27. Berrigan, *Isaiah*, 5–6, 12.

28. Berrigan, *Testimony*, 5.

29. Ibid., 221–23.

bound by absolute rules misunderstands their position. The mainspring of moral life is not the "absolutization of any human values but . . . a converted life in Christ that subsumes and often changes every natural pattern of behavior.[30] Berrigan's own clue as to how we should interpret these seemingly absolute principles comes at the end of his series of pronouncements in "An Ethic of Resurrection." "When we spread ashes at the Pentagon, we mime the death-ridden pollution of the place. The drama contains the ethic. When we dig graves on the White House lawn, we pay tribute to the empty grave of Easter, even as we show forth the universal grave to whose brink humanity is being pushed. *The drama is the ethic*."[31] What could be plainer? The Christian is called upon to participate in a drama. Ethics is mimesis. Berrigan links these dramatic actions with such classic moral engagements as Gandhi's march to the sea to gather salt in defiance of British imperial laws.[32] Principles are, at best, stage directions. The drama is the ethic. Here we see a shift from ethics as the pronouncement of moral principles to ethics as the performance of the truth. Berrigan takes as his model Jesus before Pilate. The truth, if it is to set us free, must undergo a trial. A similar drama is enacted in Gandhi's *satyagraha*.[33] In the passion of Jesus the drama focuses on death as a social method: "The ethic of Jesus . . . ," Berrigan affirms, "issues from the ever so slight edge He grants to life. He grants the edge in the 'life versus death' conflict of the Easter hymn (better, He was the edge) from the edge."[34]

An ethic of resistance stems from a life with an edge, lived on the edge. Berrigan's ethic of resistance, Gathje argues, is less optimistic about the possibilities for radical social transformation than that of liberation theology.[35] There is, after all, the miming of the Fall which is the fate of all empires. "The empires rise, the empire does unutterable harm in the world, then the empire declines and falls."[36] I mentioned earlier Gathje's argument that Berrigan's ethics of resistance is specifically different from Hauerwas's countercultural Christian ethics. Both speak of the church as a community of resistance that sustains an alternative way of life. Both see the hankering for efficacy as a temptation to abandon discipleship. But Berrigan is committed to ac-

30. Cahill, *Love Your Enemies*, 211–13.

31. Berrigan, *Testimony*, 223; italics added.

32. Ibid., 224.

33. Gathje, "Cost of Virtue," 161–63; Berrigan, *No Bars to Manhood*, 45–47.

34. Berrigan, *Testimony*, 220.

35. Gathje, "Cost of Virtue," 155, 288–89. Gathje sees a change in Berrigan's thought as the Vietnam War ground on symbolized in the shift of the prominence of Teilhard de Chardin to that of Dietrich Bonhoeffer. Ibid., 143.

36. Berrigan, *Testimony*, 175–76.

tions which are both public and political and which, in the words of a recent Protestant manifesto of resistance, "hold up a picture not just for the church but also for the world."[37] Gathje sees the Berrigans as sectarians neither in their theology nor in their ethics.[38] Their actions also were intensely public performances, declarations of resistance directed to the whole American public. These public acts of resistance are grounded theologically in a hope against hope. "For us, all these repeated arrests, the interminable jailings, the life of our small communities, the discipline of nonviolence, these have embodied an ethic of resurrection. Simply put, we long to taste that event, its thunders and quakes, its great yes. *We want to test the resurrection in our bones.*"[39] In marvelous concision, Berrigan singles out: (a) acts of resistance, (b) alternative communities, and (c) the spiritual discipline of nonviolence as the three-pronged overcoming of death as a social method in the experience of resurrection.

THE POET'S ETHICS

We discussed earlier Mark Johnson's contention that the moral landscape is not a product of abstract reasoning but that it is metaphorically mapped. In this light, Johnson argues that the principal task of ethics is "not the formulation of moral laws, but the cultivation of the moral imagination."[40] If the landscape of reality is constantly changing, it must be mapped and remapped. Who better to do this than a poet? In chapter 1, I argued that Berrigan, the prophet, is more than a prophet. Here I want to revisit several of the poems that we looked at earlier that take us further than the

37. Cobb, foreword to *Resistance*, xii. Cobb's edited volume is presented as a challenge to liberal Christians. It recognizes that *in some respects* reform of key political institutions is not a real possibility. "In the early church," George Pixley reminds us, "Christians could not affect the imperial policies and teachings. They could, nevertheless, refuse to accept the imperial ideology and could organize their lives around different principles. . . . Similarly in Nazi Germany those Christian who joined the Confessing Church had no expectation of reforming the government. Resistance meant refusal to conform to Nazi ideas and to the practices of the too-compliant recognized churches." Pixley, "Bible's Call to Resist," 25. In such a situation, Christians are called to resist the "principalities and powers," but, in contrast to Hauerwas, they continue to practice reform through building alliances with other progressives wherever possibilities arise. Cobb, foreword to *Resistance*. In terms of possibilities for reform, Berrigan is far more skeptical than Cobb's vision of progressive Christians, and Berrigan did not practice the politics of building alliances to seek reform after the mid-'60s.

38. Gathje, "Cost of Virtue," 8.

39. Berrigan, *Testimony*, 224–25; italics added.

40. Johnson, *Moral Imagination*, xii.

commentaries on the prophets. In "Hope, That Intransitive Being," the passionate austerity of the prophet living on and acting from the edge gives way to something else: Hope "hopes for—nothing / like poetry like Zen like God." The moral life which seems to be utterly transitive—"What must I do? I must do X"—rests on something far more elusive—a radical openness shorn of specific plans or expectations. Yet we must imagine the moral agent as blissful as "a mouse in Swiss cheese."[41]

Gathje points out that the Berrigan brothers became engaged in political action first in the civil rights movement as theological liberals shaped by the teachings of the Second Vatican Council. In Daniel's case, the earlier priest-worker movement in France provided moral exemplars of *kenosis*, emptying oneself in order to respond to the world's suffering.[42] This kenotic openness is expressed in an incarnational theology which, I believe, persists throughout Berrigan's life. "To put on the universe as another body. Or to put on the Body of Christ as another (and the only) Body. One and the same investing."[43]

The lyricism of intransitive hope, it seems to me, is grounded in this incarnational theology. One marvelous poem, also examined earlier, conveys the way in which the sacred thisness of the commonplace breaks through the empire's internal and external brutality. In "Eucharist" a prison liturgy is mediated by, of all people, the warden, and the blood of Christ is shared in a cracked cup as "prisoner's pot luck."[44] Community refuses to be locked down and pot luck turns out to be the most nourishing food and drink. This poem, I suggest, conveys both Berrigan's distinctive ethics of resistance and the power of transcendence. To celebrate the Eucharist within prison walls is to deny the power of the state to isolate and sever the bonds that tie us together. It creates community in the very beastly belly of prison, the anti-community. Likewise, in "Children in the Shelter" we see that saving a child from your own country's bombs is more than an act of compassion; it is compassion in defiance of death as a social method.[45] Compassion toward those confined to the edges is compassion with an edge. The Eucharist celebrated and the child rescued are political acts, acts performed eyeball to eyeball with the "age's horrific eye." The community created beats against the prison walls.

41. *Testimony*, 226–27.

42. Gathje, "Cost of Virtue," 72–111.

43. Daniel Berrigan, *Consequences: Truth And . . .*, 42–43. Note the difference in tone between Berrigan's reflections on the prophets and their critique of empire and the incarnational theology operative in some of the more lyrical poems.

44. Berrigan, "Eucharist," 124–25.

45. Berrigan, "Children in the Shelter," 114–15.

THICH NHAT HANH: TAPPING OUR INNATE CAPACITY TO BE PEACE

Chapter 2 examined the play that Thich Nhat Hanh wrote in memory of five young graduates of his School of Youth for Social Service brutally murdered for refusing to take sides in the Vietnam War. It also focused on Berrigan's comments in his foreword to the play on the quality of inwardness expressed in this genuinely Buddhist art, a serenity that eludes our Western consciousness. Berrigan was awestruck that the Vietnamese dead might return "not as ministers of vengeance, but sacramental presences, angels, spirits of new creation?"[46] Berrigan's language reflects his own Christian viewpoint; it would be more accurate to say that the murdered youth have become—or, more precisely, continue to be—bodhisattvas. The brutal murder of these youth has torn the world's fragile web, but in Thich Nhat Hanh's play the afterglow of the dead is a benign and healing presence. In death as in life, they continually reweave the web that connects all of us. The practice of weaving, we might say, is the moral act.

Buddhist ethics must be considered within the soteriological framework outlined in the Four Noble Truths.[47] The dis-ease (dukkha) is diagnosed in the First and Second Truths and the Third Noble Truth turns our minds to our own capacity (in Mahayana teaching grounded in our Buddha Nature) to heal ourselves. A moral life comes into play as an intrinsic element of the Fourth Noble Truth—the Eightfold Path. Moral life, therefore, is developmental in character and part of a systematic training.[48] Practice, not adherence to a deontological command, anchors the moral life. To understand this argument that Buddhist ethics is a species of virtue ethics, let us look at a fuller version of the passage from Damien Keown's *The Nature of Buddhist Ethics* that I cited earlier:

> The virtues are not simply means to an end which transcends them. What is distinctive about the virtues is that they participate in and *constitute* the end. . . . The virtues are means to the gradual realization of the end through the incarnation of the end in the present. Living in accordance with the end, is . . . "a progressive articulation of the end itself. . . ." The Buddha displayed this clearly in the exercise of the moral virtues both

46. Berrigan, foreword to *Love in Action*, 7.

47. Ives, "Deploying the Dharma," 23–43.

48. King, *Socially Engaged Buddhism*, 30–31. The Noble Eightfold Path is traditionally divided into three categories: sila, samadhi, and prajna—morality, meditation or concentration, and insight. Keown sees samadhi as "a means for the promotion of and participation in the basic goods of morality and knowledge." *Buddhist Ethics*, 38.

> before and after his enlightenment—they were a necessary and central part of his life. . . . It is because of this internal relationship between virtue and the *summum bonum* that the Aristotelian and . . . Buddhist ethical schemes are teleological rather than consequentialist.[49]

In making this argument, Keown explicitly rejects those scholarly interpretations of Buddhist moral life that see it as akin to the raft that takes one to the other shore—at which point the raft is left behind. Morality (*sila*) and insight (*prajna*), compassion and wisdom are mutually supportive. Neither can be reached or sustained in isolation from the other.[50]

While Keown focuses primarily on the Theravada tradition, he sees the Mahayana tradition maintaining the same marriage of ethics and insight, wisdom and compassion. The paradigm shift in ethics that comes with the Mahayana is a shift from self-control leading to personal development to "the function of moral virtue as a dynamic other-regarding quality." In the Mahayana tradition, the "field of activity," what we might call the reach or scope of ethics, becomes infinite. The first bodhisattva vow is to liberate all sentient beings: "And this is why," an early Mahayana text proclaims, "any failing by the *bodhisattva* is extremely serious: by his failing he places the welfare of all beings in jeopardy."[51]

Moreover, the understanding of Buddha Nature has important implications for the moral life. It grounds a root confidence in our capacity to follow the Eightfold Path and removes all hints that Buddhist practice is world denying. Ultimate reality and everyday reality are "not two."[52] Because the concept of Buddha Nature radicalizes the Third Noble Truth, there is a new twist to the understanding of virtue and the training that accompanies it: the cultivation of virtue gets us nowhere. It gets us nowhere because we, like all sentient beings, are Buddhas. The cultivation of virtue is not for the purpose of creating some other state of being. "Why then do we practice?" asked Dogen. Imagine a muddy pond. Gradually the mud may settle and the water becomes clear, transparent. But it never becomes something other than what it has always been—water. Practice and realization, Dogen argues, are nondual.[53] Recall Thich Nhat Hanh's discussion with the peace activist, Jim Forest, about washing the dishes that we examined in chapter 2. We wash dishes not to get them done and out of the way. We wash dishes

49. Keown, *Buddhist Ethics*, 193–94.

50. Ibid., 108–10.

51. Ibid., 131, 155.

52. King, *Buddha Nature*, 159–68.

53. Dogen, "Guidelines for the Study of the Way," 131–43.

just to wash dishes. Every act can be part of a practice and every practice is the realization of our Buddha Nature.

Keown's argument for the interdependence of a virtuous life and an awakened life is contested by some scholars. Here we must confront the issue that the moral life is a raft that can be left aside once we have achieved true enlightenment as it is raised about Thich Nhat Hanh's ethics in particular. Darrel Fasching and Dell Dechant, in their important work, *Comparative Religious Ethics: A Narrative Approach*, take as their key to interpreting Buddhist ethics a single article by the renowned Zen Buddhist scholar, Masao Abe. In their reading, Abe argues that ethics rests on the judgment of good and evil and, as such, is a form of dualistic thinking. Dualism must be and is transcended in the experience of enlightenment. Abe uses Kierkegaard's expression, "the teleological suspension of the ethical," to convey this transcendence. Moreover, Fasching and Descant quote a very unfortunate interpretation of karma by Abe in which he seems to assign some responsibility for the Holocaust to the victims themselves—an idea that Fasching and Descant, rightly, consider abhorrent. After Auschwitz and Hiroshima, they contend, there must be a bright line separating good and evil.[54]

For our purposes, whether or not Fasching and Descant have fairly interpreted Abe is of less importance than the fact that they read Thich Nhat Hanh as drawing the same conclusions as Abe about the dualistic nature of ethical judgment. However we interpret Abe, it must be said, first, that this is a somewhat odd conclusion to make regarding Thich Nhat Hanh given his explicit development of the Fourteen Mindfulness Trainings of the Order of Interbeing that I will discuss later in this chapter. The Mindfulness Trainings are binding on all members of the Order, lay people as well as monks and nuns. Nowhere in Thich Nhat Hanh's writings is it even hinted that for some advanced practitioners they would be suspended. It is as if the Buddha, after his enlightenment experience, had dispensed with the moral requirements embedded in the Eightfold Path.

Fasching and Descant come to this conflation of Thich Nhat Hanh's position with Abe's based on their reading of Thich Nhat Hanh's signature poem, "Please Call Me by My True Names," which we examined in chapter 2. Particularly the stanza that focuses on the rape of a young girl by a sea pirate and her subsequent suicide drives their critique. In their reading, the Mahayana teaching of emptiness and interdependence enacted

54. Fasching and Descant, *Comparative Religious Ethic*, 77–80. It should be clearly stated that engaged Buddhists uniformly reject such interpretations of karma. See, inter alia, Loy, *Money, Sex, War, Karma*, 53–63. It also should be noted that the actual passages that Fasching and Descant quote from Abe, while problematic, are more nuanced than these authors acknowledge.

through compassion means that the self becomes the other—Thich Nhat Hanh becomes the sea pirate such that "the very categories of 'good' and 'evil' disappear. . . . Refusing to judge others, [Thich Nhat Hanh expresses] an enlightenment that carries him beyond dualistic judgments of good and evil."[55]

The two authors argue, moreover, that Thich Nhat Hanh's commentary on the poem would seem to exonerate the sea pirate because of his conclusion that he himself might have become a sea pirate if subjected to similar "causes and conditions." In their judgment, Thich Nhat Hanh fails to acknowledge that not everyone raised in impoverished conditions becomes a sea pirate. "Karma is rooted in choice," Fasching and Descant conclude, "not fate. That is what makes us responsible for our karma."[56] So, while Thich Nhat Hanh does not in any sense blame the victim—the twelve-year-old girl—his conclusions, these authors contend, do undermine our moral responsibility for our own actions.

Fasching and Descant are absolutely correct about one thing: this one phrase, "I am the sea pirate," is the key to Thich Nhat Hanh's ethics. In chapter 2, I argued that Thich Nhat Hanh and engaged Buddhism in general seek to enhance our sense of moral responsibility by forestalling any implicit claims to moral superiority. The poem, I insisted, is not about some abstract ethical theory; it is about my heart. Because this poem is so crucial, let me see if we can shed more light on it by contrasting this interpretation with Fasching and Descant's. The sea pirate has failed to see and to love and so have I. I am also the twelve-year old girl; the world's violence *in some sense* is shared by me. Do I then despair? No, the logic of interdependence is to empower the self as a moral actor, not to suspend the ethical. The Pali Canon puts it bluntly: "This being, that becomes; from the arising of this, that arises; this not becoming, that does not become; from the ceasing of this, that ceases."[57] We can paraphrase this famous statement of interdependence in this way: Because Charles Strain is as he is, sea pirates come to be and young girls suffer grievously. Charles Strain ceasing to be as he is now, sea pirates may also cease to be and young girls no longer suffer. To think through the meaning of the saying in this way is not to inflate my sense of efficacy—I alone do not cause sea pirates to cease their piracy—rather it is to say that my actions, my inactions, and whom I become matter. The ripples of my actions, my

55. Fasching and Descant, *Comparative Religious Ethics*, 156–58.

56. Ibid., 161.

57. *Majjhima Nikaya* 2:32; *Samytuta Nikaya* 2:28.

becoming who I am, spread out indefinitely. The Dalai Lama refers to this moral sense as an ethic of "universal responsibility."[58]

Another way to address Fasching and Descant would be to ask, "What does it mean to say that I am *not* the sea pirate?" After all, "I" have not performed such heinous actions. From Thich Nhat Hanh's point of view, in segregating myself from such evil I create a deluded perception of my own moral superiority. Ethical judgments that create such a deluded understanding fail to acknowledge the many hidden (and not so hidden) ways in which I am complicit in horrendous crimes. (Without the Vietnam War, and the inadequacy of my efforts and others' to resist it, there would not likely have been the massive exodus of the Vietnamese "boat people" to which the poem directly refers).

Sallie King has, perhaps, given more attention to this poem and to the ethics of engaged Buddhism in general than any other scholar. She argues that engaged Buddhist ethics are non-judgmental and non-adversarial but they are not suspended in the enlightenment experience.

> Since there is no fixed human self, there is no fixed thing or essence in us that would be appropriate to label "good" or "bad" in a static way, as if that defined the being of the person. Obviously the rapist has severely harmed the girl. Since causing pain is always wrong in Buddhism, *we can certainly label this action of the pirate's "wrong,"* but we cannot take this one act as defining the being or innermost essence of the pirate. . . . We have all together constructed this world . . . in which people can be born into crushing poverty and hopelessness. . . . The pirate is responsible for his actions. . . . [However,] I cannot arrogate to myself a superior place, looking down from the distance of my moral superiority upon the pirate. . . . Yet it is proper for me to regard his action as wrong (because it harmed another) and to take action to prevent such actions from occurring.[59]

"We are determined not to kill and not to let others to kill," reads the Twelfth Mindfulness Training. What could be a more blunt injunction to ethically discern which acts are to be supported and which resisted? The teaching of nondualism in Thich Nhat Hanh's case does not suspend the ethical but, on the contrary, greatly broadens its scope and intensifies my sense of moral responsibility.

> Please call me by my true names
> so I can wake up

58. The Dalai Lama, *Ethics for a New Millennium.*

59. King, *Socially Engaged Buddhism*, 27–30; italics added.

and the door of my heart
could be left open
the door of compassion.[60]

THE DHARMA TEACHER

Much of Thich Nhat Hanh's writing elaborates the dharma talks that he gives at the many retreats that he leads each year. The style is informal, laced with anecdotes, stories, and connections to contemporary circumstances, like the repeated references to forty thousand children that die each day of hunger. Aphorisms abound: "A sheet of paper is made of non-paper elements"; "Nonduality means 'not two' but 'not two' also means 'not one'"; "We interare"; "An oak tree is an oak tree. . . . If an oak tree is not an oak tree, then we are all in trouble"; "Please show me your Buddha, your American Buddha."[61] These aphorisms take us to the heart of the Buddhist Dharma but expressed in a new vernacular. Thich Nhat Hanh's aphorisms themselves limn an American—or at least a Western—Buddha.

It is important to note that a dharma talk is not a lecture, although it has a didactic purpose. Such a talk is given usually as an accompaniment to a period of meditation. Imagine Thich Nhat Hanh in brown robes seated on a meditation cushion on a raised dais with a vase of flowers to one side slowly striking a bell on his other side. The bell resounds in the silent hall. Only after the last sound waves have disappeared does he begin to speak. The dharma talk grows out of meditative silence. Like the bell, the silence resonates within the space of practice. Ethical instruction as part of the dharma talk is guidance in a practice that arises within the meditation hall. We bring all of our suffering, both personal and collective, with us when we meditate and compost it.[62] Meditative concentration and the dharma talk which completes it are the sun illuminating the compost, catalyzing the chemical process. The talk, then, leads us back into the world to alleviate suffering.

As part of this analysis of the ethics of the bodhisattva, I want to look at *Being Peace*, perhaps the classic expression of the catechism of engaged Buddhism. The talks that comprise *Being Peace* are clearly directed to an audience of peace activists. They reflect Thich Nhat Hanh's experience in the late '60s with an American peace movement full of vitriol, torn by internal

60. Nhat Hanh, "Please Call Me," 72–73.

61. Nhat Hanh, *Being Peace*, 13, 33, 45, 52, 86, 88.

62. Ibid., 46–48, 51–55.

ideological conflicts, and every bit as much directed toward victory over enemies as the Pentagon that it fought. "A fresh way of being peace, doing peace is needed," Thich Nhat Hanh affirmed, and *Being Peace* laid out an alternative—peace work as the *practice* of being peace.[63]

Oddly enough for a Buddhist thoroughly aware of the First Noble Truth and a Vienamese monk who lived and struggled through the horror of the Vietnam War, Thich Nhat Hanh begins by affirming that "suffering is not enough." Presumably peace activists are well aware of the pain and suffering wreaked by the endless conflicts across the globe. The fulcrum of Buddhist practice, as I have argued, is the Third Noble Truth—our innate capacity to wake up, to understand what is going on, within us and without, and to love. It is this capacity that grounds our efforts to *be* peace.[64]

If we are constantly churned up, thrown off kilter by the world's suffering, worried about when the bombs will explode, we are not of much use. The ideal peacemaker, Thich Nhat Hanh affirms at the beginning of his second talk, is the one person in a small boat caught in a storm who remains calm. That person practices the action of non-action. "Sometimes if we don't do anything, we help more than if we do a lot." Later Thich Nhat Hanh elaborates that mind and situation are reciprocally related. "The nature of the bombs, the nature of injustice, the nature of the weapons and the nature of our own being are the same." If we would work for nuclear disarmament, we must defuse the bombs in our own hearts. The real truth is that the world situation is a reflection of how we lead our daily lives.[65]

In this light Thich Nhat Hanh's guidance runs in two complementary directions. The first is to elaborate on our innate capacity by exploring what it means to take refuge in the Three Jewels: the Buddha, the Dharma, and the Sangha. The second is to ground a Buddhist approach to ethics in a Buddhist psychology. When I say that "I take refuge in the Buddha," Thich Nhat Hanh argues, what I mean is "I go back and rely on the Buddha in me." We should think through what it means to "go back." The prophet's resounding no, I have argued, is a way to peal our eyes back. Here the bodhisattva collects herself, returns from dispersion. "Anything that can help you wake up has Buddha Nature. When I am alone and a bird calls to me, I return to myself." The universe itself becomes the *Dharmakaya*, the body of the Dharma, so that everything—a pebble, a tree, a bird's song—can wake me up. Similarly, when we practice we are linked to the *Sanghakaya*. Buddha,

63. Ibid., 81–82. On the Buddhist peace movement during the Vietnam War, see King, "Thich Nhat Hanh," 321–63.

64. Nhat Hanh, *Being Peace*, 13–18.

65. Ibid., 21, 33, 77.

Dharma, and Sangha, in truth, are only realized in practice; *they* take refuge in us.[66]

Misperception, Thich Nhat Hanh believes, leads to feelings which cloud our minds, upset our bodies, and warp our actions. He gives the example of a man in a boat who yells repeatedly with increasing anger at another boat coming straight for him until he realizes that there is no one in the boat. Correct perception involves an awareness of how all reality dependently co-arises. When we objectify phenomena, we misperceive the way in which we are interconnected. To truly understand,we must practice seeing the ways in which my reality and that of the other are "not two."[67] Reification begins with our own reality. Thich Nhat Hanh says we must learn to contemplate "body in the body," "feelings in the feelings," and "mind in the mind." The purpose of this rhetorical repetition is to underline that we cannot truly understand anything by standing apart from it. I must learn to do this first with myself. In chapter 2 we examined the process of mindfully composting our anger. Here let us examine this process more deeply by looking at a key formulation of the process.

> If I have a feeling of anger, how would I deal with it . . . ? I would not look upon anger as something foreign to me that I have to fight, to have surgery in order to remove it. I know that anger is me and I am anger, Nonduality, not two. I have to deal with my anger with care, with love, with tenderness, with nonviolence. . . . If we annihilate anger, we annihilate ourselves. Dealing with anger in that way would be like transforming yourself into a battlefield, tearing yourself into parts. . . . We cannot destroy the energy [of anger]; we can only convert it into a more constructive energy.[68]

This commentary on dealing with our feelings says a great deal about Thich Nhat Hanh's approach to the moral life, about why being peace is the only truly effective way to make peace. First, one begins with oneself. What Sallie King said about engaged Buddhist ethics being nonjudgmental and non-adversarial must be practiced in our relationship with our own self. Second, notice the martial metaphors that Thich Nhat Hanh employs in showing us how *not* to relate to ourselves: fighting our anger, annihilating it, turning our psyche into a battlefield. These are not "merely" metaphors,

66. Ibid., 23, 32, 36.

67. As we have seen, "not two" should be understood in tandem with "not one." Thich Nhat Hanh indicates that is why Buddhists speak not of oneness but of nonduality. Ibid., 41–43.

68. Ibid., 46–47.

rather they are indicative of an understanding of nonviolence that is coherent whether we are speaking about our inner conflicts or the conflict between nations. Taking sides does not work. The energies that manifest in conflicts at all levels cannot be annihilated; they can be transformed.

I am reminded of Freud's argument in *Civilization and Its Discontents* that what we call morality is a form of coercion rooted in the superego, a form of violence. It is necessary to produce civilization, by restraining wayward impulses, but it makes us discontent—or as a Buddhist would put it, we experience *dukkha*. The point of introducing the term nonviolence into our discussion of feelings is implicitly a moral argument against Freud: (a) we must not ignore our feelings if we want to practice the moral life; (b) there can be another way in which the moral agent comes to act than through the superego's violence; and (c) the practice of the moral life is a practice of nonviolence at all levels, whether we are contemplating the body in the body, feelings in the feelings or, correlatively, my relationships in my relationships or the society in the society.

Thich Nhat Hanh's treatment of feelings also says something about his attunement to his audience. At one point he says parenthetically that in America many have come to Buddhism "not by the door of faith but by the door of psychology." Rather than disparaging this fact, Thich Nhat Hanh works with it. He acknowledges that he, too, feels alienated from this society and feels the urge to withdraw. Given the mutual interpenetration of all reality, society is not something external; it is deeply rooted in our feelings, our anxieties, our despair. If we bring society with us into the meditation hall, we also must bring practice into our everyday lives. "Do you practice smiling while cutting carrots?" Thich Nhat Hanh asks. Means and ends are not two. To make peace, we must be peace. Cutting carrots mindfully can be a practice of being peace but otherwise it seems remote from getting a Buddhist social ethics off the ground. Not so, argues Thich Nhat Hanh. Being awake means knowing the myriad ways in which our lives are intertwined with others who suffer and acting on that awareness. The nonduality of practice and enlightenment is a constantly renewed process of deepening and expanding awareness which, in turn, calls forth transformative action.[69] Taking a stand, say, by adopting a vegetarian diet and encouraging others to do so as well, does not entail taking sides, e.g., by demonizing the agribusiness industry. It, after all, co-arises with my food habits and could co-cease in its present form through my eating more mindfully. Such an

69. Nhat Hanh, *Being Peace*, 52–55, 58–59 68–69, 86–88; Nhat Hanh, *Interbeing*, 3–6.

understanding, it must be insisted, does not preclude organizing for collective as well as personal action.

THE FOURTEEN MINDFULNESS TRAININGS

When he was exiled to the West, Thich Nhat Hanh changed the name of the Tiep Hien Order to the Order of Interbeing so that it would be more intelligible to Western audiences. He also changed the fourteen precepts to fourteen "mindfulness trainings."[70] He did so to avoid connotations of commandments attached to the term precepts by Western audiences. "Mindfulness trainings are practices not prohibitions." We freely take it upon ourselves to transform ourselves. Again, we do not seek a stage when these trainings would be set aside.[71] Moral action is not obedience to a divine will nor the application of principles derived from reason. It is a response to an open investigation of reality.

Thich Nhat Hanh points out that the first seven of the trainings focus on the mind, the next two on speech, and the final five on the body. This is in contrast to the five traditional Buddhist precepts for lay people, four of which focus on the body and one on speech. The structure of each training is important. All fourteen begin with awareness. Eleven of the fourteen begin with awareness of some specific form of suffering; two with awareness of the nature of true happiness and one with awareness of what constitutes a sangha (understanding and compassion). "Aware that looking deeply at the nature of suffering can help us develop compassion and find ways out of suffering," reads the Fourth Training, "we are determined not to avoid or close our eyes before suffering." This process, in fact, epitomizes what occurs with each of the trainings. Becoming aware of the specific traits of suffering, the moral agent begins, as it were, with the First and Second Noble Truth. But in his commentary on the Fourth Training, Thich Nhat Hanh takes pains to note that the First and Second Truths must be balanced by the Third and Fourth. We must nurture and safeguard our capacity to love. "When we are peaceful and happy we will not create suffering in others. When we work to alleviate suffering in others, we feel peaceful and happy. Practice is not just for ourselves but for others and the whole of society." This, he concludes, is

70. The Fourteen Mindfulness Trainings are based on the fifty-eight precepts for both monastic and lay Buddhists developed in China and presented in the *Brahma's Net Sutra*. According to that fifth-century CE document, these trainings are "the source of all Buddhas; the root of all bodhisattvas; and the original Buddha-nature itself." Because our Buddha Nature is always present, these trainings came into being. *Path of Compassion*, 54; Nhat Hanh, *Opening the Heart*, 11.

71. Nhat Hanh, *Interbeing*, 7; Nhat Hanh, *Being Peace*, 90.

the bodhisattva way.[72] The opening clause of each of the trainings is then followed by "We are determined to . . ." or by "We are committed to . . . ," indicating that we, *as a sangha*, have undertaken an ongoing practice that in essence is a response to suffering and the assumption of responsibility to alleviate it.

In chapter 2, we saw that the first three mindfulness trainings locate the problem of suffering (dukkha) in the mind with its misperceptions and these trainings, much as the prophet's critique of idolatry, are meant as an ideology solvent. By placing the suffering caused by ideologies in the First Training, Thich Nhat Hanh focuses squarely on the dukkha rooted in the modern state and in mass movements whose utopian aspirations frequently lead to dogmatism. Ideological absolutism and rigidity are responsible for the killing of millions in the modern world. The truths that we apprehend are guiding means only. We are to practice remaining open to the possibility of new insights, new truths, and, correlatively, urging respect for the views of others by refusing to impose our views on them. This is not a bland, laissez-faire attitude, because we are to urge others to renounce fanaticism. "Compassionate dialogue," Thich Nhat Hanh comments, "is the essence of nonviolent action (ahimsa)." Nonviolence appears here as a form of non-coercive engagement. One takes a stand while being open to change deriving from new insights.[73]

The Fourth Training we have already discussed. Briefly we can summarize the remaining ten trainings. The Fifth and Sixth Trainings deal respectively with the poisons of craving and hatred or aversion. Simple, mindful living with anger composted leads us to dwell in the present moment, to savor it—the focus of the Seventh Training. The Eight and Ninth Trainings focus on non-divisive speech as a critical factor in building community and reconciling conflicts. The Tenth Training discusses how that community, once formed, engages the larger society without succumbing to partisanship. The Eleventh Training focuses on right livelihood, how we shape our work life as a mindful practice. The final three trainings conform to three of the five traditional precepts but here given an expanded focus. The Twelfth Training, corresponding to the precept not to kill, focuses on nonviolence in its many forms; the Thirteenth, corresponding to the traditional precept not to steal, focuses on social justice broadly speaking and the virtue of generosity. Finally, the Fourteenth Training, corresponding to the precept not to engage in sexual misconduct, expands the meaning of this precept to

72. Nhat Hanh, *Interbeing*, 30–31.

73. Ibid., 8, 23–29, 106.

include our overall responsibility for our relationships, for the lives that we bring into the world, and the world that we bring them into.

A principle of nonviolent transformation is at work in several of the trainings, particularly trainings that involve us in resisting the actions of others. We vow not to kill "and not to let others kill" (#12). We respect property rights but "will try to prevent others from profiteering from human suffering or the suffering of other beings" (#13). How we do that without imposing our views on others (#3) involves a delicate balance. The sangha should not be politicized, but it should take a clear stand against injustice. It should try to change the unjust situation but it should not take sides in partisan conflicts (#10).[74] Approaching these trainings involves direct experimentation using appropriate skillful means. Appropriateness refers to the dual responsibility of any form of moral direction: it should be true to the Buddha's teachings and it should be adapted to the needs of the society.[75] The multiple forms of nonviolence expressed in the trainings correspond to the nature of violence as multidimensional with each of the dimensions reinforcing the other. So, mindless consumption is a form of violence which buttresses structural violence, ranging from agribusiness practices that destroy the environment to world hunger and the exploitation of the poor to feed the rich.[76] However, the very phrase "being peace" makes it clear that with each of the trainings a personal transformation is called for. In each case, the Buddhist teaching which sees inner and outer transformation as mutually implicated is upheld.

So, what is the purpose of these trainings? When asked what he hoped to accomplish through the practice of mindfulness, Thich Nhat Hanh responded by quoting a stanza from a poem that he had written: "The work of building will take ten thousand lives / But dear one, look— / That work has been achieved ten thousand lives ago." Then he comments: "Do you need to become a Buddha . . . ? The wave does not have to seek to become water—she *is* water, right here and now. In the same way, you are already . . . a Buddha. . . . What is essential is to enter the path of practice to realize this truth and help others realize it too." To undertake a Buddhist practice is to

74. Some engaged Buddhists avoid the discourse of justice as too adversarial. Thich Nhat Hanh, however, uses the term but qualifies it by adding that we are not to take partisan stances. We will take up this issue of what sort of justice this can mean in chapter 5.

75. Nhat Hanh, *Opening the Heart*, 132–33. Thich Nhat Hanh offers another image for appropriateness and skillful means by pointing to the thousand arms of Avalokiteshvara. In the palm of each hand is an eye representing insight into the myriad forms of sufferings of others. In each hand is a different instrument signifying skillful means for addressing myriad suffering. Ibid.

76. Nhat Hanh, *Interbeing*, 47–48.

enact a paradox. On the one hand, Thich Nhat Hanh says, "The bodhisattva vows are immense." They are the work of ten thousand lives. On the other hand, he equally affirms: "The very moment we make the determination to live according to these trainings and practices, joy, healing and transformation become possible right away."[77] The work of ten thousand lives is already accomplished.

Just as Daniel Berrigan's ethics is undergirded and transformed by his sense of the Incarnation, Thich Nhat Hanh's ethics is grounded in the expansive vision of the Avatamsaka Sutra: "A student asked me, 'Thay, there are so many urgent problems, what should I do?' I said, 'Take one thing and do it very deeply and carefully, and you will be doing everything at the same time.'"[78] The aim of practice is to enlarge, to open our heart to this interpenetration and its endless ramifications. "With deep looking and deep touching; we can transform this world into the world of Avatamsaka. . . . It depends on us."[79] So, in a deep sense ethics is absorbed into a religious vision but not suspended, as Abe and Fasching and Descant have argued. Instead, our actions are seen as having infinite reverberations. Practice is far more than the self-cultivation of virtue. Each and every virtuous act is precisely an opening to the heart of the cosmos.

THE VIRTUE ETHICS OF THE BODHISATTVA AND THE PROPHET

Let us return now to the hypothesis that we opened this chapter with, namely, that Thich Nhat Hanh, the bodhisattva, and Daniel Berrigan, the prophet, although they have a broader intent than creating a formal ethics, do offer us two species of virtue ethics. Martha Nussbaum argues that the heterogeneous group of philosophers who seek to develop a "virtue ethics" are united by their attention to agents and not simply actions, to the internal springs of action and to the development of moral agency over long periods of time.[80] Since Keown juxtaposes Buddhist ethics to Aristotle's understanding of virtue, it might be helpful to view Thich Nhat Hanh in juxtaposition to Nussbaum's conscious effort to craft a neo-Aristotelian social ethics. She points to four traits that, taken as a set, distinguish in her mind this form of virtue ethics from its rivals.

77. Ibid., 51; Nhat Hanh, *Opening the Heart*, 80–81.

78. Nhat Hanh, "Sun My Heart," 136–37.

79. Nhat Hanh, *Cultivating Love*, 90, 103–4.

80. Nussbaum, "Virtue Ethics," 170.

- The internal goods sought through human action are multiple and qualitatively different. Think of the difference among friendship, meaningful work and social justice.
- Reason plays a key role in prioritizing among these goods and harmonizing them.
- Emotions and passions are "complex forms of intentionality" that can be shaped by reason.
- Our present understanding about the good, especially as developed through "pernicious fictions," shapes defective passions that must be critiqued and reshaped.[81]

Certainly Thich Nhat Hanh's Mindfulness Trainings discuss a reasonably comprehensive variety of human internal goods, from peace to justice, from patterns of consumption and simple living to forms of communication, from intimate sexual relationships to the care of our children. Yet these various goods are unified by the telos of emancipated awareness. Apart from mindfulness, the different pursuits of internal goods cannot be called virtuous.

Second, awareness—insight or wisdom (*prajna*)—is much broader than Aristotle's reason. It arises through meditative concentration (*samadhi*), as well as from the cultivation of virtue (*sila*). It goes well beyond the philosopher's discursive reason to include the way in which we eat a tangerine or drink a cup of tea. It is much closer to Aristotle's practical wisdom (*phronesis*) except that the *samadhi* that is necessary for Buddhist wisdom involves spiritual disciplines not found at least in neo-Aristotelian philosophies.

Third, Thich Nhat Hanh certainly agrees with Nussbaum's understanding of the intentionality of emotions and passions. We "compost" our anger and thereby retain and redirect its energy, but again, composting involves a wider range of spiritual disciplines (stopping, looking deeply, treating our anger with compassion, etc.) than is generally comprised in a rational critique. Fourth, Thich Nhat Hanh would agree completely that our society (as infected by the three poisons of ignorance, greed, and hatred) shapes defective passions, which when crystallized into ideologies can lead to the killing of millions. When it comes to actually reshaping our passions, the Fourteen Mindfulness Trainings are more practical and more ambitious than anything that even such a wide-ranging philosopher as Martha Nussbaum has come up with. The practice of the trainings draws upon a

81. Ibid., 180. Nussbaum develops the idea of "pernicious fictions" in *Frontiers of Justice*, 413.

two-and-a-half-millennia Buddhist tradition of healing our poisoned selves and societies. Finally, it should be noted that a basic confidence in human capacity underlies Nussbaum's neo-Aristotelian ethics and, as we have seen, there is a similar confidence to Thich Nhat Hanh's ethics grounded in the Third Noble Truth and in our Buddha Nature.

"What I am suggesting, then," Martha Nussbaum concludes, "is that the education of the emotions, to succeed at all, needs to take place in a culture of ethical criticism, and especially self-criticism, in which ideas of equal respect for humanity will be active players in the effort to curtail the excesses of the greedy self."[82] By contrast, Thich Nhat Hanh sees the training of one's emotions taking place in a community of practice in which compassion is directed toward oneself, softening the edges of criticism. The community sustains the practice; apart from a multitude of such communities, we can never hope to create a "culture of ethical criticism."

In a time of moral devolution, we have argued, a strenuous life of virtue is called for. Not coincidentally, Berrigan turned to the writings of the Hebrew prophets in order to understand the times. "Everyone goes about the appointed tasks in a tranquil, apparently responsible spirit. It is as though sleepwalkers were abroad. . . . We have the socializing of sin, its mimetic power, the passage of quite normal, quotidian activities into perilous areas: the normalization of the abnormal."[83] In such a context, the kind of cultivation of virtue through reason that characterizes Nussbaum's neo-Aristotelianism seems naïve when moral devolution is in full sway. Nussbaum's fourth point about misshapen passions is intensified; society's "pernicious fictions" appear to be perfectly rational. It is the prophet, "towering in moral stature, ardent and harsh in love, clairvoyant, fiery," who appears to be mad.[84] Sweet reason is hardly up to the task of transforming these passions in such a context. It is the prophet's ardent and harsh love that dispels the pall, removes the scales, grapples with the normalized abnormal passions. The slower work of reason that Nussbaum affirms in her third point is replaced by the prophet's lacerating denunciations. While most of us seek to cultivate multiple goods and to harmonize and prioritize among them when we must, as in Nussbaum's first and second points, the prophet follows Soren Kierkegaard's admonition: Purity of heart is to will one thing. That one thing is God's justice.

82. Nussbaum, "Compassion and Terror," 25.

83. Berrigan, *Jeremiah*, 43.

84. Ibid., 43. A case in point of a pernicious fiction masquerading as the upholding of law and order and national security would be the trial and conviction of the nonviolent Transform Now Plowshares group under federal statutes that labeled them as terrorists. See http://transformnowplowshares.wordpress.com.

In his introduction to an essay on the peacemaking church, Berrigan quotes Dietrich Bonhoeffer: "Now it will be necessary simply to hold on, to light the fires of truth here and there, so that eventually the entire structure will collapse."[85] It is hard to imagine a position further from Nussbaum's neo-Aristotelian account of virtue in its relationship to a just society than this quotation from Bonhoeffer. It hardly fits with the essentially reformist assumptions of Nussbaum's position or, at least, her presupposition that reason, not being fatally compromised, is capable of transforming the pernicious fictions which construct the unjust society. And yet. To hold on, to light fires of truth must be considered virtuous action. Virtue *in extremis*. None of the saints and martyrs that Berrigan celebrated in *Testimony: The Word Made Fresh*, from Dorothy Day to Philip Berrigan, from Dr. King to Archbishop Romero, adopted nonviolence as an abstract moral principle. Rather they came to love and to act nonviolently in the midst of a violent world—even when they themselves met with violence. "We are to stand somewhere, and let come what may," Berrigan says, capturing these remarkable lives in one pithy aphorism.[86] As the American civil rights movement's anthem put it: "Just like a tree that's planted by the water, I will not be moved." With their ruling metaphor of "cultivation," many species of virtue ethics focus on the long haul growth of moral awareness, practical wisdom. But Berrigan's saying alters our understanding of virtue ethics. Before a shoot, a wisp of a tree, can begin to grow, it must root itself and withstand the shock that that entails. If *phronesis* in Thich Nhat Hanh's vision is the opening of the doors of one's heart to the cosmos, in Daniel Berrigan's case it is the knowledge of when and where to act and the courage to stand firm "come what may."

Virtue *in extremis* is what Coetzee's Mrs. Curren comes to embrace in and through her dying body. The brutal reality of apartheid South Africa stripped the scales from her eyes. Daniel Berrigan faced the brutality of the Vietnam War and the nuclear brinksmanship of the 1980s. He, his brother Philip, and their small band of followers threw themselves into the breach and brought the wrath of the warmaking state upon themselves. In the process they stripped the scales from the eyes of more than a few. For his part, Silko's Tayo learns painfully how not to tear apart the fragile web and how to weave it anew. Thich Nhat Hanh, torn from his homeland, began the slow process of building sanghas, communities of refuge where monks, nuns, laymen and laywomen could return to themselves and learn the art and

85. Bonhoeffer, quoted in Berrigan, *Testimony*, 175.

86. Ibid.

practice of being peace. Then he offered us the mindfulness trainings to set us on the long path of virtue.

4

SOCIAL LOCATION AND SOCIAL ETHICS

The Prophet and the Bodhisattva as Nonviolent Agents

Tell all the Truth but tell it slant.[1]

—Emily Dickinson

We have weathered several decades of debate over the role of religious discourse (including religious social ethics) in public life. Much of the debate was fueled by liberal, secularist fears of religion's alleged inherent proclivity for fanaticism and, on the other hand, concerns that the liberal guardians of the gates to the public square could actually succeed in excluding those whose commitments to politics are deeply grounded in faith. Much of the debate has centered upon whether and to what degree religious thinkers would need to abandon the traditional symbols and particular narrative expressions of their religious vision in order to make the case for their understanding of the common good by adopting more generic versions of rational argumentation. Understandably, numerous religious thinkers with all sorts of political convictions have bridled against going through such a screening device in order to enter the public square.[2]

1. Dickinson, *Final Harvest*, 248.

2. For surveys of various positions in this long debate with particular attention to the issue of social ethics, see Hollenbach, *Global Face*, parts 1 and 2, and Hollenbach, *Common Good*.

In the introduction to this book, I argued that Daniel Berrigan and Thich Nhat Hanh, in their lives, actions, and in their writings, represent moral classics. David Tracy's concept of the classic was developed to end run the whole debate about "religious" versus "rational" discourse. The classic opens up for us "another realm of authentic publicness." "If the text is a genuinely classic one," Tracy insists, "my present horizon of understanding should always be provoked, challenged, transformed."[3] Tracy suggests that our reaction to a classic falls along a spectrum from mild "resonance" to a "shock of recognition."[4] I accept this distinction as a way of contrasting much of Thich Nhat Hanh's writings with Daniel Berrigan's but resonance, I believe, does not necessarily imply a less moving reaction to a classic. Think of an audience deeply attuned to the complex harmonies of a symphony orchestra. We resonate, but hardly as a mild reaction. To be sure, there are shocks of recognition in reading Thich Nhat Hanh—as when I chant, "I am the sea pirate / my heart not yet open and capable of loving." There are deep resonances at work especially in Daniel Berrigan's poetry—as when he writes of holding a Vietnamese child, "the messiah of all my tears," in his arms. But on balance our reaction to Thich Nhat Hanh's bodhisattva vision falls closer to the resonance end of the spectrum, whereas Berrigan's expression of his prophetic vision falls closer to the shock of recognition pole. Tracy is quite clear that many, if not most, classics do not offer the sort of rational argument that philosophers see as required of public discourse. The kind of truth that classics offer is one of disclosive transformation in contrast to discursive argumentation.[5] Classics invite us through the resonant or shocking power of their vision. More precisely, they *compel* us to enter a conversation, a conversation in the case of Thich Nhat Hanh and Daniel Berrigan about the very shape and contours of our moral landscape.

Some time ago, along with Dennis McCann in a work on practical theology, I argued that works written to galvanize and direct collective action take on myriad forms. These forms can be located along a spectrum that ranges from "constructing the model" (e.g., think of the function of Marx's *Das Kapital*) to "performing the vision" (in contrast, think of the form and function of *The Communist Manifesto*).[6] Clearly the constructing the model side of the spectrum is the one that theologians and ethicists located in the academy are more comfortable with. Not so thinkers directly engaged in social transformation. They recognize how people are moved

3. Tracy, *Analogical Imagination*, 102, 112.
4. Tracy, "Catholic Classics in American Liberal Culture," 203.
5. Ibid., 204–8; Tracy, *Analogical Imagination*, 134.
6. McCann and Strain, *Polity and Praxis*, ch. 7.

by the truth told from a particular slant. If we confine ourselves to the US context, we see a multiplicity of genres of classic practical discourse, none of which follows the generic conventions of, say, John Rawls's *A Theory of Justice*, but each of which, arguably, have had a lasting impact on our public life. A small sample would include: John Winthrop's sermon on board the ship Arbella, "A Modell of Christian Charity," with its "city on a hill" metaphor beloved of American presidents, Thomas Paine's *Common Sense*, Jefferson's *Declaration*, Harriet Beacher Stowe's *Uncle Tom's Cabin*, Frederick Douglass's "Fourth of July Speech," Abraham Lincoln's "Second Inaugural Speech," Walt Whitman's *Democratic Vistas*, W. E. B. Dubois's *The Souls of Black Folk*, Walter Rauschenbusch's *Christianity and the Social Crisis*, Reinhold Niebuhr's *Moral Man and Immoral Society*, Martin Luther King Jr.'s "Letter from a Birmingham Jail," Dorothy Day's *The Long Loneliness*, Rachel Carson's *Silent Spring*, and Betty Friedan's *The Feminine Mystique*. In each case, the classic not only contributed to public discourse; it decisively redefined the basic assumptions, scope, and subject matter of such discourse. Even in this small sample there is a wide variety of genres and of religious or secular traditions that informed their authors. Each work, in its distinctive way, opened up a new horizon of moral possibility for all whom it engaged in conversation.

We have already entered into a sustained conversation with Thich Nhat Hanh's and Daniel Berrigan's respective visions. However, if I am to construct a model of social ethics that draws upon these thinkers and activists whose writings seek first to engage and then to illuminate, we will need some way of interpreting, assessing and incorporating their particular "slant." I suggest that each man's social location reveals a great deal about his distinctive approach to catalyzing social transformation. Each social location, in turn, gives rise to its own form of engagement. But I cannot examine their social location and distinctive form of engagement as if from Mount Olympus. What of my own social location? Berrigan, in particular, challenges those of us whose home is the academy. In a conversation with the psychiatrist, Robert Coles in 1970, Berrigan examined the moral ambiguity of professional life. He raises a question that goes to the heart of this book: "How does one really raise ethical and political questions and explore those questions in a real way—as contrasted to an academic or intellectual way? Can someone question gross and blatant injustice from a life-situation that is tied in dozens of ways, often subtle ways to that injustice?" And then he adds, "One's position in relationship to a given society is terribly important, and bears constant watching."[7] This chapter represents a second effort to

7. Berrigan and Coles, *Geography*, 78.

come to terms with the shocking and resonant power of Daniel Berrigan's and Thich Nhat Hanh's lives and writings in shaping ethical reflection.

COMMUNITY, MOVEMENT, AND INSTITUTION: THE SOCIAL LOCATION OF SOCIAL ETHICS

In chapters 1 and 2 we saw the importance of community for both Berrigan and Thich Nhat Hanh. Philip Berrigan and Elizabeth McAlister built a community of resistance around Jonah House in Baltimore to sustain the Plowshares Movement and Daniel Berrigan has lived in a Jesuit community in Manhattan for decades. However, I will suggest that the thrust of his ethics comes from a different social location. Not so with Thich Nhat Hanh. We saw in his journal from the early '60s, *Fragrant Palm Leaves*, his numerous attempts to build community in Vietnam to sustain the efforts of fellow Buddhists activists. Virtually all of his life in exile has been devoted to building community, founding monasteries and spreading sanghas throughout the West. So, I will argue that Thich Nhat Hanh's social location is a *community* and *practice*, as we have been examining it, is the form of ethical engagement suited to community building.

In Berrigan's case, I will argue that both in his key actions and in his writings as themselves forms of engaged action, his social location is a *movement*. Action of a special dramatic kind (remember his dictum: "The drama is the ethic") is the form of ethical engagement appropriate to one kind of social movement. Clearly this is the part of my thesis that will require the most careful explanation.

Both Thich Nhat Hanh and Daniel Berrigan have deep roots within their respective religious traditions. They have more ambivalent relationships to the religious institutions of which they are a part. Particularly during the Vietnam War, those relationships became highly strained. As each man sought to engage his religious order in working for peace, he was met with rejection. But this strained relationship never led to a decisive break. Strained relationships with their respective religious institutions pale in comparison to their relationships with the modern, war-making state. Confrontation with that institution marked Thich Nhat Hanh's and Daniel Berrigan's lives decisively. Moreover, their respective social locations are on the margins not only of the state but of society. In both their lives and writings, they each in a different way imagined an alternative social world.

I, on the other hand, am deeply embedded in the social *institution* of the university and have been for virtually all of my adult life. To pretend that I live, act, and write out of a community or movement, although I have been and am involved with both, would be to misrepresent what I have chosen to be. How and where I have chosen to locate myself may affect my own slant on moral truth. So, my relationship to the life and writings of both men is dialectical. Their very social locations challenge my own. But I will affirm my choice. The form of ethical engagement that fits with an institutional location, I will argue, is *praxis*. In this chapter I will ask what those of us whose primary location is some institution (religious organization, university or school, corporation, government agency etc.) can learn from the practice of communities and the actions of those who lead movements.[8]

COMMUNITY BUILDING AS A PRACTICE

To see the connection between community-building and practice means going over some of the ground that we have already covered. To take refuge in the sangha, Thich Nhat Hanh insists, is *not* an act of devotion; it is a practice. In modern society we easily become dispersed, distracted, forgetful of who we are. Our suffering, like a rock held by a swimmer, weighs us down; we drown. The sangha is a boat that can carry our suffering. The energy generated by practice builds the boat but it is the sangha that enables us to sustain our practice.[9] The sangha's practices are sustained acts of recuperation. It is not only war that must be resisted. Modern society undermines our sense of integrity; it fragments us and separates us from others. So, Thich Nhat Hanh argues that "communities of resistance should be places where people can . . . heal themselves and recover their wholeness." At one point in his discussion with Berrigan, Thich Nhat Hanh goes so far as to say that a religious community should be a "permanent opposition."[10]

Because the weight of suffering is a collective experience, the easing of dukkha must take a communal form. Reflecting on his experience during the Vietnam War, Thich Nhat Hanh expresses this understanding in a poem entitled "Defuse Me." Each of us contains bombs inside of ourselves—explosive dukkha—and we need to take turns defusing them. We are not solely responsible for the bombs. Schools, family, even traditions play their role. The Bodhisatva Vow commits each one of us to liberate each other, in part,

8. Clearly these three forms of social location are meant as ideal types and not as exclusive standpoints. Daniel Berrigan is clearly committed to the creation of communities of resistance, and during the Vietnam War, Thich Nhat Hanh was part of a movement for peace and reconciliation. While both men came into conflict with the hierarchies of their respective religious institutions, both have remained deeply embedded in their religious traditions and their institutionalized religious practices.

9. Nhat Hanh, "Go as a Sangha," 23–24.

10. Berrigan and Nhat Hanh, *Raft*, 94, 129.

by defusing soul-mines. The narrator of the poem ends by saying, "I will also be of help / when it is your turn."[11] We saw in chapter 2 that this commitment to community as the source for overcoming dukkha arose out of Thich Nhat Hanh's own suffering. When he was unable to return to Vietnam in 1967, he saw himself as "a cell removed from its body." "But I didn't die," he goes on to say, "because I brought the whole sangha in my heart. . . . Right away I began to build a little sangha in the West."[12]

A different metaphor for the sangha takes us beyond the act of resistance to explore the nature of community itself. Thich Nhat Hanh sees the sangha, particularly the monastic sangha, as akin to a laboratory—a place for investigation, a place where individuals can look deeply into their own suffering and that of society as a whole.[13] Such a sangha can also investigate what it is that sustains community in an age such as ours. For example, the Buddhist monastic community has over centuries conducted a series of investigations about how to reconcile conflicts that can be shared with all sorts of communities including families.[14] A Buddhist practice is experimental in character; sangha building is equally experimental.

In many ways, therefore, the practice that Thich Nhat Hanh prescribes is simply traditional. Practice is a three-legged stool comprised of moral discipline (*sila*), concentration or meditation (*samadhi*) and insight or wisdom (*prajna*). We can clarify Thich Nhat Hanh's thoroughly Buddhist understanding of practice by comparing it with a Western understanding. Alasdair MacIntyre's definition of a practice is particularly helpful precisely because it can have a broader application than simply moral virtues.

> By a "practice" I am going to mean any coherent and complex form of socially established cooperative human activity through which goods internal to that form of activity are realized in the course of trying to achieve those standards of excellence which are appropriate to, and partially definitive of that form of activity, with the result that human powers to achieve excellence, and human conceptions of the ends and goods involved, are systematically extended.[15]

I think that it is clear that Thich Nhat Hanh's understanding of practice fits well with this definition. First, to take on the Mindfulness Trainings is to participate in a tradition and to engage with its evolution. Second, the

11. Nhat Hanh, "Defuse Me," 142–43.
12. Nhat Hanh, *Power*, 171.
13. Berrigan and Nhat Hanh, *Raft*, 108.
14. Nhat Hanh, *Being Peace*, 77–81.
15. MacIntyre, *After Virtue*, 175.

notion of practice-realization that we saw in Dogen and equally expressed by Thich Nhat Hanh is a radical affirmation of the conjunction of means and ends and the intrinsic connection of practice with what MacIntyre refers to as internal goods. The positing of an internal relationship of morality with the telos of Buddhist practice is the major thrust of Damien Keown's argument which we saw in chapter 3. Third, the interlocking of moral action, mindful concentration and insight/wisdom indicates a coherence to Buddhist practice that is not explicitly developed in but, surely, would strengthen MacIntyre's definition. Likewise, the coordination of the mindfulness trainings with mind, speech, and body also testifies to both the fullness and coherence of this complex form of religious-ethical practice.

SYMBOLIC ACTION AS THE SOCIAL DRAMA OF A MOVEMENT

Daniel and Philip Berrigan found a different way to challenge a culture of moral devolution. They found in the central symbol of Christianity—the cross of Jesus—in Philip's words "a metaphor for nonviolent confrontation with a criminal superstate."[16] What early Christianity referred to as the "scandal of the cross" was transmuted into scandalous actions—burning draft files with napalm, digging graves on the White House lawn, pouring blood and hammering the nose cones of nuclear missiles. As indicated earlier, my argument is that the Berrigan brothers' social location was within a movement, and the distinctive focus of that movement was (scandalous) action. The movement that they were part of grew out of Dorothy Day's Catholic Worker movement and its loose network of houses of hospitality and intentional communities. Sharon Nepstad argues that we misunderstand movements if we only think of them as mass mobilizations which like waves emerge, crest, and decline only to reemerge at a later date. Movements are not unitary in form nor do they follow such a pattern in lockstep. Quakers sustained antislavery actions for decades before the antislavery movement in England caught fire. Some types of movements are not necessarily involved in garnering mass support and in engaging in strategic actions to alter the political sphere. Instead, they engage in "the politics of moral witness." In periods unfavorable to social change, they seek a "cognitive liberation by transforming our moral frameworks."[17] While such a description fits much more closely with the kind of movement that the Berrigans

16. Philip Berrigan as quoted in Nepstad, *Plowshares Movement*, 76.

17. Nepstad, *Plowshares Movement*, 4–12; Nepstad, *Central American Solidarity Movement*, 11–12.

generated, we must also remember that during the Vietnam War they were the radical edge of the religious wing of the antiwar movement and during the '80s the Plowshares Movement was the radical edge of the anti-nuclear weapons movement. So, the movements that these brothers stimulated not only challenged the status quo through acts of civil disobedience but existed in dialectical tension with broader coalitions which sought social change through more mainstream avenucs of protest.

James Jasper, in *The Art of Moral Protest*, argues that few movements achieve their stated goals. The anti-nuclear movement of the '80s is a case in point.[18] Viewed strategically, this movement could be labeled a failure. Jaspers suggests, to the contrary, that we see such protest as akin to religious rituals, that is, as manifestations of an alternative moral universe.

> Much like artists, [protestors] are at the cutting edge of society's understandings of itself as it changes. Moral protestors are often sensitive to moral dilemmas the rest of us ignore; they sometimes generate new ways of understanding the complexities of the human condition. . . . They extend our moral languages. . . . In the face of social change, protestors are like the proverbial canaries in the mines, except that they sing out rather than quietly expire.[19]

Emphasizing the creativity of protest movements, Jasper suggests that the tactics chosen combine cognition, emotion and morality but protestors also "do what they are good at."[20]

What the predominately Catholic activists at Catonsville and in the US wing of the Plowshares Movement were good at was liturgy. Daniel Berrigan sees the prophets as exemplars of public, liturgical action, as "entrepreneurs of symbolic action." In times of mass insanity, the Plowshares activists, like the prophets, went beyond nice words to construct "liturgies of hope" rooted in the liturgical year and "in its life-death-new life rhythms." "We gather to ourselves the natural forces and primordial realities of the earth—water, fire, ashes, blood, living flora, all varied vessels and elements of life. Planted, scattered abroad, blessed, invoked, breathed upon, dug

18. For an argument that these movements pressured Congress and the Reagan administration to negotiate a more substantive arms control agreement with Russia and succeeded in derailing the MX missile proposal, see Cortright, *Gandhi and Beyond*, 152–54, 161.

19. Jasper, *Art of Moral Protest*, 14–15. In developing this approach, Jasper is explicitly contradicting, on the one hand, theorists of crowd behavior who see protest movements as irrational, and on the other, mobilization theories which see political efficacy as the dominant, rational motivation. Ibid., 234–35.

20. Ibid., 237.

up, anointed, outpoured, in the very tic and spasm of crisis, with these we seek to dramatize the truth about our condition, our violated and violating humanity.[21]"

More prosaically, Sister Anne Montgomery, who has taken part in six Plowshares actions, explains the difficulty in directly confronting entrenched power the way that the lunch counter sit-ins did in the early stages of the civil rights movement. How do you break a law which allocates billions to build and maintain a nuclear arsenal? Montgomery suggests that the way to do so is through "symbolic direct action." Particularly when the endless barrage of information actually eclipses understanding, symbols reach deep into our subconscious, touching both our fears and our hopes.[22] Several Plowshares activists point to the way in which the modern technology of war desensitizes us—a process that calls to mind Coetzee's treatment of moral devolution. In order to grasp the horror of war, the symbols must shock us into awareness. Nepstad argues that the pouring of one's own blood for these Catholic activists was also a sacramental repetition of the sacrificial act of Jesus.[23]

These actions must be seen in context. Berrigan takes pains to insist that they grew out of Bible study, prayer, spiritual retreats, and the Eucharist. In this light, the foreswearing of strategies to achieve "success," the refusal to rely on any instrumental actions to attain political goals can be read as grounded in traditional Catholic sacramental theology. Sacramental actions make visible the invisible reign of God. The Plowshares actions work *ex opere operato*. Here, too, as with Thich Nhat Hanh's understanding of practice, means and ends coincide. It is enough that the action be performed; God will take care of its outcome.[24]

In his conversations with the psychiatrist Robert Coles, while he was underground after having been convicted for the Catonsville action, Berrigan created an analogy with the role of the sacrament of baptism in the early Christian community. It served as a rite of passage to an adult faith in which one became part of a community of resistance. To be baptized was to declare one's non-cooperation with Caesar and Caesar's claims to both one's

21. Berrigan, *Testimony*, 213–15; See Berrigan, *Jeremiah*, 133–34, for a discussion of Jeremiah as an exemplar of symbolic action.

22. Montgomery, "Divine Obedience," 29–30.

23. Nepstad, *Plowshares Movement*, 62–63. Rhys Williams argues that smaller, more radical social movements that resort to shock tactics to convey their moral witness are essentially self-limiting. While they goad a select few to act, they have difficulty persuading the less committed and even greater difficulty in making compromises to achieve political objectives. "Religious Social Movements," 326–30.

24. Inter alia, Berrigan, *Testimony*, 214.

worship and one's collaboration in imperial wars. This meaning of the sacrament, Berrigan said, "haunts" him.[25] If practice flourishes in, as it builds, community, symbolic action is the cutting edge of a movement that itself cuts against the grain of socialized death. But we can also interpret these symbolic acts of civil disobedience as nested within the life of the church with its yearly reenactment of the mysteries of creation and redemption. The minor dramas of Catonsville and the Plowshares Movement find their meaning within the mega-drama of salvation history.

While this theological interpretation of the symbolic actions of Catonsville and the various Plowshares actions seems closest to the consciousness of the primary actors, Victor Turner's sociological concept of a "social drama" also sheds light on these actions as social performances. Social dramas arise in conflict situations. Their initial phase is a *breach* with the ordered structure of socialized behaviors that we call a system. In the case of the Berrigans, such symbolic acts of resistance were clearly motivated by an affirmation of what Turner calls *communitas*—the bonds that unite human beings at levels beneath the ordered system (in this case the nation state) which unite "us" by dividing us from "them." Breach precipitates crisis, "when it is least easy to don masks or pretend there is nothing rotten in the village." But in the cases of the Plowshares Movement the system will not tolerate Turner's final two stages—redress and reintegration. The laser beam of light must be shut down. The glimpse of a more universal community beyond the binaries of the Cold War or the War on Terrorism must be shrouded. What is left to these "provocateurs," then, is recourse to the root metaphor of the martyr, one who refuses to call darkness light.[26] The canary in the mine sings out.

25. Berrigan and Coles, *Geography*, 153–54.

26. Turner, *Drama, Fields, and Metaphors*, 36–41, 45–50, 71–72. In his treatment of terrorism, Mark Juergensmeyer contrasts what he calls performance violence with strategic violence. The latter is what armies do. Employing careful planning, "strategizing," and logistical coordination, they seek to overcome a foe and achieve the war's targeted goal. Performance violence, on the other hand, seeks to transform consciousness—to terrorize. While terrorism does little to actually destroy an enemy's strategic resources, it reveals vulnerability and dramatizes the consequences of the suffering that the enemy's alleged oppressive power inflicts. See Juergensmeyer, *Terrorism in the Mind of Go*, esp. 121–28. By way of analogy to these two types of violence, I suggest that we can fruitfully see nonviolent action as falling roughly into two types. We can view some social movements as strategically focusing resources to achieve a specific policy transformation—think of the civil rights movement role in leading to landmark legislation. Others, however, employ "performance nonviolence" to transform consciousness, to reveal the oppression that underlies what John Dominic Crossan calls the "violent normalcy of civilization." *God and Empire*, 29–36. The symbolic actions of the Berrigan brothers fall into this latter category.

Berrigan credits the Hebrew prophets as providing models of symbolic acts of resistance. We should recall, nevertheless, the role of Gandhi as a master of this form of symbolic action in his more than four decades of struggle against the British empire. His famous Salt March to the sea, where he scooped up sea water to evaporate into salt in defiance of the British monopoly of salt production and its tax on the sale of salt, is a case in point. Gandhi chose an example of British rule whose injustice was deeply felt. Salt, a basic element necessary for life, symbolized the empire's control over all aspects of society. The need for salt and the felt outrage over its control unified Indians across lines of caste, religion, and economic status. The march itself became an organizing tool. While it did not directly confront British rule (which would have provoked a more severe repression), it did at a visceral level undermine the empire's legitimacy.[27] Satygraha not only was firmness in pursuit of the rights of the Indian people but it revealed the ugly truth of imperial rule.

PRAXIS AND THE CREATION OF COUNTERVAILING INSTITUTIONS

Up until this point, I have tried to listen deeply to the prophet and the bodhisattva. I hope that I have interpreted their lives and works in a way that truly conveys the classic significance of both the lives and writings of Daniel Berrigan and Thich Nhat Hanh. From now on I must try to transmute Thich Nhat Hanh's social ethics of communal practice and Berrigan's movement ethics of nonviolent action into a praxis-focused ethics for institutional reform. What do Thich Nhat Hanh and Berrigan have to offer to those of us embedded, for better and for worse, in institutions and professions? First, however, recall my conversation with Daniel Berrigan at DePaul. When I tried to explain to him what I hoped to accomplish working in higher education administration, he was having none of it. So, before I present where I stand, let us look more closely at Berrigan's critique of institutions, especially the university, and of institutional agents like me.

In *Jeremiah*, Berrigan speaks of institutions, like individuals, as "fallen." They develop their own relentless momentum, resisting heroic efforts to reform them. They "ingest" humans. So, the prophet arrives to level a decisive "no" at all attempts at reform. The image of bending swords into plowshares, Berrigan argues, provides an alternative symbol for "the conversion of society, its structures, attitudes, politics and priorities," transforming

27. For a clear summary of Gandhi's understanding of *satyagraha*, see Ackerman and Duvall, *Force More Powerful*, 61–111.

"instruments of death" into "a form in accord with the holy, which is to say, the fully human."[28]

One might quibble with Berrigan's interpretation of Isaiah's symbol by arguing that it is precisely a metaphor of re-forming some aspect of life but that would be a cheap and fruitless counter-statement. Instead, let us return to Berrigan's conversations with Robert Coles in *The Geography of Faith*. In this document we find a rich and nuanced exploration by two professionals of the challenges of creating and sustaining moral integrity within their professions and the institutions in which they are embedded. Regarding the university, Berrigan confesses to having a "two-edged conviction." On the one hand, the world has invaded the college campus. Universities and professors have been "ingested" by the Beast known as the "military-industrial complex." The role of power, money, and connections in shaping the direction of higher education is a microcosm of society as a whole.[29]

And yet Berrigan can still argue that "despite my reservations, I do retain the conviction that the university is going to be a crucial proving ground for man's survival." Like the churches, universities struggle with issues of life and death but, again like the churches, they insulate us from the sufferings of the poor, the working class, and the powerless. This insulation, this refusal of solidarity corrupts the professionals who are part of such institutions. In the case of universities, faculty gain tenure and moral growth—which for Berrigan is conditioned upon what he calls "shared jeopardy"—ceases. Only if we can "move our professional life to the edge" can we redeem the promise encoded in our professions.[30] Yet most of us are so cocooned in institutions that are complicit with injustice that we are rarely able to extricate ourselves. Consequently, as we saw earlier in the chapter, Berrigan doubts our ability to see what morally is at stake. In a cocoon we are effectively blind.

Faced with such a charge, an academic like myself is liable to become defensive. Do I plead that I am part of a sangha, a community of mindfulness which in its own way is a community of resistance? Do I point to former experiences of jail time for nonviolent civil disobedience? (Surely there must be a moral statute of limitations for such special pleading.) In neither

28. Berrigan, *Jeremiah*, 173; Berrigan, *Testimony*, 16.

29. Berrigan and Coles, *Geography*, 66–67, 107. For Berrigan, the inclusion by Catholic universities of ROTC in their curricula was (and is) the concrete sign of their fatal complicity with the war-making state.

30. Ibid., 67–68, 80–81, 104–5. Certainly Berrigan moved (and moves) his own life to the edges of the church which he never fails to criticize or to love. I am not as clear regarding how this analysis of professional life applies to his relationship with his own religious order, the Society of Jesus.

case can I claim such a response with moral integrity. A more forthright and non-defensive response is called for.

Institutions matter. We do not survive in a world of seven billion apart from massive institutions that organize most aspects of our lives. Forms of action and of practice grow out of institutions—neither Berrigan's symbolic acts of resistance nor Thich Nhat Hanh's practices are possible and certainly not intelligible apart from the religious traditions and the specific religious orders in which these two have lived their lives. "We cannot even begin to make sense of what we mean by action," Richard Bernstein argues, "unless we consider how specific instances of action are embodied in the social practices and institutions that shape our lives."[31] But those institutions are also the continually modified products of our actions and practices. I believe that universities also matter and in more than one university I have been part of reform movements seeking to shape the university as what I call a "countervailing institution."

In chapter 3 we saw that Berrigan in the aftermath of Catonsville came to associate his sense of moral obligation with that of Dietrich Bonhoeffer, calling forth what I described as "virtue *in extremis*," a holding fast while and until the system came apart. When Bonhoeffer spoke of the entire structure collapsing, surely, however, he meant the Nazi regime and the way in which its ideology and actions permeated every aspect of German life, but surely not the total collapse of such institutions as agriculture, the health care system, education. Transforming involves salvaging not *creatio ex nihilo*. A commitment to human flourishing requires a commitment to building and rebuilding the institutions that sustain our lives.

What is more important for my project is that institutions frequently play a crucial role in social transformation. We misunderstand the American civil rights revolution if we see it as the result of a *movement* alone. Numerous historians have shown that the civil rights movement was inconceivable apart from the support of religious *communities*, that is, the Southern black churches. Taylor Branch, among others, has pointed out the crucial role of the NAACP and Thurgood Marshall in working with the federal judiciary. In other words, a specific *institution* leveraging change through the federal court system worked in tandem with African American churches and the civil rights movement.[32] Daniel Levine has shown that in Latin America

31. Bernstein, *Praxis and Action*, 303, 306.

32. See Branch, *Parting the Waters*. Rosa Park's action that sparked the Montgomery Bus Boycott surely was a manifestation of her own moral courage. Yet it was part of an evolving plan of the Montgomery chapter of the NAACP to challenge the system of segregation. Her case was carefully selected from a number of similar ones as best suited to prosecute in the courts. Ibid., 128–36.

during the 1970s and '80s a similar "working the linkages" occurred among an institution (the Roman Catholic Church), the grassroots Christian base communities and the liberation movement that they spawned. The institutional church provided protection and resources and trained religious leaders. These leaders worked the linkages between the institution and local communities to create a movement for social change in the hostile climate that then prevailed in many Latin American countries.[33] These are two examples of what I mean by a "countervailing institution."

One further example: the role of the Roman Catholic Church in supporting Solidarity's nonviolent struggle in Poland is well known. Less well known is the role of the Lutheran Church in the nonviolent movement in East Germany. In 1981, a youth pastor at St. Nicholai church in Leipzig began a weekly prayer service. These services became the locus in which East Germans in the decade of the '80s discussed their future. By 1989, what had started so unobtrusively under the protection of a religious institution had mushroomed into mammoth demonstrations for freedom.[34] Rhys Williams summarizes what religious institutions in particular can provide to fledgling social movements. They are well equipped to offer: (a) a cognitive framework that makes sense of injustice, (b) rhetorical traditions, (c) moral legitimacy, (d) organizational resources, and, especially, (e) motivated adherents.[35]

To make sense of the critical role of institutions in social change as attested by these examples, we need another theory of institutions and communities that does not polarize the two. We need a theory that sees institutions related to an internal, collective good and not simply as pursuing instrumental, external goods. In fact, Catholic social teaching, with its principle of subsidiarity and it understanding of the role of intermediary institutions in achieving the common good, presupposes such an understanding of institutions.[36] David Hollenbach argues that political liberalism sees the only alternative to the state and the market as the individual inhabiting the private sphere. As Tocqueville realized in the early 1840s, the isolated individual is no match for those mega-institutions. In a line of thought that stems from Jacques Maritain, Hollenbach insists that society is far more robust than liberalism's characterization. "Intermediary" institutions are

33. Levine, *Popular Voices in Latin American Catholicism*, 317–21, 335–44.

34. Friesen, "Encourage Grassroots Peacemaking Groups," 210.

35. Williams, "Religious Social Movements," 315, 317–18.

36. On the role of institutions in securing the common good, see, inter alia, Massaro, *Living Justice*, 84–92.

essential both to preserve substantive freedoms over against the pretensions of the state and the market and to forge the bonds of solidarity.

> Because humans are relational beings whose identity, worth, and dignity are attained in interaction with others, human flourishing is always public or social. Thus Catholic social thought emphasizes the multiple forms of human relationship and community in which persons are formed and nurtured. Social space is not occupied only by large institutions of government and market, on the one hand and individuals, on the other. This is evident in the tradition's stress on the importance of securing the well-being of "intermediary" institutions. . . . Society is composed of a rich and overlapping set of human communities such as families, neighborhoods, churches, labor unions, corporations, professional associations, credit unions, cooperatives, universities and a host of other associations. . . . The bonds of communal solidarity formed in them enable persons to act together, empowering them to shape some of the contours of public life and its larger social institutions such as the state and the economy.[37]

Hollenbach's language blurs the distinction that I am making here between intermediary institutions (e.g., a labor union) and communities grounded in interpersonal relationships but his intent is clear: Intermediary institutions are part of a robust civil society.

If practice is the form of virtuous engagement appropriate to a community and the performance of symbolic actions is one of the ways in which movements seek to create social change, I argue that *praxis* is the form of engagement appropriate to "countervailing institutions," that is, institutions that would foster systemic, social change. Some time ago, in *Polity and Praxis*, I defined praxis as "symbolically constituted and critically reflected action seeking to inaugurate the human good." I now would add what was explicitly developed in other parts of *Polity and Praxis*, namely, that praxis is also "strategically directed" action.[38] "Symbolically constituted" refers to the metaphors and narratives that open up a moral horizon and counter the society's "pernicious fictions;" "critically reflected" recognizes the necessity for a critical social theory that, through careful examination and delibera-

37. Hollenbach, *Global Face*, 150–54. See Tocqueville, *Democracy in America*. Tocqueville's analysis of the role of voluntary associations in preserving society from drifting into democratic despotism is classic. I will return to Tocqueville's analysis in chapter 5.

38. McCann and Strain, *Polity and Praxis*, 212, 214–17. On the genesis of the concept of praxis, see Bernstein, *Praxis and Action*, 1–83.

tion, challenges the status quo. "Strategically directed" conveys the realization that all forms of action involve the exercise of power and praxis, as an exercise of power, coordinates actions that accord with both the moral vision and the social theory to effectively promote social transformation. Praxis is what agents embedded within an institution, like a university or, for that matter, a religious institution, must undertake if that institution is to become a lever for social change.

Let us look for a moment at what praxis might entail by returning to the institution that I know best—the university. There is a burgeoning literature that views such praxis within a university context as operating within the framework of political liberalism. It falls under rubrics such as "educating citizens" or "education for democracy." These rubrics refer to a panoply of university-community engagements, including experimental pedagogies, such as service learning and community-based research, and curricula, such as community service studies and peace and justice majors. This literature envisions an engaged university as fostering in its students a range of civic virtues, helping them to form a political identity by developing specific political understandings, skills, and motivations and a sense of political efficacy.[39] This form of institutional, transforming praxis views the university as a democratizing agent. Accepting the institutions of a democratic society, it does not challenge the state's imperial pretensions. In some respects my own work, both as a faculty leader and as an academic administrator, has been to transform DePaul University into such an engaged university.[40] However, since my own praxis is influenced by moral visions such as those of Daniel Berrigan and Thich Nhat Hanh, it seeks both greater solidarity and a more cutting-edge engagement than can be reached within the framework of educating for democracy. One example of this is a fight that I have led for the university to become a "socially responsible investor."[41] From a utilitarian point of view—held by many members of university boards of trustees—the only responsible policy with regards to investments is to maximize their value. No ethical considerations regarding the corporations in which investment is made is appropriate unless their enterprise so offends common morality that it would stain the university's reputation to be associated with them. If, on the other hand, as Catholic social teaching insists, the university is an intermediary institution that can, to a degree, offset the power of the state and the market, then how it invests its

39. Colby et al., *Education for Democracy*, 16–17. See also, inter alia, Colby et al., *Educating Citizens*.

40. See Meister and Strain, "DePaul University," 101–23.

41. Strain, "In Service of Whom?"

endowment, just as how it teaches its students, must cut across the grain of established patterns of involvement in the mega-institutions of our society.

In an engaged university, at least some faculty and staff will need to go beyond established modes of professional *practice* to a form of *praxis* that shapes the institution as countervailing. I could not be true to Thich Nhat Hanh's understanding of community as a permanent opposition or to Berrigan's powerful critique of the imperial overreach of the war-making state, if I did not—as deeply embedded in an institution—try to develop such a praxis.[42] In the chapters that follow I will try to illustrate how someone engaged in praxis within an institutional context can learn from both the bodhisasttva's practice within a community and the prophet's symbolic action within a movement and yet develop a distinctive form of social ethics.

So far I have suggested that to enter fully into conversation with the lives and writings of Thich Nhat Hanh and Daniel Berrigan we must attend to their social locations and the forms of engagement that fit with them and to our own social locations and forms of engagement, as well. If we view their lives and writings in this way, as opening "another realm of authentic publicness," it is clearly the case that their main contributions to public discourse and, therefore, to social ethics are their respective visions of and lived commitment to peace through nonviolent social transformation. Given the centrality of nonviolence to the social vision of both men, we have been examining its nuances all along. Here I will pull together a few loose threads and take stock of what each man's vision of nonviolent social transformation has to contribute to a praxis-centered understanding of just peacemaking or "strategic peacebuilding." Key to this taking stock is the theoretical issue of how Thich Nhat Hanh and Daniel Berrigan each understand power.

TWO-EDGED SATYAGRAHA: HEALING THE PATHOLOGY OF POWER

In *The Kings and Their Gods*, as we have seen, it is the *pathology* of power that is dissected. One scarcely glimpses what a healthy form of power might be.

42. We participate in and benefit from a myriad of institutions on a daily basis (think of agribusiness) but we do not *locate* ourselves within them. When we do, we take on moral responsibility (e.g., to promote organic and community farming). We implicitly begin to shape our engagement as a form of praxis. I know many faculty members for whom education is a professional *practice* and only rarely an explicit *praxis*. I certainly do not want to challenge their moral integrity. They act virtuously within the social norms of the institution. However, some must act to shape the institution itself and its norms. When we do, we shift from a *practice* to *praxis*.

Indeed, Berrigan's Jesus is the ultimate contrast to these pretentious kings. His is a *kenotic* Christ, a Christ who is the very opposite of the Greek Pantocrator. Yet it is the powerless ones of history who penetrate the illusions and pretensions of empires, who glimpse the truth and hold fast to it. This is what Gandhi meant when he defined nonviolent resistance as *satyagraha*.

Earlier we saw that Berrigan defined the symbolic acts of resistance of Catonsville and the Plowshares Movement as acts of re-membering, as acts of *anamnesis*, in its liturgical meaning.[43] In *The Kings and their Gods* he expands this meaning. "The power that corrupts often succeeds in corrupting memory as well." Our sacred texts harbor more than one tradition—a corrupted and corrupting version as well as God's word. The prophet holds fast to the truth.[44] Seen from this angle, all of Berrigan's commentaries on the biblical texts are *performed*, if you will pardon the metaphor, with a two-edged sword. One edge is the challenge that the text levels against our comfortable, cocooned selves. The other is leveled against the text itself from the vantage point of the truth-seeking prophet.[45] Berrigan's prophets—as well as Berrigan as a prophet—are persons who live on the edge and act with an edge.[46]

A good place to examine this two-edged criticism and what it says about nonviolence and power is *Exodus: Let My People Go*. The Exodus story is especially loved by liberation theologians with whom I associate myself. It offers not only the hope of liberation from tyranny but of a reconstructed, just society. Political theorist Michael Walzer goes even further to suggest that Exodus, with its three motifs (liberation from oppression, wandering in the wilderness, and entry into the Promised Land), is one of the mainsprings of the Western political imagination.[47] As we saw in chapter 1, Berrigan minces no words regarding the moral failure of this story. The god of Exodus, the lowercase, pharonic god, is a murderer of children. The entry into the promised land is no less ambiguous. There are, after all, the inhabitants of the land, the Canaanites. Their only crime is to be in the way.[48] So much for the story of liberation through violent means.

But it is not only the Exodus story that requires an edgy criticism; it is also the erstwhile attempts to enact the myth. Much earlier Berrigan had criticized the support of some liberation theologians for revolutionary

43. Berrigan and Nhat Hanh, *Raft*, 1–2.

44. Berrigan, *Kings*, 192–93.

45. Berrigan, *Exodus*, 2, 47, 82–83; see Meyers, foreword to *Exodus*, x.

46. Berrigan, "Life at the Edge," 787–90.

47. Walzer, *Exodus and Revolution*.

48. Berrigan, *Exodus*, 49, 163.

violence in the name of a liberating God. This was especially borne out in a letter to Ernesto Cardenal written in May 1978. Cardenal, a fellow Jesuit and poet, had organized Christian base communities in his homeland of Nicaragua that lived their faith in resistance to the Somoza dictatorship. Cardenal had issued a manifesto in which he aligned himself with the Sandanista rebels and endorsed the "violence of a violated people." Berrigan writes with deep affection for a friend and comrade who had visited him and his brother Philip when they were in jail in 1977. He acknowledges that the "few hundred guns" in the hands of guerillas are as nothing before the "doomsday cache of nuclear horrors" of his own country. He understands the instinctive reaching for the gun in the face of massive repression and disappearances. "The big boot comes down. It destroys everything we have built. And we recoil." But to Cardenal's claim that Gandhi, Merton, even Jesus might agree with him, Berrigan's reply is a blunt "I do not believe it." Having witnessed the history of crusades, colonization, imperial crimes, are we now to have "just" wars on the Left? Killing for love of the kingdom, is it not the same old story? Christians are stuck with their Christ; it will no more do for revolutionaries to "set Him aright" than for popes or the war-making state. Berrigan concludes his letter with a declaration that he wrote while underground in the aftermath of the Catonsville trial: "The death of a single human being is too heavy a price to pay for the vindication of any principle, however sacred."[49] This last statement is an important clue to Berrigan's ethics. The commitment to nonviolence is not to an abstract, absolute principle. It is rather a form of discipleship that sees the sacred manifest in each and every human life.

If the Exodus story must be viewed with a prophet's critical eye, and if an Exodus ethics of revolutionary violence must be rejected completely, still there is no going back to Egypt. No reforming the system, no "search for an 'improved empire.'" And yet. And yet after plucking up and tearing down, Jeremiah is commanded "to build and to plant (Jeremiah 1:10)." "Something new, structures in favor of 'widows and orphans and strangers at the gate.' Constructing a new social order from the ground up."[50] What those new structures might look like, Berrigan never tells us. Power is embodied in acts of resistance and in the willingness to sacrifice oneself and not others. This is not the power to plant and to build. We are left with the dictum that the reign of God transcends every human polis, but we are not told what a somewhat-better-than-others polis might look like.

49. Berrigan, "Letter to Ernesto Cardinal," 167–70.

50. Berrigan, *Exodus*, 20–21.

Two related issues regarding the shape that nonviolence takes in Berrigan's thought and action must be considered. First, numerous pacifists, including Dorothy Day, did not see the destruction of property (burning draft files, hammering the nose cones of nuclear missiles) as justifiably nonviolent actions. Although at Catonsville and in all of the Plowshares actions great pains were taken that no physical harm come to any human beings, nevertheless the actions themselves were forceful if not aggressive. There is a double edge to the kind of nonviolence that we associate with the Berrigan brothers. Their edgy actions were not only challenging to the omnipresent power of the war-making state but also to the peace movement and especially its religious wing. Certainly they would not have dreamt of challenging someone like Dorothy Day, whose life rang solid and true, but the rest of us are a different matter. A more straightforward response is that draft files during the Vietnam War and nuclear weapons for almost seventy years are the tools of the trade of death as a social method. Do weapons of mass destruction have any "right" to exist? If we look at the record of these seven decades, can we say that our political leaders have unstintingly sought their elimination and, therefore, can we, placing our trust in them, ethically justify abdicating our own responsibility for their elimination?

The second issue is raised by James Douglass, a Catholic peace activist of long standing. Douglass challenges the moral framework that prevails among nonviolent activists which pits the individual conscience against the state. Here, all too easily, evil is externalized, located outside of the engaged self. Then it becomes even easier to see as adversaries those who in some way represent the state (police, judges, prosecuting attorneys, and prison guards) instead of seeing them as fellow human beings with all of the ambiguities of character that we possess. We thereby inflate a false ego which is of a piece with the "many such false selves magnified in national egos." "Our intentions and actions for peace lead to war if they are based on a false self and its illusions. If the purpose of civil disobedience is to 'empower' such a self, it is a personal act of war." The antidote to the self-deluding process of externalizing evil is "civil disobedience as prayer," prayer that asks that God's will (not mine) be done is also a turning inward to acknowledge that the evil we resist is more internal to ourselves than we have yet to understand.[51] If anything has characterized the US Plowshares actions, it has been this prayerful approach to the actions and their aftermath. However, as Douglass suggests, this form of self-delusion is not a problem to be solved. It is an unrelenting challenge to be transformed.

51. Douglass, "Civil Disobedience as Prayer," 93–97.

RADIANT AHIMSA OR THE PRACTICE OF BEING PEACE

Douglass's comments lead us directly to the engaged Buddhist contribution to understanding nonviolence and peacemaking. Not only Thich Nhat Hanh but all engaged Buddhists affirm the insight that there can be no "outer" transformation without an inner transformation. In fact, as we have seen with Thich Nhat Hanh's commentary on the Avatamsaka Sutra, the very distinction of inner and outer must be challenged. "I am the sea pirate" is this challenge in its most radical form. As we saw in chapter 3, the primary way in which a sangha engages the world is by being peace. Thich Nhat Hanh develops this idea further when he refers to the Sanskrit term, *ahimsa* (non-harming) to define nonviolence. Immediately he states that the practice of ahimsa begins with ourselves. We each harbor seeds of violence and of nonviolence. Even soldiers have the seeds of nonviolence within them. We cannot divide the world into two camps: the violent and the nonviolent.[52] That itself would be a form of violence. The roots of war are in our own minds and our unmindful way of living. However, we do not declare war on ourselves. "We practice like the lotus flower and the mud. The lotus flower does not think, 'I do not want the mud.' The lotus knows that it can bloom beautifully only because of the mud. We have negative seeds in us. . . . We accept ourselves. . . . The process of transformation and healing requires ongoing practice."[53]

Ahimsa focuses within and without. It includes the actions of body, speech and mind. But it also includes the action of nonaction. Again, Thich Nhat Hanh refers to the one calm person in a small boat in a stormy sea. Cultivating a peaceful presence, learning how to stop ourselves from verbally lashing out in retaliation to someone's harsh words are forms of the essential practice of nonaction.[54] "Skillful action arises on a foundation of being . . . ," Thich Nhat Hanh concludes, "and being is nonaction."[55]

Fasching and Descant have challenged Thich Nhat Hanh's concept of nonviolence as ahimsa, contrasting it with Gandhi's practice of satyagraha. In Gandhi's case, they argue, "We really do have enemies whom we must go to war against. However, for Gandhi we can go to war without picking up a gun. To love one's enemies, therefore, is not to deny that they are enemies

52. Nhat Hanh, "Ahimsa," 65–66.

53. Nhat Hanh, *Creating True Peace*, 11–12, 35–36.

54. Nhat Hanh, "Ahimsa," 69.

55. Nhat Hanh, *Opening the Heart*, 109.

but rather to love them in spite of their actions."[56] Several points should be made here in response to this interpretation of Thich Nhat Hanh. First, it is the case that Thich Nhat Hanh shied away from overt forms of nonviolent resistance during the Vietnam War. Other monks in the Vietnamese Buddhist Struggle movement led massive street demonstrations and other forms of noncooperation against the repressive South Vietnamese government and against the American involvement in the war. Thich Nhat Hanh and his followers from the School of Youth for Social Service concentrated on supporting peasants victimized by both sides during the war. They evacuated villagers caught in crossfire or established cease-fire zones so that villagers would be safe; they worked alongside peasants to reconstruct villages leveled by bombs, introduced new agricultural methods, educated about health practices, and provided medicines. They cared for war orphans.[57] In all of these activities they emphasized self-help rather than dependence on the government. Above all, their persistent calls for an end to the fighting led them to be labeled as traitors by both sides. To appeal for reconciliation was itself an act of resistance.

The second point that should be made is that Thich Nhat Hanh, like Gandhi, did see ahimsa as active resistance. As we saw in chapter 2, the poem "Condemnation" clarifies just what the focus of resistance must be: "Beware! Turn around and face your real enemies— / ambition, violence, hatred and greed."[58] Thich Nhat Hanh goes further to suggest that overcoming violence that has been embedded in structures should be a priority.[59]

Third, Sallie King argues that we can understand Thich Nhat Hanh's approach to nonviolence as organized around two principles. The first principle is clearly rooted in the Four Noble Truths. It is to stop killing as a deluded fostering of suffering or to reduce it when stopping is impossible. The second principle is a refusal to take sides while actively seeking to reconcile conflicting parties. This is based upon an identification with the suffering that is manifest on both sides in a conflict.[60] "Understanding

56. Fasching and Descant, *Comparative Religious Ethics*, 163. I will leave aside the question whether or not Fasching and Descant have correctly characterized Gandhi. I believe that they have not.

57. Nhat Hanh, *Creating True Peace*, 94–109; King, "Thich Nhat Hanh," 337. King provides a succinct overview of Thich Nhat Hanh's involvement in the struggle for peace in Vietnam. See King, "Thich Nhat Hanh," 321–63. For a broader treatment of the Vietnamese Buddhist peace movement, see Topmiller, *Lotus Unleashed*.

58. Nhat Hanh, "Condemnation," 37.

59. King, "Thich Nhat Hanh," 345–46.

60. Ibid., 342–45.

suffering," Thich Nhat Hanh affirms, "is the foundation of any good action, whether it is political, social or spiritual."[61]

There is more to this commitment to reconciling conflicting parties than the expression of compassion. Buddhism provides an understanding of truth that in many respects is akin to Gandhi's. Ideas are guiding means only. Ideologies are born when we cling to narrow perspectives elevating them to a comprehensive dogma. The first three of the Fourteen Mindfulness Trainings, as we saw in chapter 2, are designed to keep ideologies from colonizing our understanding of the world and of others. Ken Jones points out the essentially dualistic character of ideologies. They result from a process that he calls "antithetical bonding." According to Jones, individuals seek assurance through belonging to groups. Group identities are strikingly strengthened when they are constructed in opposition to an alien group. Ideologies emerge as the mental simplifications that confirm one's antithetically bonded identity. Ideas become emotionally "freighted articles of faith, formulas which serve to organize all of reality. In this formulaic, solidified version, they offer ready-made "identi-kits."[62] Chris Hedges offers a striking example of the irrational but commandeering power of this social process drawn from the conflict in the '90s in the former Yugoslavia.

> In the Balkans there were heated debates over the origin of gingerbread hearts—cookies in the shape of hearts. The Croats insisted that the cookies were Croatian. The Serbs angrily countered that the cookies were Serbian. . . . To those of us on the outside it had a Gilbert and Sullivan lunacy to it, but to the protagonists it was deadly serious. It had to be. For nationalist myths stand on such minuscule differences. These myths give neighbors the justification to kill those they had gone to school and grown up with.[63]

There is in Thich Nhat Hanh's position an ambivalence about political power. In *The Art of Power*, he argues that "what most people call power Buddhists call cravings. . . . In Buddhism we speak of the five true powers, five kinds of energy. The five powers are faith, diligence, mindfulness, concentration and insight." From his social location, Thich Nhat Hanh interprets faith as "confidence not only in ideas but in the concrete results of your practice." Faith is being on a path. "This is power," Thich Nhat Hanh insists. "You can generate this kind of power every moment of your daily

61. Nhat Hanh, *Calming Mind*, 27.

62. Jones, *Social Face of Buddhism*, 54–55, 59–60.

63. Hedges, *War Is a Force*, 32.

life."[64] In conversation with Daniel Berrigan, he praised the Buddhist peace movement in its early stages that led to the toppling of the Diem regime in South Vietnam because everyone's intentions were pure, i.e., there was no thought of seizing power.[65] Later, considerations of political power complicated the issue. Partly this aversion to political strategy and tactics was based on an understanding of the proper role of monks and of the sangha as a spiritual community. At the deepest level, however, it was the awareness that the problem of violence is ultimately a spiritual problem that infects each of us individually and society collectively. The needed transformation is only secondarily political.

NONVIOLENCE AND THE AMBIGUITY OF POWER

Nonviolent action takes numerous forms. A sangha's practice of being peace and symbolic acts of resistance within a social movement are two important types. In the next section, I will propose the *praxis of just peacemaking* as a third form. But two prior steps need to be taken. First, it is important to show that this newer form incorporates many of the traits of the other two. Most especially, it recognizes the internal relationship of means and ends. From the practice of being peace it draws the following:

- Inner transformation is necessary for outer transformation. This is a central principle of engaged Buddhism.
- Inner transformation requires a disciplined engagement, a practice. So does a genuine commitment to nonviolence as Gandhi well knew. If we wish to prevent war in the future, we must begin to transform ourselves and our children in the present. When crises develop, it is most likely too late to avoid violent conflict.
- Violence and nonviolence are located along a spectrum. Thich Nhat Hanh acknowledges that we all harbor seeds of both violence and nonviolence. Furthermore, our actions are never purely one or the other. The Lotus grows in a sea of mud.
- The Buddhist understanding of truth as guiding means coupled with the understanding that we must not cling to any "truth" functions as an ideology solvent. This solvent is particularly useful in undercutting dualistic concepts that foster "antithetical bonding."

64. Nhat Hanh, *Power*, 15–16.

65. Berrigan and Nhat Hanh, *Raft*, 80–81. See King, "Thich Nhat Hanh," 328, 349.

- Nonviolent action begins with staying in touch with suffering and looking deeply into it. Nonviolence acts to alleviate suffering. Our failure to alleviate suffering is itself a form of violence.

Similarly we can take key insights from nonviolence as symbolic acts of resistance:

- Power takes pathological forms. It puts on pretension as a magic cloak. It "apes" God.
- Symbolic acts of resistance are necessary to puncture the delusion that great power is equally good. More than petitioning the powers that be is required. A spanner must be placed in the machinery of death.
- We must become aware of the possibility of moral devolution. We need the prophet's laser surgery to remove our own moral cataracts.
- Nonviolence functions as a standard not only to critique the larger society but to filter the ambiguous traditions in which we are embedded. Even Exodus, the paradigmatic story of human liberation, is steeped in blood.

Second, any attempt to integrate these insights into a form of praxis which incorporates a political strategy must first come to terms with the challenge of those who have grappled with the persistent moral ambiguity of political power. In the American context that challenge achieved its classic form in Reinhold Niebuhr's *Moral Man and Immoral Society*. To Daniel Berrigan we can hear Niebuhr say: "The demand of religious moralists that nations subject themselves to 'the law of Christ' is an unrealistic demand, and the hope that they will do so is a sentimental one."[66] He might also suggest that the refusal to take responsibility for the exercise of power and to shoulder the moral ambiguity that comes with it is *ipso facto* a sectarian stance. Faced with Thich Nhat Hanh's understanding of compassion rooted in insight, Niebuhr would no doubt argue that the Mahayana concept of Buddha Nature represents "a romantic overestimation of human virtue and moral capacity." Niebuhr might read the vision of the Avatamsaka Sutra concerning the infinite ramifications of each act of compassion as erasing the different challenges of infusing virtue into forms of social existence that are more complex than face-to-face communities. Niebuhr would raise the issue of power in social groups. Collective power, having consolidated injustice, "can never be dislodged unless power is raised against it." Beyond the level of interpersonal relations, coercion (the assertion of power) plays a crucial role both in holding larger groups together and in pursuing justice.

66. Niebuhr, *Moral Man*, 75.

Relations between larger groups are largely determined by the distribution of power between them and not by ethical ideals or a rational appraisal of comparative need.[67]

By contrast, Niebuhr reads the "law of Christ" as a love that does not resist or coerce. "Nothing is clearer than that a pure religious idealism must issue in a policy of non-resistance which makes no claims to be socially efficacious." Jesus did not enjoin his followers to love their enemies because it would convert the latter but because they were to be perfect as their heavenly Father is perfect. Such love can only bloom within interpersonal relations. "Every effort to transfer a pure morality of disinterestedness to group relations has resulted in failure."[68] Reinhold Niebuhr, in short, represents a classic moral type that fundamentally challenges the classic expression of the prophet in Daniel Berrigan's life and work and of the bodhisattva in Thich Nhat Hanh's life and work.

What surprised me in my rereading of *Moral Man and Immoral Society*, what I had completely forgotten was the better part of an entire chapter devoted to Gandhi and this long before it became evident that his satyagraha campaigns would be successful in the face of British imperial power. Gandhi, according to Niebuhr modified the pure religious ideal of love as non-resistance by incorporating an element of coercion, thereby creating satyagraha as nonviolent resistance. Gandhi, in other words, came to realize "the necessity of some type of physical coercion upon the foes of his people's freedom." In so doing, Gandhi was acting as a political realist, all the while promoting his spiritual ideal. But this incorporation of coercive power meant that no absolute distinction between violence and nonviolence can be drawn. Niebuhr points to the children of cotton spinners in England who suffered from the Indian boycott of foreign-made clothing. Moral purity had been sacrificed for political effectiveness.[69]

For this very reason Niebuhr commends Gandhian nonviolence as an appropriate instrument of power in the hands of oppressed groups, including, he specifically suggests, African Americans. It punctures the moral conceits of the oppressor who reinforces the status quo through appeals to "law and order," but because it focuses on an oppressive system without pillorying the oppressor, it leaves the door open for a peaceful resolution of

67. Ibid., xx–xxiii, 3. For a counterargument that coercion in general and violence in particular are the opposite of power which arises only in collaboration and concert among people, see Arendt, *On Violence*.

68. Niebuhr, *Moral Man*, 263–64, 266, 268. For an argument that Jesus did not counsel non-resistance but, in fact, practiced nonviolent resistance, see Wink, *Jesus and Nonviolence*.

69. Niebuhr, *Moral Man*, 240–42, 244.

the conflict. "Nonviolent coercion and resistance," Niebuhr concludes, "is a type of coercion which offers the largest opportunities for a harmonious relationship with moral and rational factors in social life."[70]

In March 1930, shortly before he launched his famous Salt March in deliberate violation of the British law monopolizing and taxing salt production in India, Gandhi made a last-ditch appeal to Lord Irwin, viceroy for India, listing a number of grievances. He concluded his appeal by saying: "India must consequently evolve force enough to free herself from that embrace of death."[71] Here and in numerous other places Gandhi made it clear that nonviolence is anything but passive; it is the exercise of power. As an exercise of power, nonviolence cannot claim moral purity. It is likely that the boycott of British-made clothing *did* harm the children of Lancaster cotton spinners. It is also clearly the case for Thich Nhat Hanh and Daniel Berrigan, as it is for Gandhi, that no such morally superior standpoint is claimed. One does one's best, as Thich Nhat Hanh puts it, to minimize the harm done by one's actions recognizing the seeds of violence in oneself. The refusal to pick up a gun, nevertheless, is a categorical moral act which Niebuhr in his attentiveness to the forceful side of Gandhi's satyagraha neglects.

Other aspects of this presumed Niebuhrian critique of the prophet and the bodhisattva, I believe, similarly miss the mark. Both thinkers present a deeply realistic analysis of the conjunction of power, ideology, and mass murder. Berrigan's dissection of the pretensions of power is as sharp as that of any Christian realist. Thich Nhat Hanh presents a compelling narrative of the seeds of violence that we water by discriminative thinking leading to antithetical bonding. The capacity to transform oneself rooted in the Third Noble Truth only becomes manifest through practice, the following of the Eightfold Path which includes the strenuous demands of the mindfulness trainings. Here there is a profound commitment to shaping the means of action recognizing that the lotus grows in a sea of mud. Evolutionary optimism—which Niebuhr saw as the form of self-delusion of religious idealists—is not an appropriate interpretation of Buddhist practice. Berrigan's eschatological understanding of the reign of God is consistently brought into sharp conflict with the structures and the illusions of goodness perpetuated by the empires du jour. Power is exercised in the symbolic acts of resistance that flow from that eschatological vision. Much of what Gandhi meant by satyagraha—firmness in seeking the truth—is reflected in the

70. Ibid., 248–52. The Niebuhr who published *Moral Man and Immoral Society* in 1932 changed key aspects of his thinking in the context of World War II and the Cold War.

71. Gandhi, as quoted in Sharp, *Waging Nonviolent Struggle*, 103.

Catonsville Nine's and the Plowshares Movement's sense of *obedience* to the law of Christ.

Juxtaposing Berrigan and Thich Nhat Hanh with Niebuhr, I am inclined to read his interpretation of Gandhi as a reflection on the moral and political power of *movements* for social change. However, preoccupied as it is with the institution of the nation state, his theory of "immoral society" does not make sufficient room for movements as agents for social change nor for the leverage that intermediary institutions can bring to bear on the state. Likewise, his treatment of Gandhi fails to take into account the role of the *ashram*, that is, of spiritual communities in India, steeped in the discipline of nonviolence and functioning as leavens of social change. These communities played a crucial role in the success of Gandhi's nonviolent campaigns.[72] My argument in this chapter is that social change is most powerfully enacted when there is a creative interaction of communities of practice with social movements and (countervailing) institutions.

THE PRAXIS OF JUST PEACEMAKING

Earlier I defined praxis as symbolically constituted, critically reflected, and strategically directed action. To this definition I would add that a nonviolent praxis ideally integrates the practice of being peace.[73] Certainly the Berrigans and the Plowshares Movement shared with Gandhi a keen grasp of the importance of symbolic acts of visceral power. Daniel Berrigan and Thich Nhat Hanh each have a critical theory of the origins of violence. What is lacking in many nonviolent movements Gene Sharp believes is strategic direction and it is the most significant factor that could strengthen the efficacy of these movements.[74] While Sharp is concerned with developing strategies within processes of nonviolent direct action, a new approach to peacebuilding places the nonviolent waging of conflict within a larger framework.

72. On the role of communities as yeast, see Lederach, *Moral Imagination*, 91–93.

73. Some authors, like Gene Sharp, emphasize nonviolent direct action as a set of techniques (Sharp identifies 198 of them) for the pragmatic exercise of power. In most instances, he contends, nonviolence has not been grounded in religious beliefs or moral principles. A Gandhi or a King with his spiritual vision is the exception and not the rule. See *Waging Nonviolent Struggle*. While Sharp is most likely factually correct in his review of a wide range of nonviolent struggles, I see an important role for religious communities, religious wings of nonviolent movements, and religious institutions in waging principled nonviolent struggle. Such groups need more than a religious vision of peace. Thich Nhat Hanh, rightly I believe, stresses the importance of a religious practice.

74. Sharp, *Waging Nonviolent Struggle*, 434.

This framework goes by various names, most especially "just peacemaking" and "strategic peacebuilding."[75] Under either heading, nonviolent waging of conflict is part of a panoply of processes that creates a sustainable peace. Both terms suggest that the processes must be built inductively by looking deeply at what is actually occurring at various levels from grassroots endeavors to the work of international NGOs. Such efforts transcend any split between moral ideals and political strategies. Likewise, not all of these processes totally exclude violence. In fact, as "a new paradigm for the ethics of war and peace," just peacemaking posits itself as an alternative that can subsume both the pacifist and the just war ethical stances.[76]

Glen Stassen and his associates see ten processes as instrumental in creating a just peace. They range from engaging in nonviolent direct action to fostering economic development, from curtailing the arms trade to employing conflict resolution techniques, and from supporting grassroots peacemaking to strengthening the UN. Lisa Schirch, for her part, offers four umbrellas under which she clusters nineteen processes which constitute strategic peacebuilding: "Waging Conflict Nonviolently" includes a multitude of processes from monitoring and advocacy, to direct action, protests, boycotts, and other forms of non-cooperation. "Reducing Direct Violence" includes creating peace zones in areas of conflict, humanitarian intervention, peacekeeping police work and restoring the rule of law. "Transforming Relationships" involves a full spectrum of conflict resolution techniques, trauma healing, and restorative justice. Finally, "Building Capacity" involves education, economic development, and conversion of the military to a focus on human security.[77]

What both approaches have in common is a recognition that peacebuilding is a complex set of processes that proceed along a broad front. Multiple efforts are necessary to create a sustainable, just peace. Schirch even includes under the rubric of "reducing direct violence" military intervention. While recognizing that such interventions often harm civilians without securing peace and human rights, strategic peacebuilding does not rule out international policing under carefully designed constraints as one of its methods.[78]

This cluster of processes does not transform peacebuilding into a hopelessly complex, utopian project. Rather each of the multiple approaches sees the need for recognizing one's own finite contribution within a much larger framework leading, it is hoped, to more intentional attempts to coordinate actions. So, we can see the importance of the Berrigans' actions as forms of

75. See, e.g., Stassen, *Just Peacemaking*; Schirch, *Strategic Peacebuilding*.

76. Brubaker et al., "Just Peacemaking," 1–2, 34–37.

77. Schrich, *Strategic Peacebuilding*, 26, 37–39, 46–48, 51–52, 58–61.

78. Ibid., 40–42.

waging conflict nonviolently while valuing Thich Nhat Hanh's practice of being peace as contributing to a transformation of relationships in conflict situations. But no single approach is promoted as a magical solution. Strategic peacebuilding broadens our understanding of the ways in which the forms of nonviolent engagement that we have been studying can be employed. For example, Lisa Schirch agrees that rituals are central to nonviolent direct action. However, in peacebuilding efforts they can play a still larger role. Rituals can be and have been used in trauma healing, in creating safe spaces for victims of violence, in placing people in a new context not governed by the logic of violence thereby allowing opponents to develop new relationships and to "rehumanize" the other. By creating a liminal experience of time and space, an idealized peaceful experience, rituals enable opponents to imagine an alternative future by creating "a desired world using symbols, senses and a safe pathway for emotions." Through rituals as simple as sharing a meal with one another, opponents "act their way into new behavior."[79] Similarly practices such as sitting and walking meditation can create a powerful sense of community. Moreover, when practiced over time by peacebuilders, they can create what Peter Hershock calls a "liberating intimacy" with present experience, opening the person to new ways of thinking and responding.[80] Such openness and spontaneity on the part of mediators, conflict resolution teams, those guiding programs of restorative justice or members of Truth and Reconciliation commissions can play a crucial role in breaking through logjams to the resolution of protracted conflicts.

Working along the broad front of peacebuilding are many different kinds of agents: the UN, its agencies, international NGOs, including religious organizations like the World Council of Churches, a variety of communities including religious communities that provide the grassroots foundation for any enduring conflict resolution, local and national governments which must be part of a lasting solution, development agencies, Truth and Reconciliation commissions, universities providing necessary research and evaluation, and so on. Clearly many of these agents are institutions. Most of the processes intrinsic to just peacemaking or strategic peacebuilding take decades not years to accomplish. Institutions are organizations that can sustain a common purpose over long stretches of time. John Paul Lederach, in his framing of peacebuilding, is leery of the term institution. Institutions, in his view, imply bureaucratization, inflexibility, and lack of responsiveness. "How do we sustain the social capacity to support constructive change," he asks, "while consistently innovating and adapting to

79. Schirch, *Ritual and Symbol in Peacebuilding*, 58–59, 72, 84, 88.

80. Hershock, *Liberating Intimacy*.

a dynamic and demanding environment?" What are needed, he suggests, are "smart, flexible platforms" that can combine permanence of purpose with responsive innovation. A platform does not turn in upon itself, as if its purpose was to perpetuate itself. It exists to launch something. The metaphor that Lederach uses to describe such "process-structures" is a river. From a great height you do not see a river's movement; you see its form and structure. From the middle of a river it is all dynamic change without a vision of its ultimate shape.[81] The trick is to see and act in both dimensions simultaneously. For my part, I am less leery of seeing institutions as part and parcel of any strategic praxis of peacebuilding because I have been part of an institution that has repeatedly reinvented itself. What we need are institutions that are like rivers. As I have just suggested, there is plenty of room for the prophet and the bodhisattva within the multiple approaches of strategic peacebuilding. What, for example, would a Truth and Reconciliation commission be without the truth-telling prophet or the bodhisattva's reconciling kindness? But river-like institutions are also needed.

We have covered a large piece of ground in this chapter. I have argued that we get a unique perspective or "slant" on different models of social ethics by understanding the social locations of their authors and the forms of social engagement that follow from those locations. In the case of Thich Nhat Hanh that social location is the sangha or community and the appropriate form of nonviolent engagement is ahimsa along with *the practice of being peace*. In Daniel Berrigan's case, his social location is at the cutting edge of the peace movement and the chosen form of nonviolent engagement is *symbolic acts of resistance*. I, on the other hand, am embedded in an institution and the appropriate form of nonviolent engagement of agents embedded in isntitutions is *the praxis of strategic peacebuilding*. In many historical contexts social change was brought about through the interaction of communities, movements and institutions.

These distinct forms of nonviolence are based on different understandings of power. A social ethics that deals with the issue of power cannot avoid dealing with Reinhold Niebuhr's classic treatment in *Moral Man and Immoral Society*. While I believe that Niebuhr's critique of religious idealism largely does not apply to either Thich Nhat Hanh or Daniel Berrigan, the praxis of strategic peacebuilding can include both of their forms of nonviolent engagement and simultaneously address Niebuhr's understanding of the moral ambiguity of power. To truly make good on this claim, however, we need to develop an understanding of social justice informed by our tutelage at the hands of the prophet and the bodhisattva.

81. Lederach, *Moral Imagination*, 126–28.

5

COMPASSION AND JUSTICE

Social Ethics and Capability Theory

"You gringos," a Salvadoran peasant told an American visitor, "are always worried about violence done with machine guns and machetes. But there is another kind of violence that you should be aware of, too. I used to work on a hacienda. My job was to take care of the dueño's dogs. I gave them meat and bowls of milk, food that I couldn't give my own family. When the dogs were sick I took them to the veterinarian. When my children were sick, the dueño gave me his sympathy but no medicine as they died."[1]

—Cited in N. Scheper-Hughes, *Death without Weeping*

All violence is injustice.[2]

—Thich Nhat Hanh, *Calming the Fearful Mind*

Any social ethics for the twenty-first century must incorporate a theory of justice. We are keenly aware of how structures impinge on our lives, how systems—political, economic, cultural, and ecological—shape and oppress us. Salvadoran peasants teach us profound truths about structural violence.

1. Scheper-Hughes, *Death without Weeping*, 230.
2. Nhat Hanh, *Calming Mind*, 101.

For many, if not most of us, the idea of justice first dawns in an intuitive sense of injustice. It is profoundly unfair when children die from hunger and disease and dogs go well fed. All types of injustice, the Salvadoran peasant might have said, are acts of violence. Thich Nhat Hanh's saying, on the other hand, connects our task in this chapter with the discussion of the types of nonviolent action in chapter 4. We do not develop our understanding of justice in the context of a mythical state of nature. We must develop it with constant awareness of immense suffering, systemically imposed, and of the pathology of power, ideologically undergirded, that generates the myriad forms of violence that tear apart human communities. Developing a model of justice congruent with the insights of the prophet and the bodhisattva is the task of this third attempt to distill an ethics of peace and justice from the actions and writings of Daniel Berrigan and Thich Nhat Hanh.

Robert Schreiter, writing about the need for liberation theology to reinvent itself after the collapse of state socialism as a viable political economy, suggests five tasks for a future theology geared to praxis. Such a theology must first be an act of *resistance*, catalyzing a struggle against oppression. Its second task is *denunciation*, identifying the structures of oppression. Identification must be accompanied by a *critique* that unmasks the pathology of power. The fourth task is *advocacy* of specific projects to change the status quo. The final task is *reconstruction*, shaping a vision conducive to human flourishing.[3] What Schreiter suggests as the tasks of any liberation theology, I will argue, applies even more to a model of justice geared toward praxis.

If we review the positions of Daniel Berrigan and Thich Nhat Hanh in light of this construction of the tasks necessary to evolve a religiously grounded theory of justice, it seems obvious that Berrigan performs the first and second tasks in profound ways. But it is equally true of Thich Nhat Hanh. Recall how Thich Nhat Hanh portrays the mindful practice of sangha-building as a form of permanent opposition to the corrosive individualism of our time. Moreover, Thich Nhat Hanh is surely speaking with a prophetic voice when he denounces all violence as injustice. I also believe that Berrigan's critique of idolatry and its intrinsic connection with "death as a social method" is, at least, an embryonic critical social theory. We can say the same for Thich Nhat Hanh's critique of ideology in the first three mindfulness trainings as they are supplemented, as we saw in chapter 4,

3. Schreiter, *New Catholicity*, 109–10. Praxis, which I defined in chapter 4 as symbolically constituted, critically reflected and strategically directed action to inaugurate the human good, can be seen in Schreiter's terms as being born in the space that connects advocacy and reconstruction. Another world must be strategically as well as symbolically and critically envisioned. It goes without saying that this also entails the internalization of the first three tasks outlined by Schreiter.

by Ken Jones's treatment of antithetical bonding and Chris Hedges's delineation of the social processes that lead inexorably to war. But what of the fourth and fifth tasks?

In terms of advocacy it seems clear *whom* Berrigan is advocating for—the poor, the marginalized, the excluded, and the victims of war. Thich Nhat Hanh, in true Mahayana form, advocates for all living beings.[4] But *what* they advocate for is not nearly as clear. Given their roles as prophet and bodhisattva, the work of social reconstruction lies beyond their calling. Berrigan, in particular, is quite pessimistic about the possibility of constructing a just society. Recall his criticism of reform movements which, in his mind, seek a new and better Egypt, obviating the need for an exodus. We also looked at his clearest take on the issue of social justice in *Isaiah: Spirit of Courage Gift of Tears*. A just society cannot come to pass through evolution or revolution. It can only emerge through God's action. And yet justice is demanded of the nations even as they ruthlessly cut down God's servants, those who advocate for justice.[5] Such pessimism (a true Christian realism Berrigan might say) is spiritually sustained by hope against hope in a God who acts in ways beyond our ken. Contrary to this harsh theology, I argue that the logic of the fall need not (does not) dominate the historical process. This conviction, Pope John Paul II said in *Sollicitudo Rei Socialis*, is "based on the Church's awareness of the divine promise, guaranteeing that our present history does not remain closed in upon itself but is open to the Kingdom of God."[6]

While some engaged Buddhists shy away from justice language as too adversarial, too rooted in the retributive justice of the law court, Thich Nhat Hanh makes bold use of it, especially in the Fourteen Mindfulness Trainings.[7] Two mindfulness trainings call us to be aware of the suffering caused

4. In *Living Buddha Living Christ*, 79–80, Thich Nhat Hanh speaks out against the idea of God's preferential option for the poor. I believe that he is reacting to a simplistic version of the concept which would seem to suggest the exclusion of the non-poor from God's love. Think of the option for the poor as the *locus* where God's all-encompassing love goes to work. If you would align yourself with God's unconditional love, then align yourself with the poor, the marginalized, and the excluded.

5. Berrigan, *Isaiah*, 117–18.

6. John Paul II, *Sollicitudo Rei Socialis*, #47. Berrigan's pessimistic reading of history is counterbalanced by his lyrical poems which are suffused by a faith in the incarnation.

7. Sallie King points out that engaged Buddhists have frequently eschewed justice discourse although they have in most cases adopted human rights discourse. For some engaged Buddhists the overtones of retribution and the adversarial atmosphere of the courtroom carried by justice discourse are alien to an ethic riveted in compassion. Nevertheless, King argues that all engaged Buddhists affirm some version of economic justice. After tracing the complexities of engaged Buddhist positions on multiple forms of justice, King sums things up by saying for these thinkers "justice language . . . is not sufficient. . . . Justice must be interpreted with compassion and mercy." The latter are

by social injustice and oppression. The Eleventh Training recognizes that this injustice is a form of violence and it is directed against nature as well as society. In the Thirteenth Training we begin with an awareness of the suffering caused by social injustice, then we vow to prevent anyone from exploiting another living being and yet we are to do this by cultivating loving kindness. Thich Nhat Hanh links the Thirteenth Training with the Fourth, Fifth, and Twelfth Trainings. The Fourth focuses on our hearing the cries of the world; the Fifth encourages us to "free ourselves from a destructive social and economic machine"; and the Twelfth links our vast expenditures on arms and the military with lack of funding to alleviate hunger, to cure diseases and to eradicate illiteracy. The Ninth and Tenth Trainings suggest how we should do this, that is, by speaking out against injustice but without using words that divide (#9) and taking a stand against injustice without taking a partisan position (#10)—a challenge, I have suggested, that works like a Zen koan.[8] So, exactly one half of the mindfulness trainings are explicitly tied to confronting social injustice and the other seven could easily be shown to be linked as well. The interwoven threads of this tapestry of practice include perception and awareness, speech, acts of resistance, the development of individual lifestyles, and collective engagement.

Both Berrigan and Thich Nhat Hanh present challenges which I cannot claim to honor fully. The spiritual task of responding to their challenges continues indefinitely. But I also acknowledge the importance of the fourth and fifth tasks set by Schreiter. It is not enough to advocate *for* living beings; some constructive vision must also be advocated: advocacy leading to reconstruction. Again, here is Schreiter speaking of a theology geared toward praxis:

> Without . . . a horizon of utopia and prophecy it becomes difficult to focus, mobilize and sustain a struggle for a different kind of world. That different world must be able to be imagined, in however indistinct a fashion . . . in order for people to risk the present for the sake of a different kind of future. . . . Present evil can be denounced without a clear concept of an alternative good, but a praxis to eliminate the evil cannot be undertaken without some *telos*. Exodus from Egypt is not possible without the hope of a Promised Land; otherwise, it is only an exodus to die in the desert.[9]

---

non-negotiable Buddhist values that "may sometimes be in conflict with the rhetoric of justice." King, *Being Benevolence*, ch. 7; see esp. 202, 206, 213–14, 218–19.

8. Nhat Hanh, *Being Peace*, 93, 97–102.

9. Schreiter, *New Catholicity*, 103.

I believe that Schreiter has it right. Given the current state of political conflict and ideological rigidity in the United States and the scope of the challenges that we face, I believe that it is premature to offer a full-fledged blueprint for the reconstruction of society. However, we can offer a *model* of justice, a sketch of a *matrix* for developing new forms of praxis and of *vehicles* for carrying them forward. This provisional sketch will be built in stages. First, we will look at the "pro-social values" of empathy, benevolence and compassion and their role in elaborating a relational model of person-in-community. Second, following Martha Nussbaum, this understanding of the self will be used to revise the reigning social contract theories of justice. Compassion, in particular, arising out of our shared vulnerabilities, is the motivating force in our quest for justice that both pushes back the frontiers of justice and supplements or, more precisely, supersedes our quest for and practice of justice. Third, building upon these insights, I will present the "capability theory" developed by Amartya Sen and Martha Nussbaum as the model of justice that bears the clearest and deepest affinity with the vision of a just and peaceful world that we have been developing in previous chapters. Fourth, we will examine how one engaged Buddhist movement, the Sri Lankan Sarvodaya movement, seeks to reconstruct society through an alternative model of rural development. However, given both Daniel Berrigan's life of activism and Thich Nhat Hanh's fostering of an engaged Buddhism, I owe it to these forbearers to do more than articulate a theory of justice. The theory must be aligned with new forms of praxis. So, responding to Schreiter's challenge, I will propose a vision of "global civil society" as a matrix for developing the praxis of just peacemaking and of transnational advocacy NGOs (TANGOs) and transnational advocacy networks (TANs) in collaboration with countervailing institutions as, for the present, the best vehicles for carrying that praxis forward.

PROSOCIAL VALUES AND A RELATIONAL MODEL OF PERSON-IN-COMMUNITY

Let's begin at an empirical level, namely, with how social justice is conveyed in many universities. The engaged universities that I discussed in chapter 4 have created "service learning" programs that integrate work in community organizations with classroom learning. I also have taught such courses for the past fifteen years. However, such programs are promoted with an understanding of justice that I find problematic. In virtually all of the literature on engaged learning, the pedagogical process is seen as moving students "from charity to social justice." Invariably charity is construed as patronizing, as lacking in respect for the other or for her strengths, and as fostering a non-reciprocal relationship. Justice is seen as the polar opposite. Charity, in this rendition, bears almost no resemblance to the Christian virtue of *caritas* or the Buddhist virtue of compassion (*karuna*).[10] In my judgment, this ubiquitous treatment of justice versus charity presents a false dichotomy that misrepresents the process of moral development and undermines moral action. Here I present an alternative understanding focused on the relationship of compassion and justice.

Let's begin with a scene from one of American literature's classic expressions of compassion and indictments of injustice. It is the climactic scene in *The Adventures of Huckleberry Finn*, where Huck, having traveled the Mississippi River with Jim, a runaway slave, confronts the realization that two con men, the King and the Duke, have sold Jim back into slavery. Huck draws on the only social theory available to him that tells him that Jim is property and he properly, that is, by divine right, belongs to Miss Watson. Huck recognizes that his duty before God is to write a letter to Miss Watson so that she can reclaim what is rightfully hers. But having written the letter and having felt absolved of sin, Huck begins to remember the friendship, and the reciprocal acts of kindness that he shared with Jim, singing and laughing as they floated down the river. "Somehow," Huck concludes, "I couldn't seem to strike no places to harden me against him." So, faced with the awful specter of divine judgment, Huck says, "All right, then, I'll go to hell," and tears up the letter.[11]

One of the most memorable scenes in all of American literature, to be sure, but what bearing does it have on the task of constructing a new model of justice? In the first place, Huck's experience reminds us that we are all socialized into frameworks which convey some sense of justice and injustice that, in many cases, are religiously legitimated. More importantly, those frameworks that we may take for granted as true can be horribly wrong. We need the prophet's denunciation and critique. But Twain offers us a clue as to how we might right this wrong. In *Huckleberry Finn*, those who are motivated by self-interest turn out to be frauds, thieves, and murderers.

10. This theory of a linear development employs the classic rhetorical strategy of juxtaposing a debased form of one concept (charity) over against a vaguely stated, but positively inflected alternative concept (justice). Because of the prevalence of this comparison of charity and justice, I have often wondered whether the term "charity" can still be used or whether negative connotations are permanently stuck to it. Here I will focus more directly on the dialectic of compassion and justice. See further Strain, "Moving Like a Starfish."

11. Twain, *Adventures of Huckleberry Finn*, ch. 31, 167–68.

By contrast Huck, Twain's moral exemplar, is motivated by empathy and friendship. He cannot harden his heart against Jim.

Huck lacks an alternative, even if inchoate, theory of justice that he could appeal to in order to resist not only the laws and mores of the antebellum South but also its theology. Yet Huck has one thing that he can rely on, his empathy for Jim. Martin Hoffman argues that empathy appears to be hardwired in human beings. It is a result of natural selection in a species that is intrinsically social. It undergoes a complex developmental process that begins at a preverbal and preconceptual stage. Expressions of empathic distress can be seen in infants only a few days old, for example, in crying that mirrors another infant's crying. Early in their second year, young children begin to act on these feelings by seeking to comfort other toddlers in distress. When the young child begins to realize that she is a self who is distinct from the suffering other, empathy becomes sympathy or compassion while still retaining its affective charge.[12] At still later stages, cognitive processing begins to play a key role. "Each stage combines the gains of the previous stages. At the most advanced stages, one is exposed to a network of information about a victim's condition, which may include verbal and nonverbal cues from the victim, situational cues, and knowledge of the victim's life condition." Each kind of cue is processed differently, with empathy aroused largely by nonverbal cues. Knowledge about the victim will be processed through more complex cognitive processes including role taking and introspective processing.[13]

Adult interventions with young children focused on sharing toys, on understanding how another child may be reacting to the child's actions,

12. Hoffman, *Empathy and Moral Development*, 4–6, 64–65, 70–72, 88, 274. Primatologist Frans de Waal supports Hoffman's argument concerning the evolutionary roots of empathy and the multilayered character of prosocial emotions. Whereas we consider sympathy or compassion "as a single process, as something that you either have or lack . . . , in fact it consists of many different layers added by evolution over millions of years. Most mammals show some of these—only a few show them all." Certain mammals—apes, elephants, whales, and dolphins—besides humans, move beyond empathic distress to active sympathy, including providing consolation and "targeted helping" grounded in perspective taking. The emotional repertoire that we share with these mammals can be viewed as like a Russian doll. For de Waal, the fact that we share this repertoire does not devalue our humanity. "If being sensitive to others were truly limited to our species, this would make it a young trait, something we evolved only recently. The problem with young traits is that they tend to be experimental. . . . Linking empathy to our frontal lobes, which achieved their extraordinary size only in the last couple of million years, denies how much it is part of who and what we are. Obviously, I believe that empathy is part of a heritage as ancient as the mammalian line." *Age of Empathy*, 43, 88–89, 96, 100–101, 108–9, 208–9, and passim.

13. Hoffman, *Empathy and Moral Development*, 5–7.

serve to develop a basic sense of justice as fairness and reciprocity. Bonding empathy with such moral principles helps to correct empathic bias toward those who are familiar and compensates for its over or under arousal. While moral principles educate empathic feelings, the latter, Hoffman says, have an enduring role to play. "Abstract moral principles learned in 'cool' didactic contexts . . . lack motive force. Empathy's contribution to moral principles is to transform them into prosocial hot cognitions—cognitive representations charged with empathic affect, thus giving them motive force."[14]

Hoffman expands this analysis by arguing that "caring," when it is elevated to a philosophical ideal, grounding an entire social ethics, is itself an abstract moral principle which needs to be charged with empathy to have motive force. Mature adults have empathically grounded principles of both caring and justice. In given situations they may opt for one or the other but to see caring and justice as exclusive alternatives misreads the complexity of our moral lives.[15]

Hoffman uses an example from psychiatrist Robert Coles' study of the moral lives of children during the era of the struggle for civil rights to illustrate the complex bonding of empathy with caring and justice, an example that takes us beyond Huck's purely empathic response. A Southern white teenager initially joins a crowd harassing a black teenager who is integrating their school. However, the quiet dignity of the black teenager leads his white counterpart to feel bad for him while attributing the cause of the injustice to meddling federal judges. Empathy and caring, however, lead him to intervene when the harassers threaten physical violence. The white teenager then develops a friendship with the black teenager. Finally, he comes to the conclusion that segregation is unjust and must be ended.[16]

This example coheres with an argument that Martha Nussbaum makes in *Frontiers of Justice*, namely, that our benevolent inclinations can be warped by "pernicious fictions" that abound in our public culture. Our emotional life is socially shaped including the way emotions choose their "objects, their modes of expression, the norms they express, [and] the beliefs about the world they embody." But if our benevolent emotions can be misshaped, they can be reshaped. "If we are made aware of another person's suffering in the right way, we will go to his or her aid. The problem is that most of the time we are . . . not led, through an education of the imagination, to picture these sufferings vividly to ourselves. . . . It seems that the

14. Ibid., 10, 17–18, 23, 221, 238–39, 241–42.

15. Ibid., 222–26, 267–70.

16. Ibid., 107–8.

extension of benevolence is at least possible and that people's concepts of what they owe to self and others are actually very fluid."[17]

REVISING SOCIAL CONTRACT MODELS OF JUSTICE

Nussbaum's argument for the malleability of prosocial emotions and, in particular, for a common fund of benevolent emotions undergirds her neo-Aristotelian critique of social contract theories of justice.

> For the social contract tradition, the idea of mutual advantage is central: parties depart from the state of nature in order to gain mutual benefit. . . . [My] capabilities approach feels free to use an account of cooperation that treats justice and inclusiveness as ends of intrinsic value from the beginning, and that views human beings as held together by many altruistic ties as well as by mutual advantage. Together with this, it uses a political conception of the person that views the person . . . as *a political and social animal, who seeks a good that is social through and through*. . . . The good of others is not just a constraint on this person's pursuit of her own good; *it is part of her good*. . . . The person leaves the state of nature . . . because she cannot imagine living well without shared ends and a shared life.[18]

Nussbaum's Neo-Aristotelian understanding of the self as a political and social animal is congruent with Catholic social teaching, which sees our social nature as mirroring the Trinitarian God who is pure relationality. It is also congruent with the Buddhist understanding of interdependence and the mutual interpenetration of all living beings. In Nussbaum's eudaemonistic theory, fully human flourishing is only possible in common.[19]

Nussbaum's argument about benevolent sentiments and their education leads us to an additional point. She advocates not merely an understanding of sociability as an intrinsic good (we are *social* animals) but also an awareness of our vulnerability as mortal, bodily beings (we are social

17. Nussbaum, *Frontiers of Justice*, 411–13. Nussbaum defines empathy as the imaginative reconstruction of another's feelings. *Upheavals of Thought*, 327–35. This definition is problematic in light of Hoffman's more nuanced presentation of a complex empathic process. Imaginative reconstruction would seem to require more complex processing than infants (or certain other animals) are capable of but who do experience empathic distress at another's pain. She does acknowledge psychologists who see a closer connection between the two and, moreover, see a close connection between compassion and helping behavior. Ibid., 331.

18. Nussbaum, *Frontiers of Justice*, 156–58; italics added.

19. Ibid., 85–86, 91.

animals). Social contract theories presuppose fully functional, autonomous and roughly equal adults who freely adopt a political system. For many individuals throughout their lives and for all of us during significant chunks of our lives, we are, to the contrary, dependent, vulnerable, existing in asymmetrical relationships with caregivers. Infants and children, the elderly, people with physical or mental disabilities are citizens, too, as are their caregivers and deserve support adequate for them to lead the fullest human life possible.[20]

Nussbaum argues that the emotion that arises when I recognize another as suffering from what are shared vulnerabilities (think of the Buddha's triad of suffering from illness, old age and mortality) is compassion. Emotions for her are cognitive in character and compassion specifically involves the judgments, first, that the harm suffered by the other is serious, second, that it is in some sense undeserved, and third, that "some sort of community between myself and the other" exists, or what she calls the "eudaemonistic judgment" that this being is important to me, "an end whose good is to be promoted."[21]

Both Christians and Buddhists will take issue with Nussbaum's second judgment. Agapic love is unconditional as the parable of the Prodigal Son insists. Likewise, in dharma talks Thich Nhat Hanh frequently uses the example of the right hand aiming for a nail with a hammer and hitting the left hand instead. No faultfinding on either side (I'll take you to court, right hand); no attempt at moral justification (You got in the road, left hand). Rather, an immediate recognition that the other's suffering is my own—the self/other distinction in the Buddhist understanding of compassion is overcome as being the root of ignorance.[22] Bluntly stated, compassion challenges the implicit stance of moral superiority in the judgment of deserved or undeserved suffering.

In response to critics who emphasize the untrustworthiness of emotions such as empathy and compassion in leading to moral principles undergirding a just social order, Nussbaum spends a great deal of time discussing the need to educate compassion especially by providing children with stories that stretch their imagination of the conditions of others. To bring this about requires "a culture of ethical criticism" through which our egoistic self—with its fears, envies, and jealousies, which thwart our empathic sensibilities—is challenged. The ideal of the adult male, as "self-sufficient,

20. Ibid., 87–89, 96–102 and passim.

21. Nussbaum, *Upheavals of Thought*, 301–21.

22. Nussbaum will acknowledge that one may have compassion for one who is culpable if the punishment greatly exceeds the crime, or if circumstances qualify the perpetrator's culpability. Ibid., 312–14.

controlling, dominant," an ideal that requires repressing our fears and denying our vulnerabilities, in particular, needs to be overcome through educating our imagination.[23]

Daniel Berrigan and Walter Brueggemann insist that it is not merely a question of substituting better stories for those that warp our emotions in order to educate benevolent emotions. It is a question of resurrecting the imagination itself. "We need to ask not whether [another world] is realistic or practical or viable," Brueggemann insists, "but whether it is *imaginable*. We need to ask if our consciousness and imagination have been so assaulted and coopted . . . that we have been robbed of the courage and the power to think an alternative thought."[24] Before we can imagine another world, we must imagine that another world is possible and imagine ourselves as the kind of people that could create it. The prophet's yes, following all too slowly his no, affirms this enduring possibility in the teeth of socialized death.

There is a dialectic at work here, however. If our compassion needs to be educated in order to extend itself beyond the small circle of family and friends and to release it from the grip of pernicious fictions, it is compassion that provides the motive for expanding the frontiers of justice. Compassion includes the excluded. The parable of the Prodigal Son is not only a parable of unconditional love; it is also a parable about the limits of distributive justice. The eldest son has a clear sense of justice as a fair discrimination between those who deserve rewards and those who do not. The troubling question the parable raises is this: Why is the eldest son not like his father? As implicitly critical of the eldest son's narrow view of justice, the father's love is compassion with an edge. Recall our discussion in chapter 1 of Berrigan's poem, "Children in the Shelter." I called both the act and the telling of the story of Berrigan carrying a Vietnamese child into a bomb shelter as they escaped from American bombs falling on Hanoi compassion with an edge. Likewise, in the midst of war, the work of Thich Nhat Hanh's students from the School of Youth for Social Service in helping peasants rebuild bombed-out villages was compassion with an edge. Such acts revealed the profound injustice of war. How do you educate students not just to extend the scope of compassion but to allow themselves to be transformed by examples of compassion with an edge? What sort of understanding of justice can we come to if we open our minds and hearts to the koan at the heart of the parable of the Eldest Son? Or, for that matter, the parable of the Sea Pirate?

23. Nussbaum, "Compassion and Terror," 24–25. See also *Frontiers of Justice*, 408–15.

24. Brueggemann, *Prophetic Imagination*, 39; italics in original. See also 40, 59–60.

A clear case in which this dialectic of compassion and justice is at work in Nussbaum's writings is her treatment of people with physical or mental disabilities. This is an area where Nussbaum seeks to push back the "frontiers" of justice. Traditional social contract theories, based on the myth of the fully functional, autonomous person, as we have seen, do not take into account human vulnerabilities. To be cared for in times of need is a basic right that needs to be met if one is to live a life with dignity.

> A satisfactory account of human justice requires recognizing the equal citizenship of people with impairments, including mental impairments, and appropriately supporting the labor of caring for and educating them. . . . It also requires recognizing the many varieties of impairment, disability, need and dependency that "normal" human beings experience, and thus the very great continuity between "normal" lives and those of people with life-long impairments.[25]

The scare quotes around "normal" represent the work of empathy and compassion that dissolves such a morally bankrupt distinction between "normal" persons and—what?—"abnormal" persons. By pushing back the frontiers of *justice*, Nussbaum demands that a just society must not exploit the compassion of caregivers. They too have a life to live and, to begin with, their loving work should be considered as work and adequately compensated.[26] So, for example, the tendency in our society to assume that caregiving will be relegated to women who act out of sacrificial love like stay-at-home moms or to low-paid day care and nursing home workers not only raises issues of basic justice but exploits and thereby corrupts compassion.

Those thinkers who ground their understanding of social justice in Catholic social teachings will welcome this deepened understanding of compassion and justice but, following John Paul II, will want to see the synthesis of compassion and justice giving birth to solidarity. In his 1987 encyclical, *Sollicitudo Rei Socialis*, Pope John Paul described the overcoming of the moral obstacle to the development of all as "above all a question of *interdependence*, sensed as a *system* determining relationships in the contemporary world, in its economic, cultural, political and religious elements, and accepted as a *moral category*." It is this shift to seeing interdependence as a

25. Nussbaum, *Frontiers of Justice*, 98–99.

26. Ibid., 100. Nussbaum recognizes that there is a gender issue involved, in that most of the caregiving for those with impairments is by women who, in caring for a family member, are not compensated at all or who, in institutional settings, are often compensated at minimum wage levels.

moral category that John Paul characterized as a conversion of the heart. Then he went on to add:

> When interdependence becomes recognized in this way, the correlative response as a moral and social attitude, as a "virtue" is *solidarity*. This then is not a feeling of vague compassion, or shallow distress at the misfortune of so many people, both near and far. On the contrary, it is a *firm and persevering determination* to commit oneself to the *common good*: that is to say, to the good of all and each individual, because we are *all* really responsible for *all*.[27]

The transformation of the sheer fact of interdependence into the virtue of solidarity is to be applied at the collective level, as well. In international relations it means shifting from mutual distrust to collaboration and abandoning all forms of imperial domination. Such solidarity for the Christian, the pope insists, is rooted in communion with the Triune God.[28]

For their part, engaged Buddhists are less likely to stress a shift from a "feeling of vague compassion" to solidarity. Compassion grounded in awareness of specific forms of suffering—as presented, for example, in the Fourteen Mindfulness Trainings—is hardly vague. A persistent cultivation of the concrete awareness of suffering in its multiple forms, both personal and collective, leads to resolve. The first of the Bodhisatva vows, "Livings beings are numberless, I vow to liberate them all," conveys this resolution as does its conceptual underpinning that awakening is achieved by each together with all or not at all. I mentioned earlier that the Tenth Mindfulness Training ("A spiritual community should . . . take a clear stand against oppression and injustice and should strive to change the situation without engaging in partisan conflicts") represents a koan for me. Gandhi's *satyagraha*, firmness in the truth while treating all parties as ends in themselves, is one way of addressing it. True solidarity crosses borders. The Hebrew prophets' focus on the widow, the orphan, and the stranger at the gate was a declaration of solidarity with those who fell outside the structures of a patriarchal society. Jesus' practice of what John Dominic Crossan calls "open commensality," men and women, tax collectors and sinners eating together, transgressed his society's "vertical discriminations and lateral separations." His was a radically egalitarian challenge to the social order as reflected in who is invited to the table and who is not.[29] In short, Jesus' solidarity subverted all forms of partisanship.

27. John Paul II, *Sollicitudo Rei Socialis*, #38; italics in original.

28. Ibid., #39–40.

29. Crossan. *Jesus: A Revolutionary Biography*, 69.

Finally, both Christians and Buddhists will say that compassion supplements or, more precisely, supersedes justice. Justice can do much but it stops short of addressing our need for friendship or our need for forgiveness, for someone to share our grief over the loss of a loved one or the need of the dying for a caring presence. Such compassion is the manifestation of our Buddha Nature. Likewise, Berrigan's experience at St. Rose's Hospital for the dying poor nicely captures the linkage and dialectic of justice and compassion. On the one hand, the nonviolent warrior for justice saw in this place a challenge to our prevailing models of justice. "In any sane scheme of things . . . would not free medical care be free to all?" Yet St. Rose's offered more: Compassionate care so that those cast aside could die well. "With what a sense of refreshment, self-restoring, I came to St. Rose's. Slowly I sensed that an atrophied sixth or seventh sense was coming to life; a sense of recognition." At St. Rose's, something more than justice was provided and that something was the presence of the reign of God.[30]

So, compassion motivates the search for justice; it pushes back the frontiers of justice and reveals the limits of justice. Acting with compassion and seeking justice together lead to the firm commitment of solidarity. Hoffman's and Nussbaum's discussions of empathy and care culminating in the discussion of compassion and solidarity reveal a rich array of prosocial emotions that is obscured in treatments of "charity" as a debased form of relationality. Unlike Nussbaum, those who view education for social engagement as a linear movement "from charity to social justice" miss entirely the dialectic of compassion and justice, and consequently do not grasp the full meaning of solidarity. So, now we come back to the central issue of this chapter, only now restated. What model of justice is congruent with this ethos of compassionate caring? What sort of justice could the prophet and the bodhisattva embrace?

HUMAN RIGHTS AS HUMAN CAPABILITIES

Nussbaum calls her alternative to social contract theories of justice "capabilities theory." She states clearly that she conceives it as a species of human rights theory.[31] She developed the theory in collaboration with economist and Nobel laureate, Amartya Sen. Initially the theory was presented as a critique of and an alternative to the prevailing Western model of development which focused exclusively on GDP growth as a measure of social progress. As a crude utilitarian calculus GDP says nothing about the distribution of

30. Berrigan, "Where Death Abounded, Life," 171–73.

31. Nussbaum and Faralli, "New Frontiers of Justice," 155.

economic goods but, more importantly, one social good (wealth) hardly heals all social ills. So, Sen and Nussbaum offer their "capabilities approach" as a form of human development or what Catholic social teachings would call integral development. This approach asks a simple question, "What is each person able to do and to be?" It is a resolutely outcome-based approach but one which treats each person as an end: Aggregate calculations, like GDP, miss how different persons and all of us at different stages of our lives need different resources in order to be able to live a life of dignity as a being of intrinsic worth. When we ask the question of what capabilities are necessary for a life of dignity, the answer is many different capabilities. "The capabilities approach is resolutely *pluralist about value*: it holds that the capabilities that are central for people are different in quality, not just in quantity; that they cannot without distortion be reduced to a single numerical scale; and that a fundamental part of understanding and producing them is understanding the specific nature of each."[32] Tied to this idea of plural social goods is Nussbaum's argument that a society may not trade off a superfluity of one good for a deficiency of another.

Nussbaum incorporates a specific list of capabilities that trump all other considerations in estimating the justice or injustice of a given society. The capabilities approach is not only a means for normatively evaluating human development; it also suggests *which* capabilities are so intrinsic to a human life with dignity that it cannot be actualized without their basic development. As a species of human rights theory, the central capabilities must be achieved by all at a minimum *threshold* if the society is to be considered just.[33] Based on extensive experience working with women and women's advocacy organizations in India *and* through cross cultural dialogue, Nussbaum lists ten capabilities that are essential to a human life able to be lived with dignity. These combine both the development of internal capabilities and the social, political, and economic conditions necessary for their actualization:

- *Life*, including the removal of social causes of premature death.
- *Bodily health*, including adequate nourishment and shelter.
- *Bodily integrity*, including security from violent assault.
- *Senses, imagination, and thought*, including their development through education and a guarantee of the freedom to express them.

32. Sen, *Development as Freedom*, 58–63, 104–7; Nussbaum, *Creating Capabilities*, xi, 18–19, 4–6.

33. Nussbaum, *Creating Capabilities*, 24–25, 27–28, 32, 40, 62–63.

- *Emotions*, including not having one's emotional development warped by abuse or fear.
- *Practical reason*. "Being able to form a concept of the good and to engage in critical reflection about the planning of one's life."
- *Affiliation*, including freedom to associate with others, freedom of assembly, "having the social bases of self-respect and non-humiliation."
- *Other species*, including living in a respectful relation to nature and other living beings.
- *Play*, including the leisure to live a creative and enjoyable life.
- *Control over one's environment*, including the right to political participation, freedom of speech, and the right to acquire and hold property.[34]

In *Women and Human Development*, Nussbaum defends her list of rights from the cultural relativists. She argues for what David Hollenbach calls "dialogical universalism," an overlapping consensus developed through ongoing cross-cultural interchanges. Such a list is contestable and revisable.[35]

Nussbaum singles out affiliation and practical reason as critical to securing the other capabilities. Affiliation is obvious given her understanding of human beings as social animals. Fostering relationships grounded in mutual recognition and respect, as well as protection of privacy in all social spheres, grounds each of the basic entitlements. Practical reason supports the freedom to choose and to plan one's own model of the good life.[36] For example, enabling a hungry person to feed herself is not only making a lasting impact, it is restoring that person's dignity and recognizing that freedom of agency is intrinsic to a life of dignity.

This list fulfills one of what I see as the requirements of a theory of justice for our time, namely that it include an argument for basic rights. Rights discourse is the moral vernacular of our time and it has been employed by courageous resisters in every corner of the globe. What I mean by "the moral vernacular of our time" has been nicely captured by Samuel Moyn in *The Last Utopia*:

> When people hear the phrase "human rights," they think of the highest moral precepts and political ideals. And they are right to do so. . . . The phrase implies an agenda for improving the world, and bringing about a new one in which the dignity of

34. Ibid., 30, 32–34.

35. Nussbaum, *Women and Human Development*, 34–80; *Frontiers of Justice*, 296–98. See also Hollenbach, *Claims in Conflict*, 130–33.

36. Nussbaum, *Creating Capabilities*, 39–40.

> each individual will enjoy secure international protection. It is a recognizably utopian program. . . . It promises to penetrate the impregnability of state borders, slowly replacing them with the authority of international law. It prides itself on offering victims the world over the possibility of a better life. . . . Human rights in this sense have come to define the most elevated aspirations of both social movements and political entities—state and interstate. They evoke hope and provoke action.[37]

In our time, if we are to both denounce the injustice of the present and to advocate for a different future, we will inevitably speak of human rights. Around the utopian idea of human rights, numerous practical movements have emerged pushing into new areas of humanitarian concern.[38]

If we want to foster this movement, we must constantly reinvent it. Nussbaum's list is more than a contribution to theories of justice. As evidenced by her close work with women's advocacy NGOs in India, it is an *intervention* in the history of the human rights movement. Not only does it go beyond civil liberties to articulate social and economic rights—many formulations, beginning with the UN's Universal Declaration, do that—but it also emphasizes women's rights and it links the cause of human rights to a transformation of Western models of development. It has the potential, at least, to shape new forms of praxis.[39]

There are a number of good reasons to adopt Nussbaum's model of justice in order to elaborate a social ethics informed by the prophet and the bodhisattva. First, Nussbaum locates her model squarely within the social contract tradition. As such, it does not claim to be a full-blown definition of the good life. Rather it specifies minimal conditions necessary for a life that is worth living. Both Buddhist and Christian traditions present their own robust understandings of a good life. Such visions are not preempted by a minimalist approach to social justice.

Pluralism is further protected by the incorporation of civil liberties within the list of capabilities. Moreover, items on the list can be implemented in a variety of ways through the agency of different social institutions.[40] What we are presented with is not a hardened ideology but a self-limiting model which functions as guiding means (upaya), particularly in expanding the frontiers of justice.

37. Moyn, *Last Utopia*, 1.

38. Ibid., 7, 41–42, 121, 132, 145, 148–50, 155, 157–58, 220–23.

39. See Nussbaum, *Women and Human Development*.

40. Nussbaum, *Frontiers of Justice*, 70–71, 78–80. Nussbaum sees the state as the necessary guarantor that basic rights have been met but it is not necessarily the agency that delivers them.

Nevertheless, second, it is the ways in which Nussbaum transforms social contract theory that are most important for our purposes. The lever of this transformation is her concept of human beings as *political animals*. We are social beings, part of whose good is found in living well with others. Prosocial values are biologically grounded. Basic empathy, properly tutored, becomes benevolence and compassion. So we form societies with others not only out of self-interest but in pursuit of an intrinsic good. Social institutions, of all sorts, are less necessary constraints on our freedom than ways through which we intersubjectively realize freedom.

Third, for Christians who believe in "God's preferential option for the poor" or Buddhists who recognize that life is suffering, Nussbaum's recognition, in conjunction with other feminist ethicists, that we have basic needs that must be met if we are to live a life worth living and that we are vulnerable beings who are supported for significant portions of our lives in asymmetrical relations of dependency is of central significance. The fiction of the autonomous, self-sufficient individual who enters a social contract simply to maximize its own interests ultimately is a pernicious fiction. A corollary to this emphasis on human vulnerabilities is that an ethics of care and an ethics of justice are interdependent. In asymmetrical relations of dependence, care takes on central importance. Yet, justice demands that both the one cared for and the caregiver be adequately supported so that they both are capable of a fully rounded and dignified life.[41]

Fourth, Nussbaum focuses on what we can call the emotional and imaginative foundations of a healthy life in society. A healthy social matrix in Nussbaum's estimation requires cultivating the imagination in ways that counter pernicious fictions which propagate the antisocial emotions of shame and disgust and which foster stigmatization and humiliation.[42] Viewed from this angle, Berrigan's *Sorrow Built a Bridge* that records his experiences with gays dying of AIDS during the period when stigmas prevailed was more than a journal of compassion. It was a counter-narrative that resisted a pernicious fiction and thereby functioned to restore our emotional capacity for living well together.

Fifth, both Daniel Berrigan and Thich Nhat Hanh would welcome an understanding of justice that does not obscure the role of prosocial emotions in the theory and practice of justice by lacing the term "charity" with pejorative connotations. Instead prosocial emotions but especially compassion play a political role which includes expanding the "frontiers" of justice.

41. Ibid., 66–67, 88–89, 168–71, 413; Nussbaum and Faralli, "New Frontiers of Justice," 152–53.

42. Nussbaum, *Frontiers of Justice*, 412–13. On this topic see, Nussbaum, *Hiding from Humanity*.

Compassion needs to be educated or, as Thich Nhat Hanh would put it, mindfully trained. One form of that education is to equip it with a theory of basic capabilities that enable us to live a dignified life.[43] Yet, it is compassion that, Nussbaum argues, breathes life into morality and into the legal systems that bind us together. Quoting Walt Whitman, she says, "To hold men together by paper and seal or by compulsion is no account / That only holds men together which aggregates all in a living principle, as the hold of the limbs of the body. . . ."[44]

Compassion, even when ill-developed, gives us "an ethical core to work with, a promising imaginative basis for the extension . . . of concern."[45] This imagination of the other as intrinsically linked to one's own good is the cognitive dimension of compassion and accords well with the Hebrew prophets imagining a time when the widow, the orphan, and the stranger at the gate will be cared for. Where Nussbaum turns to the arts and especially to literature to nurture and expand the empathic imagination, Thich Nhat Hanh will suggest that ultimately this requires a *practice* that roots compassion within our daily activities and fosters a constant awareness that we "inter-are."

Sixth, by focusing on multiple conditions of a life worth living, Nussbaum implicitly expands our understanding of what it means to be impoverished. There can be no simple solution, then, to poverty. The capabilities list fleshes out what Catholic social teaching means by "integral development." All of the capabilities must be developed. Rights correspond to what a Buddhist recognizes as the conditionality and emptiness of our existence. We do not flourish on our own, apart from a complex matrix through which we become capable of a complex actualization. Given this complexity, it is reasonable to assume that no single social institution can enable us to become capable in this complex sense. Contributions from multiple intermediate institutions are necessary to achieve integral development.

Finally, there is a degree of optimism in Nussbaum's model of justice that accords more with socially engaged Buddhism and with the universalist emphasis in Catholic social teaching than it does with Berrigan's dark vision grounded in a hope against hope. Her optimism is rooted in her understanding of our intrinsic sociality and in an understanding of compassion and the role of education in shaping us as cosmopolitan moral agents. While I welcome this optimism, I must also say, having spent more than

43. Nussbaum, *Upheavals of Thought*, 399, 403.

44. Whitman, "By Blue Ontario's Shore," as cited in ibid., 404.

45. Nussbaum, *Upheavals of Thought*, 414; see also 425–33. See also Nussbaum, *Cultivating Humanity*.

forty years teaching at the university level, that I am not quite as sanguine as Nussbaum about the role of education in general and the humanities in particular to transform the "pernicious fictions" that distort our public life. Racism (to the degree that it has been checked while certainly not overcome), especially as it was cemented in the ideology and legal system called Jim Crow, was not transformed by education but through a prophetic voice. While Dr. King can certainly be seen as a public educator, his voice was far closer to Isaiah than to Socrates. Moreover, voice alone did not alter racist structures. It required the praxis, i.e., (recalling our earlier definition), the symbolically constituted, critically reflected, strategically directed actions of a prophetic community.

What I take away from this critique of Nussbaum's optimism is that while models of justice are essential to an elaborated social ethics, they must be buttressed, first, by a critique of the reigning ideologies and, then, by praxis. So we need, for example, Berrigan's dissection of imperial power as the practice of "death as a social method." Likewise, the praxis that the model of justice clarifies and supports will feed back into our reflections on the model itself.

SARVODAYA: A BUDDHIST VISION FOR RECONSTRUCTING SOCIETY

What might it look like if Nussbaum's model of justice were being implemented on the ground? Engaged Buddhism offers one example, the Sarvodaya movement in Sri Lanka, that bears some affinity with Nussbaum's capability approach and offers a concrete model that "another world is possible." Sarvodaya, which means "the awakening of all," was started in 1958 by a high school teacher, A.T. Ariyaratne, who wished to provide his students with an experience of Gandhian selfless service. What began as a "service learning" project matured into an alternative to the Western model of development. In this alternative the rural village is seen as the heart of the nation. The awakening of these villages—Sarvodaya has organized fifteen thousand of them—is to produce the collective awakening of the nation.[46] Ariyaratne combined Gandhian principles of nonviolent social change with an interpretation of Buddhist teachings that stressed collective awakening. So, the First Noble Truth was translated as "There is a decadent village." The roots of this social suffering were seen in the three poisons which foster a social system based on egoism and competition. The liberation that is

46. Macy, foreword to *Buddhism at Work*, xi; see also 7–8. See also Bond, "A. T. Ariyaratne," 121–46.

sought is political and economic as well as cultural and spiritual. Key to this collective awakening is the Shramadana or work camp where organizers bring the village together—including the children—and lead a process of discernment about what needs to be done. The village as a whole then organizes and carries out its task, whether it is digging a well, building a school or creating a community garden to meet children's nutritional needs. The slogan of Sarvodaya is "We build the road and the road builds us."[47]

This positive Gandhian-Buddhist vision aims at village self-sufficiency in meeting a set of basic human needs—ten in all, ranging from a clean environment and balanced nutrition to continuing education for all and the meeting of cultural and spiritual needs. There must be integral development of all dimensions of a human life. Sarvodaya hopes to build a "no poverty / no affluence" society. Sarvodaya is also based on a comprehensive critique of the Western model of development focusing on the three dimensions of economics, power and consciousness. The Western model provides an economic order that widens the gap between rich and poor, fosters an unsustainable way of life, and creates both envy and despair in the minds of vast numbers of poor people. Power is centralized in the hands of a Western educated elite and violence is used to maintain that power. These two dimensions foster a consciousness of suffering and deprivation. The centers of power turn the resulting collective anger outward, promoting bigotry, wars, and ethnic hatred based on the delusion that "we are different." In Sri Lanka's case this malign process led to two decades of civil war with the Tamil minority—a war that Sarvodaya opposed by organizing massive peaceful gatherings that brought together different ethnic and religious groups to meditate together. Sarvodaya's strength as a model is its vision of another possible world and its huge success in organizing Sri Lankan rural villages. It is more than a theory; it is, indeed, Buddhism at work.[48]

The example of Sarvodaya takes us several steps beyond Nussbaum's model of justice. First, as a *theory*, Sarvodaya concretizes a model similar to Nussbaum's by tailoring it to the needs of rural villages and explicitly contrasting itself with Western models of development that have served to create mass exodus from rural locales across the Third World. Second, it offers a *Buddhist-inspired framework* (i.e., grounded in the Four Noble Truths)

47. Bond, *Buddhism at Work*, 9–10, 14–16, 19–21. See also http://www.sarvodaya.org.

48. Ibid., 27–42, 49–50, 95–96. While it may slow the rural-to-urban exodus, however, it was not as designed to deal with the worst expanses of slums which ring the cities of the Third World. In 2002, Sarvodaya began emphasizing *Nagarodaya*, its urban awakening program in recognition that a collective awakening of liberation must address the needs of the urban poor. Ibid., 110.

for understanding why villages fail to thrive and how collective liberation might come about. Third, through the Shramadana, it offers a *method of organizing* villages that emphasizes self-reliance. Finally, as a *movement*, it provides a carrier, or, in Buddhist terms, a "vehicle" for actualizing the theory. If we compare Sarvodaya, then, to the set of tasks that Schreiter offered for a social model geared toward praxis, Sarvodaya clearly goes beyond the tasks of resistance, denunciation, critique, and even advocacy to actual reconstruction. More importantly, it has addressed the issue of how to put its model into practice.

PREPARING THE WAY FOR RECONSTRUCTING EMPIRE

Schreiter's own examples of social locations where theology and social ethics are called to the task of reconstruction are post-Soviet Eastern Europe and post-apartheid South Africa.[49] I suggest that reconstruction is premature in "our" social location or, more precisely, my own location as an American citizen at the heart of empire.[50] Empires oppress. They commandeer the lion's share of multiple goods leaving weaker states unable to ensure basic capabilities for all of their citizens. Overweaning hubris leads empires to collapse unless, that is, they disentangle themselves from the twisted cables of power. Our empire has not yet reached the stage of collapse and, I will argue in chapter 6, it still is utterly deluded by the myth of its own exceptionalism.[51]

In such a historical context it is easy to see the vital necessity of the prophet's denunciation coupled with symbolic acts of resistance. If we shift to the bodhisattva's perspective, it becomes clearer than ever that we are not the people that we need to be to take on the empire whose toxic fumes fill our lungs. Violence fills our airwaves as it rages on our streets. The violence of retribution pervades the systems that mete out "justice." Callous neglect of forty-five million Americans who live in poverty poisons our collective

49. Schreiter, *New Catholicity*, 101, 103–4.

50. I will take up what I mean by this description of my social location in chapter 6. Until then, I ask that we work with an intuitive understanding of the severe ambiguities in America's global role.

51. We can trace this myth all the way to John Winthrop's sermon, "A Modell of Christian Charitie," in 1630 on board the ship Arbella before it even landed at what was to become the Massachusetts Bay Colony. Through his famous metaphor of "a city on the hill," Winthrop set apart his ragtag group of followers from all human societies that had gone before as providentially designated by God to be a beacon, a model for the rest of humanity. See Cherry, *God's New Israel*, 39–43.

psyche. For engaged Buddhism there can be no outer revolution without inner transformation. So, building spiritual communities is a practice necessary to prepare for future reconstruction of society. We are, in short, a long way from taking up the task of reconstruction.

Nevertheless, it is important for a model of justice that has concrete weight as opposed to merely theoretical cogency to move us beyond resistance, denunciation and critique to somewhere between advocacy and reconstruction. The next step beyond Nussbaum will be, I suggest, something less than a full-blown model for social reconstruction, as articulated in practice by Sarvodaya. It will be an empirically grounded theory of how social transformation to implement a model of justice like Nussbaum's might come about as well as a specification of the historical *matrix* that could generate social forces (communities, movements, institutions, and networks) that might be or become the *vehicles* for social transformation. Given the unripeness of our historical context, this will only be a provisional sketch. But such a sketch could well encourage us to risk moving to specific forms of praxis that cohere with our understanding of justice.

The sketch itself, to be sure, because it commits us to a particular reading of history with its complex welter of social forces entails a risk. With this in mind, I begin with a recent example of nonviolent overcoming an empire that will lead directly to my own provisional sketch of social forces that open a horizon of social transformation. I mentioned earlier the chill that descended over all of Eastern Europe when, in 1968, Soviet tanks crushed the fledgling efforts of party leadership in Czechoslovakia to create "socialism with a human face." Two years later Polish workers in the Gdansk shipyards went on strike over raises in food prices. They streamed out of the shipyards and, rioting, they trashed the Communist Party headquarters. Soldiers quickly corralled the strikers, killing several workers. The frost in Eastern Europe turned to ice.

In the decade that followed, both workers and intellectuals drew the lessons from these experiences. First, a direct challenge to a totalitarian power structure would not work. So, Polish workers sought only the right to organize independent unions, not to change the Soviet system. Second, violent confrontation would only draw worse repression. Third, workers, intellectuals, and students would have to act in solidarity. Fourth, allies needed to be found in "countervailing institutions"—in the Polish case this would be the Catholic Church.[52]

52. As an *institution*, the Catholic Church in Poland was a visible sign of resistance to the Communist regime. As a *community*, it provided Poles with a sense of a collective identity that was separate from the ideologically enforced identity of a Communist society. Likewise, Solidarity played a complex role as both an embryonic *institution*

Key intellectual-activists, Adam Michnik in Poland, Vaclav Havel in Czechoslovakia, and Gyorgy Konrad in Hungary, went a step further. They called for the formation of "parallel structures" outside of political control. "Because power is still totalitarian," Michnik said, "whereas society isn't any more; it is already anti-totalitarian, it rebels and sets up its own independent institutions, which lead to something we could call civil society in Tocqueville's sense. That is what we tried to build: civil society."[53] Solidarity, the independent union, was a case in point. So also were the "flying universities" in Poland that offered uncensored lectures in apartments eluding as much as possible central control. In the terms that we developed in chapter 4, "working the linkages" among empowering communities, social movements, and countervailing institutions brought about a birth of civil society. Such examples of self-organization were instances of what Havel called "living in truth," living without being compromised by the blandishments of power. As in Gandhi's India, withdrawing cooperation from empire, seeding new social organizations without attempting to slay Goliath, led eventually to the crumbling of imperial rule. The Soviet system turned out to be more Oz than Goliath, only the mirage of power.[54]

Michnik's reference to Alexis de Tocqueville, I believe, is of key importance. In his classic *Democracy in America*, Tocqueville with acute prescience detailed both the form of oppression to which democracies are vulnerable and the antidote to that proclivity. Where feudal society was hierarchical, organic, and structured through mutual obligations between lords and serfs, Tocqueville saw democracy as egalitarian, atomistic and, in a thousand ways, communicating the message, "You're on your own." The type of person that emerges with democracy is the individual, a person, Tocqueville takes pains to note, who is not—initially at least—egoistic but simply self-absorbed, wholly engaged in a private pursuit of happiness with family and a few friends. Such a person only rarely tunes in to public affairs. As a result, a unique form of despotism may arise which even preserves the forms of democracy. An immense protective power, "it does not break men's wills but softens, bends and guides." Periodically the people awaken and elect their benign rulers and then return to their solitary preoccupations. "They console themselves for being under schoolmasters by thinking that they have chosen them themselves."[55]

(an independent union) and as a *movement* that united Poles across multiple sectors of industry and society.

53. Adam Michnik, as cited in Schell, *Unconquerable World*, 195.

54. For this entire history, see Schell, *Unconquerable World*, 186–215, and Ackerman and DuVall, *Force More Powerful*, 113–74.

55. Tocqueville, *Democracy in America*, 506–8, 692–93.

As individuals, we are powerless over against the mega-institutions of the modern world, but Tocqueville saw an antidote in Americans propensity to form associations. "As soon as several Americans have conceived a sentiment or an idea that they want to produce before the world, they seek each other out, and when found, they unite. Thenceforth they are no longer isolated individuals but a power conspicuous from the distance whose actions serve as an example; when it speaks, men listen." The associations that Tocqueville refers to include well-institutionalized political associations that are part of a federal system such as the decentralized institutions of local government, but he points to a much broader range of associations "to give fetes, found seminaries, build churches . . . hospitals, prisons, and schools." Such associations are self-initiated and sustained. They are formed based on one's own vision joined with that of others, not ideologically imposed. Taken together, they form a civil society that Vaclav Havel and others celebrated as a way to live in the truth. Central in Tocqueville's mind is not only the power generated by associations but, above all, their educative function.

> [Associations] provide a thousand continual reminders to every citizen that he lives in society. . . . At first it is of necessity that men attend to the public interest, afterward by choice. . . . By dint of working for the good of his fellow citizens, he in the end acquires a habit and taste for serving them. . . . Feelings and ideas are renewed, the heart enlarged and the understanding developed only by the reciprocal action of men upon one another.[56]

The Eastern European dissidents had no choice under Soviet rule but to create, as best they could, a civil society in the cracks and crevices of the system. Our context is somewhat different. Many still hold out the hope that reform may come from within the political system or that the market can self-correct in contrast to Berrigan who would certainly suggest that Tocqueville's nightmare has come true. Earlier I aligned myself with John Cobb and his colleagues who are willing to form alliances with other progressives if and when possibilities for social change occur but who recognize the need to resist the headlong destructive course of the industrial growth society and its militaristic counterpart.[57] This option leaves the door of reform-

56. Ibid., 512–13, 515–16. Clearly some associations evolve into institutions. Tocqueville also had in mind social movements as part of civil society when he discussed the role of associations. He was astounded when he first heard that one hundred thousand men had committed themselves to forming the Temperance Movement. Ibid., 516.

57. Cobb, foreword to *Resistance*, x–xiii.

ism open just a crack. At the same time we need to heed Dr. King's sober analysis in his "Letter from a Birmingham Jail" that those in power, those who oppress others, rarely transform themselves voluntarily; there must be countervailing pressure.[58] "Working the linkages" among communities, movements, and countervailing institutions can provide such pressure. For this conjunction to occur, however, there must be a matrix that can sustain all three forms of social life. Both states and markets are powerful forces that are not likely to be the sources of social transformation. I do not believe that, in this context, either will function as a *matrix* of social change in Tocqueville's double sense of both empowering and educating ordinary people to take hold and shape a viable future. Does this mean that Nussbaum's theory of justice and her list of capabilities as human rights are inconsequential, a sheer exercise in idealism with no purchase on historical reality? I will argue here and in the following two chapters that the matrix for countervailing power may well be civil society and not only in its domestic versions but through the efforts of transnational organizations that together constitute "global civil society" (GCS). At present, this seems to me our best bet not only to provide a holding action against the destructive forces of the imperial state and the industrial growth society but also to promote, on a thousand fronts, the changes that are needed if we are to leave a habitable, reasonably just future for our children and grandchildren.

GLOBAL CIVIL SOCIETY AS A MATRIX FOR JUSTICE AND HUMAN RIGHTS

Margaret Keck and Kathryn Sikknik argue that the problem with traditional international relations theory is that it sees states as the sole actors on the international stage. Consequently, it cannot explain huge changes like the collapse of the Soviet Union. Traditional international relations theory does not see who the agents were that created such huge transformations.[59] Adam Michnik pointed to the role of an inchoate, domestic civil society as a key force in the transformation of Eastern Europe. But these civil society groups found crucial allies in transnational advocacy NGOs (TANGOs) like Helsinki Watch (which later became Human Rights Watch) and transnational institutions like the Catholic Church. Alliances among these groups formed transnational advocacy networks (TANs) whose moral politics contributed to the transformation of Eastern Europe.

58. King Jr., "Letter from a Birmingham Jail," 291–92.

59. Keck and Sikkink, *Activists Beyond Borders*, 204, 213.

Similar patterns can be seen whether we focus on current forms of strategic peacebuilding or on the three areas—human rights, women's rights and environmentalism—that Keck and Sikknik point to as having developed the most robust TANs. First, there are many more players than nation-states on the international stage. No longer are crucial issues raised and negotiated by states alone. Religious, academic, and legal groups and NGOs of all stripes have made their voices heard. Second, these groups have formed strategic alliances with intergovernmental agencies, UN agencies, and select nation-states. Third, the current phase of globalization has fostered linkages between local communities and TANs, linkages that never before were possible. It goes without saying that the enhanced technologies of communication that are intrinsic to this phase of globalization have produced a "democratization of information" that has equipped both local NGOs and TANs with a formidable lever for social change. Finally, these shifts have forced scholar-activists to rethink how, where, and by whom social change comes about.[60]

John Keane sees such social forces arising out of a new matrix called "global civil society" (GCS) that is diverse, complex, and highly interactive.[61]

> Global Civil Society is neither a static object nor a fait accompli. It is an unfinished product that consists of sometimes thick, sometimes thinly stretched networks, pyramids and hub and spoke clusters of socio-economic institutions and actors who organize themselves across borders, with the deliberate aim of drawing the world together in new ways. These non-governmental institutions and actors tend to pluralize power and to problematize violence; consequently their peaceful or "civil" effects are felt everywhere.[62]

60. Lederach and Appleby, "Strategic Peacebuilding," 26–27. See also Clark, "UN-Civil-Society Interactions," 60.

61. Some authors dispute the term "global" because there are numerous countries which have yet to be included in this "society of societies." They prefer the term "transnational." I, however, while recognizing the distinction, will use the terms interchangeably. Sanjeev Khagram and coauthors describe several levels of transnational associations: international NGOs (INGOs), also transnational advocacy NGOs (TANGOs) with members in three or more countries. At a deeper level transnational advocacy networks (TANs) link loosely related TANGOs for purposes of information exchange; transnational coalitions coordinate tactics to create transnational campaigns (e.g., the successful campaign to ban landmines); and transnational social movements mobilize numerous NGOs for joint action across borders. Khagram et al., "From Santiago to Seattle," 6–9.

62. Keane, *Global Civil Society?*, 8. This definition overlooks the ideological conflict among different normative definitions of GCS. Mary Kaldor offers five definitions. The first two, *Societas civilis* and the bourgeois society version are previous historical

Keane's definition straddles the empirical-descriptive versus normative divide. This is especially true regarding the pluralizing of power and the problematizing of violence. "Civil" is to be understood in two senses: (a) non-governmental and (b) promoting civility.

> [GCS] is marked by a strong and overriding tendency to both marginalize or avoid the use of violence. . . . [GCS] more or less observe[s] the rule that non-violent respect for others overrides any consideration of their national identity or skin colour or sex. . . . Its extra-governmental institutions and forms of action are marked by . . . respect for principles of compromise, mutual respect even power-sharing among different ways of life.[63]

Normative definitions recognize that terror networks, drug cartels, sex traffickers, and the like also inhabit the spaces in which GCS proliferates but these are seen as parasitic and ultimately destructive of the globalized society that allows them to grow alongside of "civil" associations. Mary Kaldor emphasizes that GCS cannot flourish apart from the rule of law including an evolving international law and the presence of states that see their self-interest reflected in a multilateral, collective system and which together form a "humanitarian regime . . . that has the capacity to uphold human rights in practice when states fail to do so." This capacity for a form of humanitarian intervention that safeguards civilians and brings war criminals to justice is part of a security framework without which, Kaldor argues, GCS cannot flourish. But, she hastens to add, "It is more like policing than war fighting."[64]

---

definitions which identify civil society with, respectively, the public monopolization of violence to create order and the world of commerce, social classes, and welfare. The neoliberal version sees a voluntary "third sector" replacing government functions in support of an order more amenable to global commerce. The postmodern version criticizes civil society as a Western imposition but sees the possibility of a plurality of global civil societies including nationalist and fundamentalist versions. Finally, the activist model emphasizes self-organization outside of the normal political sphere for purposes of constraining the power of states and markets and for promoting emancipation. Kaldor identifies her approach, as do I, with the activist model. However, Kaldor does recognize the presence within GCS of organizations that reflect both the neoliberal and the postmodern ideological versions. Kaldor, *Global Civil Society*, 6–12, 106–7. There is a difference among those who see the institutions of the market as part of civil society and those who do not. In this discussion I will focus on GCS as a third force beyond the state and market.

63. Keane, *Global Civil Society?*, 13–14.

64. Kaldor, *Global Civil Society*, 109–10, 132, 134–38. Kaldor's focus on "human security" in contrast to "national security" will be discussed further in chapter 6.

Keane, for his part, sees GCS as, by definition, a space within which heterogeneous forms of life, ethical systems, and types of action can flourish, engage with, and contest one another as they also challenge states. But the condition for such flourishing, for Keane, is the categorical acceptance of GCS itself as a "common framework of intelligibility" that allows these organizations, institutions, networks, and movements to coexist peacefully.[65] As a "bottom-up" process, GCS provides a new force that can challenge and negotiate with centers of political and economic authority through processes of "campaigning, lobbying, and struggling for a new generation of rights, including gender, the environment and peace at global, national and local levels."[66] Transnational advocacy networks have been effective in the three areas just mentioned by combining: (a) "information politics," gathering and widely disseminating expert knowledge, for example, of human rights abuses, (b) "symbolic politics," graphically framing issues, for example, by circulating photos of civilians maimed by landmines, (c) "leverage politics," working with allies to bring pressure on states as we have just seen in the case of Eastern European dissidents working with Helsinki Watch to document human rights violations in the Soviet empire, and (d) "accountability politics," monitoring whether or not states live up to their treaty commitments and, where necessary, "naming and shaming" the violators.[67] A fifth politics, "coalition politics," has been pursued in some campaigns of TANs. In such cases TANs build partnerships with intergovernmental agencies, the UN and like-minded states. An example of coalition politics was the campaign to ban landmines which we will examine in chapter 6.[68] Jackie Smith suggests that TANs pursuing these forms of moral politics provide a voice to groups that otherwise are not represented or are underrepresented in international forums. They are especially important in offsetting the power

65. Keane, *Global Civil Society?*, 201–3.

66. Kaldor, *Global Civil Society*, 142–43.

67. Keck and Sikkink, *Activists Beyond Borders*, 16–25.

68. Such alliances have shown the potential of TANs to enhance the efficacy of the United Nations itself. In June 2004, a Panel of Eminent Persons on United Nations-Civil Society Relationships presented a report that made valuable recommendations for enhancing and regularizing the ways in which NGOs become accredited by the UN and interact both with the General Assembly and various agencies as well as how the UN should collaborate with local NGOs on UN sponsored projects. Clark, "UN-Civil-Society Interactions," 64–68. For the report itself, see www.un-ngls.org/orf/Final%20 report%20-%20HLP.doc. On immediate efforts to implement the report, see http:// www.un-ngls.org/orf/UNreform.htm. Roger Coate discusses the emergence of what some have called a "third UN" beyond the member states and the various UN agencies. This third UN is comprised of a diverse set of interactions and partnerships of the UN with civil society. "Growing the 'Third UN,'" 153–68.

of international organizations such as the World Bank, the International Monetary Fund, and the World Trade Organization that disproportionately represent the Global North.[69]

Keane, however, cautions us not to think of GCS as "something like a world proletariat in civvies," that could ever become a pure utopian movement. GCS is far too messy and complex for that.[70] Nevertheless, TANGOs and TANs can point to significant changes in public consciousness. In a 2000 report, Human Rights Watch pointed to an important transformation in "public morality" that was brought about to a great degree through the efforts of human rights TANs:

> The progress made . . . in standing up to crimes against humanity represents more than a doctrinal qualification of the prerogatives of sovereignty. Behind the advances in international justice and the increased deployment of troops to stop atrocities lies an evolution in public morality. More than at any time in recent history, the people of the world today are unwilling to tolerate severe human rights abuses and insistent that something be done to stop them.[71]

Such reframing of the norms that people apply to international issues, Keck and Sikknik insist, must be done in a way that resonates with existing norms. For example, TANs have been effective when they reveal the chasm that exists between states' declarations of rights and their actual practice.[72] Likewise, environmental TANs have been more effective when they have reframed their issue in human rights terms as, for example, when deforestation of the Amazon has been framed as a violation of indigenous peoples' rights. The same has been true of TANs focused on development issues.[73]

69. Smith, "Economic Globalization and Strategic Peacebuilding," 261–64. As their power has grown, TANGOs and TANs have been challenged by governments and corporations which ask how representative these organizations are and to whom they are accountable. See Clark, "UN-Civil-Society Interactions," 68.

70. Keane, *Global Civil Society?*, 65, 75. We might think of GCS as akin to the interstate system, i.e., as a process for moving multiple vehicles of change in multiple directions at once but with a common trait of peaceful purpose in contrast to the way that the warmaking state constrains social life.

71. As cited in Kaldor, *Global Civil Society*, 132. It would be easy to cite examples from even more recent history where this public morality flagged or even became dormant. Just as surely, counterarguments can be given that underline Human Rights Watch's position. This underscores the general point that GCS is always a work in progress.

72. Keck and Sikkink, *Activists Beyond Borders*, 204–6.

73. Sikkink and Smith, "Infrastructures for Change," 34; Nelson, "Agendas, Accountability and Legitimacy," 135. Although I have emphasized the role of TANs in

Framing issues is typically a first step. After putting an issue on the global agenda, TANs seek allies among intergovernmental agencies and like-minded states. Through an iterative process of public debate and policy dialogue, a sufficient consensus is built for some change in global policy or for an international treaty. "Such global policy networks have shaped responses to issues as diverse as landmines, poor-country debt, climate change, affordable treatment of AIDS and gender relations."[74] GCS represents an emergent force in international politics. None of its gains are irreversible. In fact, Kaldor sees the 9/11 terror attacks and the subsequent US response as creating a vicious circle that feeds on itself and like a black hole tears at the peaceful evolution of GCS.[75] Nevertheless, GCS does provide spaces within which TANGOs and TANs can flourish. Not only do they provide new centers of power and leverage grounded in a moral politics but the very nature of a moral politics emphasizes the educative role that Tocqueville saw as crucial to the countervailing role of voluntary associations.[76] Given the salience of human rights discourse among many TANs, they, potentially at least, provide a means by which we could move from Nussbaum's theory of justice to praxis. GCS functions as a matrix generating new organizations, movements, and networks which invent new forms of praxis which, in turn, expand the matrix. As I suggested, this is a provisional sketch of what might be the matrix in which new vehicles for change, offering new forms of praxis might emerge. It sketches not a utopian vision but an empirically grounded possibility for a hopeful future.

---

the rise to prevalence of human rights discourse, it is important that we recognize that they function well only in tandem with strong *domestic* NGOs. Keck and Sikkink point out that campaigns against human rights violations in Argentina and Chile were more successful than in Guatemala because of the strength of domestic NGOs in Argentina and Chile and their comparative absence in Guatemala. *Activists Beyond Borders*, 206.

74. Clark, "UN-Civil-Society Interactions," 64.

75. Kaldor, *Global Civil Society*, 148–55.

76. GCS, as Keane has argued, opens a highly interactive space. TANGOs and TANs pursue different goals and frame in different ways the norms that are at stake. Consequently, TANs and TANGOs educate one another. Charles Call points out that human rights TANs originally were silent on the rights of women, gays, and other groups. They had to be challenged and pressured to expand and reframe their human rights discourse. With the articulation of new norms, new forms of praxis arose. This high degree of interactivity is part of what is meant by seeing GCS as a matrix of new forms of power. "Human Rights Practitioner's Perspective," 125–27.

CONCLUSION

This chapter began with the cry of one of billions of the oppressed. I used Schreiter's model of a full-blown theology or social ethics geared toward praxis with its five functions (resistance, denunciation, critique, advocacy, and reconstruction) to assess how far Daniel Berrigan and Thich Nhat Hanh could take us in responding to that cry of the oppressed. Then I examined the interaction between compassion and justice challenging the model that views moral maturity as a linear development from "charity to social justice" and that, consequently, misses the dialectic of compassion and justice in creating a social ethics geared toward praxis. I offered Martha Nussbaum's capability approach to justice as a species of human rights theory as best attuned to this understanding of compassion and justice while preserving the best in the social contract tradition. Yet creating a new theory of justice is not enough. A transition from theory to praxis must be made. For that to occur there needs to be a matrix that can spawn new forms of praxis and a vehicle to carry them forward. After studying Sarvodaya, a Buddhist model of rural development, as one successful model that completes Schreiter's full trajectory of tasks, I offered "a provisional sketch" of what in a more global context could guide the transition from theory to praxis. As a first step, we examined the interaction among communities of resistance, movements and countervailing institutions giving rise, for example in the case of Poland's nonviolent revolution, to civil society. Expanding that Tocquevillian insight, I suggested that GCS might well be the matrix and emergent TANGOs and TANs, especially in the areas of human rights, women's rights, and environmentalism, might be the vehicles for carrying forward new forms of praxis leading to social change.

This completes part 2 of this book, in which we first looked at Daniel Berrigan and Thich Nhat Hanh as embodying and expressing two different types of virtue ethics. Second, we examined Berrigan as located on the cutting edge of the peace movement and Thich Nhat Hanh as a community builder, as well as my own social location within an institution, and analyzed the implications of these social locations for social ethics. Third, we looked at the dialectic of compassion and justice in this chapter.

Recall that in chapter 3 we looked at Native American novelist Leslie Marmon Silko's image of the world as a fragile spider web. Her hero, World War II veteran Tayo, suffers from what we call today PTSD but, as John Dominic Crossan puts it, his illness is more sociosomatic than psychosomatic. His healing has to comprehend all that he has gone through, all that he has witnessed in a worldwide war. With the help of a Navajo healer, Tayo must descend into the heart of darkness of twentieth-century history.

In Tayo's nightmare, evil appears as "whirling darkness" that initially possesses the European colonizers but eventually all races. "Then they grow away from the earth / then they grow away from the sun. . . . / They see no life. . . . / They fear the world / They destroy what they fear." The final pattern of destruction comes from "rocks with veins of green and yellow and black," from the uranium mines of northern New Mexico.

> Whirling
>   whirling
>   whirling
>   whirling
> set into motion now
>   set into motion.[77]

Tayo's nightmare is one from which we all must awaken. The next two chapters take up two facets of this apocalyptic scenario. Chapter 6 will deal with the American empire, mesmerized by its own power to destroy or, as Berrigan puts it, under the rule of Lord Nuke. Chapter 7 will confront the issue of the fundamental threat to the biosphere brought about by our own mindless ravaging of the earth.

77. Silko, *Ceremony*, 135, 137–38.

Part III

APPLYING THE SOCIAL ETHICS OF THE PROPHET AND THE BODHISATTVA

6

DISMANTLING THE EMPIRE

American Militarism and Just Peacemaking

History is a nightmare from which I am trying to awake.[1]

—Stephen Daedalus, in James Joyce, *Ulysses*.

Hope is not like a lottery ticket you can sit on a sofa and clutch, feeling lucky. . . . Hope is an ax you can break down doors with in an emergency; . . . hope should shove you out the door, because it will take everything you have to steer the future away from endless war, from the annihilation of the earth's treasures and the grinding down of the poor and the marginal. Hope just means another world might be possible, not promised, not guaranteed."[2]

—Rebecca Solnit, *Hope in the Dark*

Two voices deeply opposed; both decidedly true. If we are to err, however, let it be on the side of hope. We can wield hope's ax; others have done so. In many of our lifetimes, after all, a tidal wave of justice has risen more than once, sweeping away a nightmarish system: the dismantling of colonial empires in the aftermath of World War II; the civil rights revolution in the

1. Joyce, *Ulysses*, episode 2.
2. Solnit, *Hope in the Dark*, 5.

United States in the 1950s and '60s; the collapse of the Soviet empire in the late '80s and early '90s; the end of apartheid in South Africa in the '90s. In most cases, the transformation was largely wrought by nonviolent means.

Yet, we must honor young Stephen's message if we are to facilitate wise Rebecca's hopeful vision. Chalmers Johnson has written a trilogy of books dissecting America's military empire. The second of these is entitled *The Sorrows of Empire: Militarism, Secrecy, and the End of the Republic.*[3] The sorrows that Johnson has in mind are conveyed in the subtitle: Our military empire threatens us with the end of our republic. Sorrowing is a good place to begin. Recall our earlier discussion of Abraham Heschel's contention that the Hebrew prophets participated in the divine pathos. Grieving the repression of compassion as our nation puts on the armor of Mars is important. It is part of waking up from the nightmare.

What nightmare we may ask? We have dreamed our way through more than a decade of constant warfare with still more conflicts on the horizon but we have, we must confess, done so without waking in a cold sweat or, at least, not often. "[We] are reduced," Berrigan says, "to the state of moral zombies sleepwalking the world. This is the truth of our condition, verified on every hand. Blind, deaf and, worst of all, heartless." In this state we taste "before death, the death named despair."[4]

The Hebrew prophets knew one thing with blinding clarity and one thing only: God's judgment on "empire as such." With that insight came a raft of corollaries: recognition of the process of moral devolution, a sure grasp of the idolatrous essence of imperial ambition, feeling in one's bones the wounds inflicted by empire, foresight into the inexorable dynamic of imperial rule. No need for a vengeful God or an enemy at the gates. "The contradictions, animosities and opposites strain and stretch the imperial fabric; it falls in a rotten heap."[5] Even as we move beyond the prophets' and Berrigan's preference for symbolic acts of resistance, we must internalize the prophet's one clear truth.

First, we must examine the case for America as an empire in which the "sorrows of empire" have already appeared. Second, we will ask what kinds of virtue the prophet and the bodhisattva nurture for those of us confined in the belly of the beast. Third, we will situate the prophet's and the bodhisattva's responses to empire along a spectrum of approaches that claim to lead us to a just peace. Finally, we will look at some transnational movements

3. The three works are: *Blowback: The Costs and Consequences of American Empire*; *The Sorrows of Empire: Militarism, Secrecy, and the End of the Republic*; and *Nemesis: The Last Days of the American Republic*.

4. Berrigan, *Isaiah*, 14, 33.

5. Berrigan, *Jeremiah*, 188; Berrigan, *Isaiah*, 101–2.

and advocacy networks that have proven that it is possible to constrain imperial overreach.

This is the first chapter of two that apply what we have learned from the lives and works of Daniel Berrigan and Thich Nhat Hanh and from the effort in part 2 to develop more formal ethical approaches building upon their moral insights to crucial issues that we face. Applied ethics by its very nature calls forth a variety of strategies which confront key forks in the road at numerous stages. There will be differences in how we interpret our historical context and how we characterize the issues that we face. Second, while we may agree about some of the major features of Berrigan's and Thich Nhat Hanh's ethical positions, surely there will be important differences with my own synthesis of those positions with those of others such as Martha Nussbaum whose theory of justice we discussed in chapter 5. Third, the underlying assumption of this book—its warp, if you will—is that no single moral vision and praxis, however classic, is adequate to the complexities and ambiguities of the two issues that I will address. So, the following two chapters will juxtapose the prophet's and the bodhisattva's stances with several alternative diagnoses of and prescriptions for resolving the issues that we face. Neither my choices of dialogue partners nor my sorting through of their strengths and weaknesses is incontestable. Fourth, applied ethics, wending its way through these different forks, will result in a variety of strategies for action. Finally, how we envision a transformed society is crucially important and, certainly, the moral imagination opens a wide horizon of possibilities. The route that I take will differ from yours. At best, I can offer only *a* model that may illuminate your pathway.

WHAT EMPIRE? WHAT SORROWS?

The Founders, beginning with George Washington, were leery of foreign entanglements. James Madison saw the instruments of imperial rule—standing armies engaged in endless warfare—as a mortal threat to republican government. Despite the actual conquest of a continent, Americans were generally averse to thinking of their nation as an empire. For a brief period, the acquisition of overseas colonies in the aftermath of the Spanish-American War led some, like Senator Albert Beveridge of Indiana, to speak of imperialism in positive terms. However, there was also a fierce debate during this period over whether or not America should become a colonial empire. Throughout much of the twentieth century, "empire" remained a term of opprobrium. When Ronald Reagan coined the term "evil empire" to characterize the Soviet Union, it should not be inferred that he thought of America as a "good empire." For Reagan and most Americans that would have been an oxymoron.[6]

With the collapse of the Soviet Union between 1989 and 1991, and especially since September 11, 2001, a reevaluation of the concept of empire has been underway, especially by the ideological movement that came to be called "the neo-conservatives." They picked up the rhetoric of empire and polished it to remove the tarnish. "We are not just any hegemon," argued Charles Krauthammer, a primary exponent of the neo-con ideology in the popular media. "We run a uniquely benign *imperium*. This is not mere self-congratulation: it is a fact manifest in the way others welcome our power."[7] Leaders on the left and the center followed suit. Madeline Albright, Secretary of State under President Clinton, referred to America as "the indispensable nation."[8] Michael Ignatieff, a human rights advocate, joined the neo-conservatives arguing that "we" have a duty to intervene with force when people are oppressed by their own governments. "Empire," he asserted, "is a precondition for democracy."[9] Ignatieff coined the phrase "Empire Lite" and went on to dampen the anxiety of the Founders over the role of imperial pretension in subverting republican government.

> Ever since George Washington warned his countrymen against foreign entanglements, empire abroad has been seen as the republic's permanent temptation and its potential nemesis. Yet what word but "empire" describes the awesome thing that America is becoming? It is the only nation that polices the world through five global military commands; maintains more than a million men and women at arms on four continents; deploys carrier battle groups on watch in every ocean; guarantees the survival of countries from Israel to South Korea; drives the wheels of global trade and commerce; and fills the hearts and minds of an entire planet with its dreams and desires.[10]

In response, a number of historians and political theorists have disputed not the facts cited in this quotation from Ignatieff but his sanguine interpretation. They have argued, in essence, that George Washington got it right. Chalmers Johnson's trilogy is a good place to begin. The title of one of the chapters in Johnson's *Nemesis: The Last Days of the American Republic*, "Comparative Imperial Pathologies: Rome, Britain, and America," conveys

6. Johnson, *Sorrows of Empire*, 42–45, 67.
7. Krauthammer, as cited in Bacevich, *New American Militarism*, 83.
8. Albright, as cited in Bacevich, *Washington Rules*, 141.
9. Ignatieff, as cited in Bacevich, *New American Militarism*, 25.
10. Ignatieff, as cited in Johnson, *Nemesis*, 73.

succinctly Johnson's analysis. Part and parcel of the neo-conservatives' recuperating the ideology of imperialism has been the creation of sanitized versions of the *Pax Romana* and Great Britain's colonial empire. Apologists like Niall Ferguson see the latter as a civilizing force unparalleled in spreading the Western rule of law. The torch, he insists, has been passed on to America. Johnson strips away the veneer that hides the reality of imperial rule. "All empires, it seems require myths of divine right, racial preeminence, manifest destiny or a 'civilizing mission' to cover their often barbarous behavior in other people's countries." These apologists for civilizing empires, replies Johnson, never consulted the victims of their imperial conquerors. He then goes on to cite chapter and verse regarding British massacres of subjugated peoples and the destruction of thriving indigenous industries, like Indian textile production. These and other factors led to the collapse of village institutions, in turn, generating widespread famine. Britain even fought two wars in China to force the importation of opium produced in India, thereby becoming the world's "most successful drug cartel."[11]

Turning his attention to the other model of a "benign hegemon," Johnson argues that the advocates for American imperialism have drawn the wrong lessons from history. Through a series of conquests, Rome consolidated its hold over all of Italy and Sicily. It extended its dominion to North Africa, Asia Minor, Greece, and Gaul. The acquisition of an empire required the Romans to shift from an occasional mustering of citizen-soldiers to a standing professional army garrisoned around the empire enforcing exploitative rule. With the support of his army, Julius, the general, crossed the Rubicon to become Caesar. When his nephew Octavian consolidated power and became Augustus, the institutions of republican life survived in name only; the reality was a military dictatorship. With Rome's military success arose the arrogant belief in its indispensable civilizing role. There was nothing "benign" about Roman rule. Little Israel knew firsthand the iron fist of imperial rule. John Dominic Crossan points to the three times (4 BCE; 66 CE; 132 CE) that Roman legions garrisoned in Syria marched south to quell rebellions in the Jewish homeland destroying whole cities in the process.[12] What was to become an image of redemptive suffering in Christianity, execution by crucifixion, was in practice an instrument of state controlled terrorism. Military rule relying on mercenary soldiers, however, had its cost. Imperial overstretch eventually led to Rome's collapse.[13]

11. Johnson, *Nemesis*, 71, 76–77, 79, 82–83.

12. Crossan, *God and Empire*, 109–10.

13. Johnson, *Nemesis*, 63–70; Johnson, *Sorrows of Empire*, 15.

Johnson makes a case for America as a military in contrast to a territorial empire. The evidence for this assertion is largely what the proponents of empire concede, or, rather, what they trumpet: Over 737 military bases scattered in 130 countries, the unequaled superiority of the US military, its confrontational presence at most if not all of the globe's trigger points from the Korean DMZ to the Persian Gulf, and its well over one hundred military operations since the end of the Second World War. And there is the more sinister side of this empire—the dozens of covert operations by the CIA to overthrow or destabilize "unfriendly" regimes, the training at the School of the Americas of Latin American soldiers who became the notorious death squads in Latin America's dirty wars of the 1970s and '80s, a shift of America from pushing a global legal order enforced in treaties to a unilateralism that refuses to sign new treaties and abides by the ones that it has ratified only when it suits its interests.[14]

Referring to his first work on American imperialism, Johnson defines "blowback" as "retaliation for the numerous illegal operations that we have carried out abroad that were kept totally secret from the American public. This means that when the retaliation comes—as it did so spectacularly on September 11, 2001—the American public is unable to put the events in context. So they tend to support acts intended to lash out against the perpetrators, thereby most commonly preparing the ground for yet another cycle of blowback."[15]

Consider blowback as the first of the sorrows of empire brought about by the goddess Nemesis, the punisher of hubris, overweening pride. Johnson adds four more sorrows to the list. First, there will be endless wars, a fact of imperial rule that in terms of sheer numbers of military operations is surely underway. Well before the current conflicts with Iran and North Korea heated up, Johnson suggested that weaker nations would seek weapons of mass destruction to counterbalance the overwhelming military superiority of the United States. Second, there will be a loss of constitutional rights. Congress, he argues, has already abdicated its constitutional obligation to be the sole branch of government to declare war. Third, what Vaclev Havel, following Gandhi, called "living in the truth" will be supplanted by propaganda and disinformation that glorifies war and warriors. Finally, and almost certainly, imperial rule will bankrupt our society. There will be guns but no butter, as infrastructure decays, children's education is shortchanged and we shred what remnants remain of the social safety net. "We are on the cusp of losing our democracy," Johnson concludes, "for the sake of keeping

14. Johnson, *Sorrows of Empire*, 1–3, 68–69, 73–77, 151–85.

15. Johnson, *Nemesis*, 278.

our empire. Once a nation is started down that path, the dynamics that apply to all empires come into play—isolation, overstretch, the uniting of forces opposed to imperialism, and bankruptcy. Nemesis stalks our life as a free nation."[16]

THE NEW AMERICAN MILITARISM

Andrew Bacevich, a self-designated political and cultural conservative, is an ex-career army officer, having served in Vietnam and lived through the transition from soldiers defamed to idolized. He knows the brutal costs of war having lost a son to the war in Iraq. Bacevich is no convert to pacifism. He argues that his service defending against the threat of a Soviet invasion of Western Europe was an honorable one. Not so today's preemptive wars or wars to topple hostile regimes. In *Washington Rules: America's Path to Permanent War*, Bacevich describes himself as having spent one-half of a lifetime comfortable with orthodoxy and deferent to authority. In other words, as "a slow learner." As a career army officer, Bacevich spent considerable time posted in Germany anticipating a Soviet *blitzkrieg* from the East. Shortly after the fall of the Berlin Wall, leading a group of officers, he was in the former East Germany where, by sheer chance, they stumbled upon a Russian military exercise. Transfixed, the group watched tank maneuvers only to see an armored vehicle sputter and burst into flames. This was the feared Soviet juggernaut? "Now," Bacevich concludes, "I started however hesitantly to suspect that orthodoxy might be a sham. I began to appreciate that authentic truth is never simple and that any version of truth handed down from on high—whether by presidents, prime ministers, or archbishops—is inherently suspect." Ever so slowly questions took over. "How could I have so profoundly misjudged the reality of what lay on the far side of the Iron Curtain. . . . Yet that was the lesser half of the problem. Far worse than my perceiving 'them' was the fact that I had misperceived 'us.'"[17]

In a spate of books, Bacevich charts his education. It centers on a demystification of what he calls America's Credo, the belief, shared by both liberals and conservatives, that America alone has the mission—for many, a divine commission—to spread its values, institutions, and way of life across the globe. This belief, Bacevich insists, is "hardwired in the American psyche."[18] America is the "redeemer nation." In fulfillment of this credo America has increasingly turned to military means projected globally, a

16. Johnson, *Nemesis*, 279; Johnson, *Sorrows of Empire*, 285.

17. Bacevich, *Washington Rules*, 3–4, 6, 10.

18. Bacevich, *Limits of Power*, 78.

force that is prepared to intervene anywhere on that globe in furtherance of the nation's sacred mission.[19]

Bacevich's grounds his critique of what he calls "the new American militarism" in an analysis of the twentieth century as "an age of massive conceits, devised by ideologues who entertained heady dreams of bending history to suit their will." Utopian dreams plus hubris yielded catastrophe. Not only Communism and National Socialism succumbed to dangerous delusions, Bacevich traces a similar American utopian impulse to Woodrow Wilson and his mission to end all wars by remaking the world in the image of America.[20] The US Senate constrained Wilson's ambitions, and internal and external conditions similarly curbed the ambitions of subsequent presidents, but the utopian impulse remained.

With the end of the Cold War, the major constraint on American ambitions to spread its way of life across the globe evaporated. Overlapping this geopolitical seismic shift was a transformation of the collective understanding of the military, its functions, and its status in the minds of both decision makers and the American public. The result was a "misbegotten marriage" of the new American militarism with "eschatological ambition." "The key point is this: at the end of the Cold War, America said yes to military power. The skepticism about arms and armies that formed the original Wilsonian vision . . . vanished."[21]

Four transformations have led to the emergence of the new American militarism. The first is a vast expansion of the scope and costs of defense and a reconfiguration of the purpose of the military. By one recent estimate, the US share of global military spending is 41 percent. The United States spends more on defense than the next fifteen nations combined. Such estimates do not include the budgets of the CIA, Homeland Security, or Veterans Affairs.[22] Nor do they include veteran benefits or the interest on the share of the national debt incurred by defense spending. When added together, these multiple budgets easily exceed a trillion dollars. More important for Bacevich is that the mission of the military has changed from defense against potential aggressors to "global power projection." Through its bases in foreign countries, twelve attack carrier groups and rapid deployment capabilities the US military asserts its supremacy *everywhere*. Far more than

19. Bacevich, *Washington Rules*, 12–15. See Tuveson, *Redeemer Nation*.

20. Bacevich, *New American Militarism*, 9–11.

21. Ibid., 5–7, 14.

22. Heeley, "U.S. Defense Spending," n.p.

our embassies and diplomats or development aid, this presence declares to friends and any potential foes who we are and what we are capable of.[23]

The second manifestation of the new American militarism is "the normalization of war." Bacevich quotes Madeline Albright as famously asking then Chairman of the Joint Chiefs of Staff, Colin Powell, "What's the point of having this superb military . . . if we can't use it?"[24] Surely, Bacevich concludes, she need not have been concerned because military operations have mushroomed since the end of the Cold War. Policymakers have come to see coercion as "an all-purpose tool" and the just war criterion of war as a last resort has gone by the boards.[25]

The third transformation leading to the new American militarism is "a new aesthetic" of war. With the implementation of high tech weapons systems, war is now seen as clean, surgical. It is no longer Kurt Vonnegut's slaughterhouse or the bloody entangling and all-corrupting spider web revealed in films like *Platoon* and *Apocalypse Now*. CNN brings us war-as-spectacle to be watched on our home entertainment systems in the comforts of the family room.[26] Fostering the illusion of the "surgical strike," drone technology further distances us from the bloody face of war and obliterates the just war distinction between combatants and non-combatants.

Finally, Americans have reevaluated the soldiers themselves. Instead of being victims themselves corrupted by war they have become the paragons of virtue, representing the very best in the American way of life. This raising of the profession onto the highest of pedestals Bacevich sees as emerging in tandem with the eclipse of the ideal of the citizen-soldier. Instead of viewing our patriotic duty as actually *serving* in the military it has been transformed into unqualifiedly *supporting* our troops.[27]

Bacevich traces the eschatological partner in this misbegotten marriage to Wilson's conviction that God wills the universal sway of American values and principles. We could just as easily follow a thread that begins with John Winthrop's sermon on board the Arbella on its way to the new world in 1630 with his famous proclamation that the new colony would be "a city upon the hill," called to be a beacon to all humankind. The thread links Winthrop to the Founders belief that America represented a *novus ordo seclorum*, a new order of the ages. The myth of a redeemer nation was later expressed in the nineteenth-century doctrine of manifest destiny. The

23. Bacevich, *New American Militarism*, 16–18.

24. Albright, as cited in ibid., 24.

25. Bacevich, *New American Militarism*, 19, 211.

26. Ibid., 20–21.

27. Ibid., 23–24, 26–29, 108.

thread wended its way only after almost three hundred years to Wilson.[28] On the first anniversary of 9/11, President Bush articulated this assumption of an eschatological agency when he stated: "The ideal of America is the hope of all mankind." "That hope still lights the way," he continued, "and the light shines in the darkness and the darkness will not overcome it."[29] Bacevich does not underscore the blasphemy of this proclamation. There is a deep irony in the fact that a born-again president expropriated phrases in the prologue of John's gospel referring to the divine Word and used them to articulate America's sacred mission. Eschatological ambition could hardly be more audacious.

The solidification of the new American militarism as the central component of American international relations required the triumph of a new, Neo-conservative ideology. This ideology evolved in two phases. The first generation of Neo-conservatism emerged in reaction to the defeat in Vietnam and the multiple movements of the '60s which attacked traditional authority structures. Bacevich unveils the core assumptions of these founders: the West faces a uniquely evil and implacable foe in Communism and it must not be appeased. Military force is indispensable in confronting evil. Isolationism must be rejected as a dereliction of duty; the foe is everywhere and must be confronted everywhere.[30] The ideology of this first generation of Neo-cons could be called apocalyptic militarism—apocalyptic in its externalization of evil, its faith in violence, its call for vigilant, endless struggle, and its willingness to entertain a nuclear holocaust as a military option.

When, against all expectations, the Soviet empire collapsed, a new generation of Neo-cons emerged. The first Gulf War for this generation demonstrated America's military supremacy, a fighting force unmatched by any of the legions of previous empires. These ideologues were unqualified millennialists. In their vision, the post-Soviet era created a Hobbesian world that requires an imperial power to maintain order. Simultaneously, there was a unique opportunity for America to propagate its ideals and institutions globally. As with the first generation of Neo-cons, military power is the preferred instrument for spreading these ideals and institutions.[31]

Conservative? Hardly. From Bacevich's viewpoint these new neo-cons had outdone the utopian fantasies of the Left. All that remained was to

28. For these and other examples, see Cherry, *God's New Israel*; see also Tuveson, *Redeemer Nation*.

29. President George W. Bush, as cited in Bacevich, *New American Militarism*, 12. Just as Rome required an imperial theology, America has produced its imperial theology.

30. Bacevich, *New American Mililtarism*, 69–71, 73–78.

31. Ibid., 81–87.

demonstrate these assumptions and principles on the battlefield. The Iraq War was to be only act 1, scene 1 of a democratizing-through-force that would, in a resurrection of domino theory, spread throughout the Middle East. "We may willy-nilly find ourselves forced," argued Norman Podhoretz, the grandfather of neo-conservatism, "by the same political and military logic to topple five or six or seven more tyrannies in the Islamic world."[32] The Iraq War produced no domino effect, as US forces became bogged down in an eight-year struggle against a persistent insurgency.

It would be dangerously naïve to assume that the United States in the Obama era has decisively broken with the Wilsonian paradigm. While dialing back on the eschatological rhetoric, President Obama has retained the core belief in American exceptionalism. In justifying US intervention in the 2011 Libyan civil war, for example, he argued that brushing aside America's responsibility as a leader among nations "would have been a betrayal of who we are. Some nations may be able to turn a blind eye to atrocities in other countries. *The United States of America is different*."[33]

In the updated edition of *The New American Militarism*, Bacevich argues that the four signs of militarism may have morphed in the Obama era but they remain in force. Obama added "a constellation of secret drone bases" to the more than seven hundred military bases on foreign soil that Chalmers Johnson decried.[34] General George Casey, Army chief of staff, in the run-up to the 2008 election told Congress that the United States had entered an "era of persistent conflict." This was what Casey called the "new normal" that Obama had inherited.[35] Simultaneously with the winding down of the war in Iraq, the theatre of the "war on terror" was expanded into Pakistan, Yemen, and Somalia. Finally, war as spectacle and the new ethos of supporting our troops as a replacement for actually serving in the military was borne out in, of all places, a Budweiser advertisement that read: "Here's to the heroes. . . . Please raise your Budweiser and join us in honoring those who keep our nation safe and free." The ad promised a donation to support families of fallen soldiers every time a major league batter hit a

32. Podhretz, as cited in ibid., 95.

33. Ben Feller, "Obama's Libya Speech Strongly Defends Intervention," *AP/Huffington Post*, March 28, 2011, http://www.huffingtonpost.com/2011/03/28/obama-libya-speech-_n_841311.html; italics added. This statement should not be read as implying that Obama simply followed suit established by his predecessors. In fact, he did seek the United Nations Security Council's approval and acted in concert with NATO allies. Nevertheless, some in Congress felt that he had ignored the War Powers Act.

34. Bacevich, *New American Militarism*, 229, 232.

35. General George Casey, as quoted in ibid., 234.

home run.[36] So, watching your favorite team at a sports bar and drinking a Bud was cast as an act of patriotism!

Bacevich's conservative critique in *The New American Militarism* of the misbegotten marriage is implicitly theological. In later works, Bacevich offers a more explicitly Niebuhrian critique of America's utopian delusions. Reinhold Niebuhr, Bacevich argues, saw with "uncanny accuracy and astonishing prescience" the looming tragedy of America as a great power. An authentically Niebuhrian interpretation recognizes that history, its convoluted course and its meaning, always exceed human comprehension. So, the dream of managing history is intrinsically misleading, a mortal threat. With the dream comes hubris, an excessive confidence in American power—or, for that matter, human power as such—to reshape history, to create a global order in its own image and likeness. True security lies not in the exercise of power but in accepting in practice its inherent limits.[37]

Hubris reached one peak with the Bush doctrine of preemptive warfare with its conceit that war can be controlled, kept within tightly managed boundaries. Niebuhr saw such warfare not only as morally wrong but as utterly mad. We must, he said, "resist such ideas with every moral resource." Preemptive war that had been viewed in Niebuhr's day as a crackpot idea had now become official policy. Against this doctrine, Bacevich calls for a commitment to the criteria of the just war tradition.[38] Bacevich's prognosis is as bleak as his diagnosis. Empires rarely wake up in time. They trust in false solutions, seeking security from Chalmers Johnson's "blowback" by further expansion of the national security state. Quoting Niebuhr, Bacevich concludes that this Sisyphean task "adds a touch of pathos to the tragedy of our age."[39]

36. Bacevich, *New American Militarism*, 236.

37. Bacevich, *Limits of Power*, 6–7, 119, 121–22. Bacevich largely draws upon one critical text by Reinhold Niebuhr in *The Irony of American History* which focuses on pretentious claims to control and direct the historical process.

38. Bacevich, *Limits of Power*, 163–65.

39. Reinhold Niebuhr as cited in Bacevich, *Limits of Power*, 182; see also 84–96. Both Chalmers Johnson and Bacevich argue for a return to constitutional checks and balances to offset the imperial presidency. Bacevich in particular stresses just war principles that justify military action only for defensive or, in rare cases, humanitarian purposes. He offers clear guidelines for reining in runaway defense budgets. These prescriptions for dismantling the empire make common sense that both conservative constitutionalists and radical reformers could accept. The problem is that they lack a domestic carrier of social change, a movement, or advocacy network that would galvanize the American public and exert sufficient pressure on the government to change its suicidal course. See Chalmers Johnson, *Dismantling the Empire*, 194–96 and Bacevich, *New American Militarism*, chapter 8.

THE REIGN OF "LORD NUKE"

The history that Bacevich traces began with the utopian aspirations of Woodrow Wilson. Garry Wills, however, sees the rise of the imperial presidency, let loose from constitutional restraints on the power to declare war, as inextricably tied to the Manhattan Project and the dawn of the nuclear age. The Bomb created an age of anxiety; it placed the nation on a perpetual emergency footing. It "redefined the government as a National Security State, with an apparatus of secrecy and executive control." Within one decade of Hiroshima, the US had amassed an arsenal that could obliterate one hundred ninety-two thousand Hiroshimas.[40] The reign of what Berrigan calls "Lord Nuke" was ascendant. Like any god, this lord demanded our soul, dictated our emotional life to be one of perpetual fear and anxiety, and decreed our passive acquiescence. Something more than the ideological war between East and West was in play, Berrigan insists. "Something else: something more mysterious, awesome, biblical is at work; the age-old claim of death in the world."[41]

Like a comet, the Bomb, coursing through Cold War America, pulled a long tail with it. Deploying the Bomb required an ever-expanding number of bases on foreign soil and an arms race to create, first, SAC bombers, then nuclear submarines, intercontinental ballistic missiles, and military satellites to deliver the Bomb. Foreign military bases, in turn, frequently required directly supporting unsavory dictators. Moreover, safeguarding the Bomb required secrecy. The Manhattan Project was the exemplar of secrecy and executive control. Even Vice-President Truman was unaware of the project before he suddenly became commander-in-chief. With the onset of the Cold War, the Bomb fostered the rise of a byzantine complex of intelligence agencies engaged in spying and increasingly in covert operations. Secret from whom? Certainly not from the countries like Iran where the CIA engineered the overthrow of a democratically elected leader in 1953 nor like Cambodia where we conducted secret bombing campaigns during the war in Indochina. Rather, secret from the American people. Keeping secrets from the American people meant that presidents and heads of agencies had to lie and repeatedly engage in cover-ups.[42]

The president who had sole control of the use of the Bomb could not be expected in a time of perpetual emergency to engage in lengthy consultations with Congress, let alone wait upon their declaration of war. "This

40. Wills, *Bomb Power*, 1, 42.

41. Berrigan, *Dwell in Peace*, 340–41.

42. Wills, *Bomb Power*, 42–44, 137–40, 152–54, 157–60.

was in effect a quiet revolution. It was accepted under the impression that technology imposed it as a harsh necessity. . . . The nature of the presidency was irrevocably altered by this grant of a unique power."[43] Simultaneously, any president becomes "a prisoner of his own power." Early in President Obama's first term, Wills described the President as an "entangled giant." Wills was surprised only by the rapidity with which the new administration became chained to the imperatives of the national security state.[44]

EMPIRE: THE NORMALCY OF CIVILIZATION'S VIOLENCE

Bacevich and Wills with their diagnoses, respectively, of the new American militarism and the national security state focus on the pathologies of America as the currently reigning empire. My former colleague, Jesus-scholar John Dominic Crossan, takes on imperialism as such in *God and Empire: Jesus against Rome, Then and Now*. It makes sense to turn to the Hebrew and Christian scriptures to understand the pathology of empire, according to Crossan, because of a very basic "geopolitical truth." Israel's "Promised Land was simply the cockpit of empire." As each imperial rooster leapt into the pit to contest its predecessor, tiny Israel was in the way: Assyrians followed by "the Babylonians, the Persians, the Macedonians, the Greco-Egyptians, the Greco-Syrians and finally the Romans."[45]

In Crossan's analysis, imperialism co-arises with the civilizations that emerged on the fertile plains of the earth's great rivers. Civilization with its walled cities, its self-justifying historical records, and its religious legitimation of hierarchical order presupposed the domestication of people, as well as plants and animals. Structural violence in the forms of social stratification, slavery, patriarchy, and inequality of wealth, as well as the systemic use of direct violence to coerce those within as well as to subdue those outside the city's walls, are endemic to civilization. "The point I wish to emphasize," insists Crossan," is that imperialism is not just a here-and-there, now-and-then, sporadic event in human history, but that civilization, as I am

43. Ibid., 45–47.

44. Wills, "Entangled Giant," *New York Review of Books*, October 8, 2009, http://www.nybooks.com/articles/archives/2009/oct/08/entangled-giant/?pagination=false&printpage=true. As I finish this manuscript in the summer of 2013, revelations of the National Security Agency's monitoring of millions of phone records of American citizens without probable cause make it clear just how entangled President Obama has become in the web of the national security state—as are all Americans. We are caught in a web woven, as Wills argues, since the end of World War II.

45. Crossan, *God and Empire*, 73, 82.

using that term, has always been imperial—that is, *empire is the normalcy of civilization's violence*. . . . If you oppose empire-as-such, you are taking on what has been the normalcy of civilization's brutality for at least the last six thousand years."[46]

Crossan spends a good deal of effort in dissecting Roman imperial theology which focused on Augustus as Son of God. Religious legitimation was and is a key ingredient in the maintenance of imperial rule. That legitimation undergirds its social hierarchy, its economic exploitation, and its military iron fist. No less a poet than Virgil depicted the climactic battle in the civil war between Octavian and Marc Antony as a battle between the forces of civilization and those of barbarism. Standing shoulder to shoulder with Augustus were the gods of the nation, Venus, Neptune, and Minerva, in opposition to "monstrous gods of every form and barking Anubis." The *Pax Romana*—in reality only the lulls between a succession of wars—was a divinely ordained "peace through victory."[47]

The Hebrew and Christian scriptures present an alternative: God's call to pursue justice through nonviolence leading to genuine peace. But these scriptures also and repeatedly revert to framing their own imperial theology with its vision of a God of retributive violence. The core texts for both Jews and Christians, texts that have framed our political as well as our religious identity, are thoroughly ambiguous.[48] Imperialism arrogates all that is sacred; the very words intended to liberate must be sifted, again and again, to uncover some semblance of truth. Civilization's normalcy of violence, the Jewish and Christian scriptures reveal, is an invasive species.

Normalcy, Crossan hastens to add, is not destiny. Civilization's imperial violence is a virus which constantly mutates but it is not part of our social DNA. Human beings invented civilization; human beings can uninvent it. Crossan sets a first-century Jewish monastic community near Alexandria and a Catholic monastic community that endured for half a millennium on an impossible island off the west coast of Ireland in explicit contrast to empire as the normalcy of civilization's violence. Such communities physically separated themselves from urban power centers and overthrew hierarchical social patterns by creating egalitarian communities. Rendering to God what is God's, they renounced Caesar's coins.[49]

At the end of his disturbing inquiry into civilization's violence, Crossan envisions human history as three tectonic plates ceaselessly grinding

46. Ibid., 30–34; italics added.

47. Ibid., 15–25.

48. Ibid., 94–95 and passim.

49. Ibid., 36–47.

against one another. In the center is the largest plate—what "some have called Macroparasitism . . . but I call Civilization itself." To one side is Nihilism, society governed, as the twentieth century repeatedly demonstrated, by mass murder, offering, as Crossan puts it, "peace through death." To the other are the utopian efforts of all ages.[50] Crossan's image of plate tectonics suggests that, unlike many monastic communities which simply shake the dust of civilization off their collective sandals, a transformative community must be a community with an edge pushing hard against civilization's normalization of violence. It is also clear that Crossan sees a different role for utopian social movements, like the early Jesus movement, than Bacevich. The differences in their exemplars of utopianism are also clear: In Crossan's analysis, Jesus performed symbolic acts of nonviolent resistance. As we saw in chapter 5, nowhere were these actions more powerful than in his practice of table fellowship. Drawing on cross-cultural anthropology, Crossan sees the way we eat together, our pattern of "commensality," as a microcosm of the prevailing social structure. But by practicing "open commensality," eating with whores (i.e., unattached women) and "tax collectors and sinners," Jesus defied the very way that imperial civilization colonized human bodies in one of their most basic functions. Embodying the reign of God, open commensality challenged social barriers and hierarchies and thereby the normalcy of civilization's structural violence.[51] The disastrous utopian movements of the twentieth century, on the other hand, all too quickly adopted civilization's normalcy of violence and succumbed to the delusion that through mass murder they could control the course of history.

THE PROPHET'S GRIEF VERSUS DEATH AS A SOCIAL METHOD

The prophet grieves. Grieves for the lost lives and the squandered resources. Grieves for foreclosed futures. Grieves for the future suffering of grandchildren from "blowback" or the collapse of empire. Grieves for her own deeply compromised moral integrity, wounded by the daily conscious or unconscious acts of complicity. Recently, I happened upon a website that detailed American casualties of our wars in Iraq and Afghanistan. The site focused on three persons. One was a young woman whose face was so clear, so fresh that it sparkled with gentle life. And she is gone, utterly gone. Never to have children, never to read to a grandchild. For what? For that moment, at least,

50. Ibid., 240.

51. Ibid., 118–20, 131–34.

I grieved. Grief—maybe a spark of anger—at least a beginning, a listening for a liberating word.

Grief is the first sign of resurrection from moral numbness. Judith Butler argues that "grievability" is the sign of a life regarded as a life, a life not consigned to the waste bin. Grievability acknowledges our common precariousness; our lives can be lost. But historically precariousness has led to domination by one group seeking to secure its life from precariousness at the expense of another. Modern warfare, in which civilians disproportionately suffer, has its own way of channeling grief.

> The shared condition of precariousness leads not to reciprocal recognition, but to a specific exploitation of targeted populations; of lives that are not quite lives, cast as "destructible" and "ungrievable." Such populations are "lose-able," or can be forfeited, precisely because they are framed as being already lost or forfeited. . . . Consequently, when such lives are lost they are not grievable, since, in the twisted logic that rationalizes their death, the loss of such populations is deemed necessary to protect the lives of "the living."[52]

So, when Madeline Albright was confronted with the deaths of, perhaps, five hundred thousand Iraqi children because of the economic sanctions enforced throughout the 1990s that supposedly targeted the Hussein regime, she said: "It is a hard choice but I think . . . it is worth it."[53] While hardly a statement that an Iraqi parent would make, Albright is very clear: one does not grieve "collateral damage."

Albright's comment takes us to the heart of the matter: Not only are the dead children rendered invisible in death as in life but *our* emotions have been shaped by a political framing. Butler argues that resistance to the political framing of whom we may grieve and whom we may not is as old as Sophocles' *Antigone*.[54] Yet public demonstrations of grief by the Hebrew prophets in the teeth of the granite face of power predate *Antigone* by several centuries. So, Berrigan sees in the grief of the prophet Joel "the exorcistic virtue of the Word . . . the setting back of the power of death." "But of mourning [the empire] knows nothing; for mourning would bring to the fore words and wordlessness, thoughts too deep for tears . . . , acknowledgment of guilt, the will to reconcile . . . , purpose of amendment publicly proclaimed."[55]

52. Butler, *Frames of War*, 14–15, 31.

53. Albright, as cited in Bacevich, *Washington Rules*, 142–43.

54. Butler, *Frames of War*, 38–39.

55. Berrigan, *Minor Prophets*, 90, 98. In the cases of the wars in Iraq and Afghanistan,

I suggest that the prophet's grief can be contagious and that it is the single most important contribution that the prophetic tradition offers to the confrontation with empire. As we saw in chapter 1, our first inclination might be to say that it is the prophet's anger that fuels resistance. From a Buddhist standpoint, however, anger most often weds itself to dualistic projections: we place the source of anger outside of ourselves, however we construe "ourselves." Anger fixates blame. So, Thich Nhat Hanh advises us to compost our anger. Shorn of lashing out in mindless blaming, anger becomes grief. Grief transforms the shame that we feel, if we are morally awake at all, at the war crimes that have been committed in our name. Shame stains. Like Lady Macbeth, we try desperately to wipe away the blood. But simply crying out "not in my name" will not work. From the Buddhist standpoint of interdependent coarising (Charles Strain being as Charles Strain is, these crimes have come to be) I cannot hide behind a wall of spurious moral purity. No cheap grace, no easy forgiveness. I grieve over my deeply rooted complicity, the damage done to my own soul.

Emotions are cognitive in character, as Martha Nussbaum maintains. They establish a moral horizon. Grief, mindfully embraced, I suggest, is a virtue that will expand the moral horizon ultimately to include all those made to suffer in endless wars. The compassion that underlies grief—the loss of the other as the loss of self—Buddhists insist can be trained. Emotions, thus shaped, lend existential weight to ethical reflection. Possible decisions and actions become live options. If the Hebrew prophets grieve God's flight from a temple built on a pyramid of human suffering, what might it mean to grieve an empire that practices "death as a social method?"

THE BODHISATTVA'S WITNESS

In the midst of a civil war in Vietnam in which both sides were backed by rival imperial powers, Thich Nhat Hanh and the students from his School

---

deliberate efforts by the government to control the images of the war presented in the media, including discouraging the presentation of images of flag-draped coffins of American soldiers, so as not to undermine further support for the wars, meant that, as a nation, we have failed to grieve our own lost men and women. Antigone, you will recall, grieves her soldier-brother. It is not simply Afghan and Iraqi civilians that we have not mourned but our own soldier-brothers and sisters. This point hit me with seismic force when I read a single sentence in a paper by a veteran who was a student in my class in spring 2012: "I have yet to experience a veteran being treated as anything other than a ghost." How can we grieve a ghost? They are neither alive nor dead. The dead have not been laid to rest and the living not restored to life. Antigone stakes her life on the importance of grief to the living as well as the dead. Creon, the ruler, turns his back on his dead nephew—and sets in motion a chain reaction of tragic deaths.

of Youth for Social Service practiced the "politics of reconciliation."[56] The very creation of community which acted to heal those harmed by war was as much a prophetic act as those of monks who led demonstrations against the South Vietnamese regime and even the symbolic acts of resistance of those who immolated themselves. As with Jesus' practice of open commensality, community building was a rejection of the normalcy of civilization's violence.

In the face of imperial atrocities, Thich Nhat Hanh prescribes a process of mindful attention to what is going on within oneself and in the world. Zen master Bernie Glassman provides a more detailed look at this process in the three principles for his Zen Peacemaker Order. The first principle is "not knowing." When we ask ourselves, "What can we do to dismantle the American empire?," the first and most important response is, "I don't know." Any other response is dishonest and betrays the seriousness of the issue. The second principle is to bear witness. Glassman has conducted meditation retreats at Auschwitz, among drug addicts in Zurich and the homeless in New York, and on the steps of the Capitol—all locations of great suffering or immense injustice. We need to let the enormity of the harm done and our connection with it sink in. Only then does Glassman suggest that we can actualize the third principle, which is healing.[57]

Kishitigarbha, perhaps, crystallizes the bodhisattva's tranquility in the midst of immense *dukkha*. He doesn't do much; he simply liberates a sufferer by taking her place in one of the many, many Buddhist hells. While flames lick around him, he remains unperturbed. Kishitigarbha knows what it means to share another's pain. In *The Reluctant Fundamentalist*, Pakistani author Mohsin Hamid's main character, speaking to an unnamed but threatening American, says of post-9/11 America that "as a society, you were unwilling to reflect on the shared pain that united you with those who attacked you. You retreated into myths of your own difference, assumptions of your own superiority and you acted out these beliefs on the stage of the world."[58] Sharing pain with our attackers? That demands a lot. The bodhisattva knows that mindful awareness of shared *dukkha* may be the only way to transform the impossible command to love one's enemies into genuine compassion.

In chapter 3, I suggested that the first three of the Fourteen Mindfulness Trainings function as an ideology solvent. From an engaged Buddhist standpoint the pretense of ultimacy conveyed in the discourse of American

56. Chan Kong, *Learning Love*, 72, 86.

57. Glassman, *Bearing Witness*, 66–90.

58. Hamid, *Reluctant Fundamentalist*, 168.

values as the "light of the world" is a powerful collective delusion. The failure to illuminate the human suffering that spreads in the wake of the "lightbearers" is the sign of something gone terribly wrong. To declare one's nation a "benign hegemon" without ever listening to the families of those whose deaths are termed "collateral damage" is to will ourselves collectively deaf. The transformation of war into a sound and light show, a spectacle not fouled by blood and gore, is to be blinded by a mirage. Mindfulness means bearing witness to the full suffering that war produces. Compassion opens our ears and cuts through the mirage that hides the reality of war. Where the prophet denounces the hubris of empire, the bodhisattva dissolves its hardened ideology.

JUST PEACEMAKING: THE NEW PARADIGM FOR THE ETHICS OF WAR AND PEACE

In *God and Empire*, Crossan makes a crucial distinction between matrix and background when discussing Jesus, Paul, and early Christianity. A background serves to set a subject in relief but has no internal connection with the subject whereas a matrix is in constant and reciprocal interaction with the subject. The Roman empire, Crossan insists, was the matrix for Jesus, Paul, and early Christianity.[59] Our discussion of Johnson, Bacevich, and Wills provides perspectives on our own imperial matrix. An ethics of war and peace offered by an American that does not come to terms with this matrix is fatally abstract. We hazard our ethical construction from within the belly of the beast. This means that if the prophet's "no" does not continually echo in our mind, then, it seems certain, we are being cocooned, wrapped in gauze, turned deaf and dumb, and absorbed into the belly's wall. Without the bodhisattva's mindfulness, however, we all too easily lose awareness that we and the beast "inter-are."

In chapter 4, I discussed "just peacemaking" or "strategic peacebuilding" as the appropriate praxis for one who is located within powerful institutions. Glen Stassen and his collaborators make the case in *Just Peacemaking* that their ethics of war and peace represents a third paradigm in contrast to pacifism and just war theory. In our contemporary context, they argue, just war theory can label terrorism as always wrong but it says nothing about how to prevent it. Pacifism courts withdrawal when it condemns all violence without draining the swamps that incubate violence. Just peacemaking is grounded not in ideals but in actual practices that construct peace from multiple angles. Rather than pitting pacifism and just war theory over

59. Crossan, *God and Empire*, 1–2.

against one another, it seeks a common ground in actual practices of peacebuilding. Its strength lies in its inductive as well as its dialectical approach. "Just peacemaking theory specifically rejects basing ethics on ideals outside of empirical history, and bases its ethics instead on what practices are actually proving to decrease the number of wars in real history."[60]

Just peacemaking supports the practice of nonviolent direct action and so makes room for the prophet. Emphasis on the role of grassroots voluntary associations and on cooperative conflict resolution clearly can be strengthened by the bodhisattva's community building spirituality. Many of the other initiatives from fostering sustainable economic development to strengthening the UN and its programs speak to the necessity for countervailing institutions. As we saw in chapter 4, Lisa Schirch suggests four umbrellas under which the various processes of strategic peacebuilding or just peacemaking can be clustered: (1) waging conflict nonviolently, (2) reducing direct violence, (3) transforming relationships, and (4) building capacity.[61] Resistance is not enough; nor is reconciliation. New structures must replace the old which fueled the conflict. Ultimately, just peacemaking seeks to create a "global civic culture" comprised of governments linked with international agencies and NGOs of all sorts through which ordinary citizens can work to goad states toward peaceful behaviors, sustain international collaborations and mediate conflicts. In short, as we discussed in chapter 5, just peacemaking presupposes a global civil society as the matrix out of which arise those groups which commit themselves to building peace.[62]

However, something is missing from these practices of strategic peacebuilders, namely, the need to alter the matrix out of which Americans, at least, act. I believe that the first step in a lengthy process of transformation is to dismantle our military empire.[63] Apart from a concerted practice of dismantling our own empire, initiatives to prevent war, resolve conflicts, and build peace elsewhere become Sisyphean tasks. In chapter 4, I argued that the prophet and the bodhisattva adopt different forms of nonviolent

60. Brubaker et al., "Just Peacemaking," 1–2, 11–15.

61. Schirch, *Strategic Peacebuilding*, 26 and passim.

62. Schroeder, "Work with Emerging Cooperative Forces," 161–63; Friesen, "Encourage Grassroots Peacemaking," 208–9.

63. I distinguish here between transforming a matrix and dismantling a military empire. Matrices, like ecological systems, cannot be taken apart piece by piece. However, our military empire can be challenged and taken apart bit by bit. Dismantling itself might be viewed as an overly utopian goal. However, as I suggested in the opening paragraph to this chapter, many of us who have lived through the second half of the twentieth century have witnessed the dismantling of more than one empire and of numerous autocratic regimes.

action. We can juxtapose both of these (see table 6.1) with just peacemaking and just war theory. This table represents the variety of positions with which just peacemaking not only seeks to remain in dialogue—it is open to dialogue with any position—but those with which it would form an alliance to dismantle the empire.[64]

Table 6.1

Bodhisattva	Prophet	Just Peacemaking	Human Security	Classical Just War
Ahimsa Being peace Politics of reconciliation	Symbolic acts of resistance Satyagraha Social movement politics	Waging conflict Nonviolently Reducing direct Violence Transforming relationships Building capacity	R2P Humanitarian intervention Reconfigured military Development	Defensive wars Humanitarian intervention Restoration of constitutional checks and balances Politics of limits

The bodhisattva represents the practice of *ahimsa*, non-harming, and the politics of reconciliation, whereas the prophet represents the practice of symbolic acts of resistance and a social movement politics. Someone like Andrew Bacevich, who professes classical just war theory, believes that America should engage in military action only as a last resort and for defensive purposes or for humanitarian intervention in cases of egregious violations of human rights as last resorts. He calls for the restoration of constitutional checks and balances, a curb to wildly excessive spending on the military and the promotion of a politics of limits versus a politics of eschatological ambition.

There is one new approach to war and peace represented on this spectrum that we have not yet discussed. This approach that focuses on "human security" is worth a brief analysis because it zeros in on how the American empire exercises its military might. As with just peacemaking theory and practice, the proponents of human security call for a paradigm shift in our thinking about and approach toward war and peace. "We need to make a core shift," argue Mary Kaldor and Shannon D. Beebe, "from focusing on traditional threats to focusing on conditions-based vulnerabilities." In their case the shift is away from the conventional use of the military to safeguard

64. Hence it does not include neo-conservative militarism nor a crusade theory of warfare.

territorial integrity or national security to the protection of vulnerable persons and communities. Vulnerabilities include not only the threat from a foreign enemy or internal repression but also conditions of poverty, hunger, and illness which breed collective fears and conflict. "Human security recognizes the interrelatedness of security in different places. Violence and resentment, poverty and illness . . . travel across the world through terrorism, transnational crime or pandemics."[65]

The concept of human security was first articulated in 1994 by the United Nations Development Program. It was part and parcel of a significant broadening of the concept of development from the previous narrow focus on GDP and it represented a clear departure from the theory and praxis of the national security state. In a globalized world both GDP as a measure of well-being and the traditional understanding of national security misapprehend how human lives are placed in jeopardy. Reframing security to focus clearly on the protection of individuals and peoples reinforced the involvement especially of transnational NGOs advocating for the human rights of endangered peoples.[66] Kofi Anan, while Secretary-General of the UN, articulated the principle of "Responsibility to Protect," which calls for the international community to intervene when a state is unwilling or unable to halt genocide, ethnic cleansing, or crimes against humanity.[67]

The human security approach, while recognizing the need to address the conditions of want and fear that breed violence, focuses much more on how to reconfigure militaries to confront the "new wars" of the twenty-first century.[68] "New wars" are primarily directed against civilians; they are

65. Beebe and Kaldor, *Ultimate Weapon*, 4–5.

66. Ahmed and Potter, *NGOs in International Politics*, 156.

67. Beebe and Kaldor, *Ultimate Weapon*, 285–87. Crystalizing an extensive process of consultation, Anan took pains not to pit "outside" intervention against state sovereignty: "State sovereignty implies responsibility, and the primary responsibility for protection of its people lies with the state itself. Where a population is suffering serious harm, as a result of internal war, insurgency, repression or state failure, and the state in question is unwilling or unable to halt or avert it, the principle of non-intervention yields to international responsibility to protect." Anan, as cited in Smith, "Strengthen the United Nation," 174. Canada and Norway, along with a number of mid-sized states, have taken the lead in creating a "Human Security Network" which views and addresses international issues from a human security perspective. The Network has endorsed the concept of the Right to Protect and has pushed for such limitations on the instruments of warmaking as a small arms treaty. Williams, "New Approaches in a Changing World," 282–85.

68. Beebe and Kaldor, *Ultimate Weapon*, 79–80. The United States chose to fight an unconventional attack on 9/11 by non-state actors through a conventional war against two states. In so doing, it fundamentally misunderstood the nature of the conflict that it faced. Because of the lethality of conventional as well as nuclear military technology,

more often conducted by non-state actors ranging from paramilitary death squads to terrorists, from rebels to transnational criminal organizations. Counterinsurgency approaches are ostensibly designed to meet the challenges of new wars, but they place a premium on defeating the enemy not on protecting human lives. It should be the other way around argue Kaldor and Beebe. In addition to counterinsurgency, other forms of warfare (e.g., drone warfare) communicate clearly to occupied peoples that their lives are of lesser value than American or European lives. "We don't need to have the 82nd Airborne escorting kids to kindergarten," Condoleezza Rice once insisted. On the contrary, Kaldor and Beebe argue, that is what the 82nd Airborne should be doing in a conflict situation; better yet, they should be training local military and police to escort the children. The inability of children to attend school for fear of attack or the danger of landmines, or because they lack money for books, or because they must take care of younger siblings while both parents work is a primary symbol of human insecurity. Accessibility to education is key to human development. Civilian control which subordinates the role of the military to such larger goals is key to the human security approach.[69]

Now, let us come back to the table (6.1). The point of this juxtaposition is my contention that each approach to peace has something (more than one thing) to contribute to our discussion and, more importantly, to the practice of just peacemaking. Andrew Bacevich's dissection of the mesmerizing power of the new American militarism and his critique of neo-conservative eschatological hubris are as challenging as—and for many more credible than—the prophets' denunciation of empire. Whereas the prophets' approach, and Berrigan's in particular, is attuned to what Crossan calls the normalcy of civilization's violence and Thich Nhat Hanh's Mindfulness Trainings dissolve any ideology, Bacevich's critique is directed against

conventional warfare between symmetrical powers would be an unprecedented bloodbath. Iraq and Iran's war in the '80s is a case in point. But the military is still configured and trained to fight this type of war. Ibid., 9, 19, 34–35. High-tech weapons—like the ultra-expensive F-22--are of no use in any of these new wars. "So what is the ultimate weapon?" Beebe and Kaldor ask. "It is a mindset that recognizes the essential equality of human lives." This sounds obvious, but counterinsurgency warfare's failure to protect civilians and, especially, the casual acceptance of "collateral damage" results in more recruits for the enemy. Ibid., 195–97.

69. A human security approach in contrast to counterinsurgency warfare treats the protection of human lives as an end in itself, as its first principle. This involves the preservation of human rights even in the midst of conflict, the creation of safe spaces where legitimate political authority can be established, a bottom-up approach that involves people in devising their own secure arrangements, multilateral interventions under international law, and clear civilian control over strategic efforts, including military involvement, in establishing security. Ibid., 79–80.

the particular form of imperial ideology (or, as we have seen with President Bush's proclamations, imperial *theology*) that prevails in the United States today. Bacevich could also be expected to cast doubt on human security's contention that some other purpose for the military than pure defense of the nation is called for. The human security approach shares with just peacemaking a focus on the multiple factors that place human lives in jeopardy. But it pays more attention to the proper use of force as part of the "responsibility to protect."[70] Just peacemaking includes the practice of nonviolent struggle and the politics of reconciliation in its ten initiatives.[71] From the just peacemaking perspective, then, each of the other perspectives has something vital to contribute to the creation of effective just peacemaking initiatives. As I see it, just peacemaking must eschew labeling or put-downs that one view or the other is not Christian or Buddhist enough or that the others are not sufficiently realistic. As I have indicated, its approach focuses on *practices* and not a single practice. If the resulting ethics is not sufficiently pure, so be it. Orthopraxis can be as dangerous as orthodoxy.

However, this does not yet resolve the issue of America's military empire. The combination of Bacevich's Niebuhrian attack on neo-conservative eschatology and both Berrigan's and Thich Nhat Hanh's fully elaborated theories *do* get at its ideological legitimation. They strip away the mask of the "benign hegemon." But what can actually dismantle the military empire? And, to be sure, dismantling is far more preferable, as Chalmers Johnson demonstrates, than the alternative which is imperial collapse.

WORKING THE LINKAGES

Chapter 4 drew on Daniel Levine's concept of "working the linkages" in his discussion of the dialectical relationship among the Latin American Christian base communities, the Catholic Church as a countervailing and protective institution and movements of resistance against Latin American military dictatorships of the mid 1970s through early 1990s. Similarly we focused on the spiritual role of the Southern African American churches, and the work of the NAACP within the legal system in supporting the American civil rights movement. The Catholic Church in Poland also worked in

70. I do not want to suggest that these positions do not have thoughtful criticisms to make regarding each other. Just peacebuilders, for example, have emphasized that a strong focus on security can lead to a virtually exclusive emphasis on state building that overlooks injustice and the necessity for reconciliation on the ground. Richmond, "Conclusion: Strategic Peacebuilding," 354, 356.

71. See chapters 1 and 3 in Stassen, *Just Peacemaking*.

tandem with Solidarity in the successful resistance to Soviet rule. Chapter 5 turned to Alexis de Tocqueville's interpretation of the role of domestic voluntary associations that constitute civil society in resisting the insidious spread of "democratic despotism." That chapter expanded Tocqueville's analysis to suggest that an embryonic "global civil society" might become a matrix spawning various forms of just peacemaking. In fact, the proliferation of non-governmental organizations working on strategic peacebuilding on all levels from the local to the international is one key element in a paradigm shift away from a narrow concept of peace as the cessation of conflict between warring parties toward the concept of a just peace.[72] In this chapter, I will argue that transnational advocacy NGOs (TANGOs) and the transnational advocacy networks (TANs) that they form—working in tandem with domestic efforts—may serve to dismantle America's military empire *over a very long haul.*

How can we understand this process? An example of working the linkages that focused on government violations of human rights comes from the "dirty war" in Argentina. After the military coup in March 1976, thousands of Argentinians were disappeared by the military junta. Relatives of the disappeared who became known as the Madres gathered spontaneously to protest the government's actions. Their courageous resistance movement drew allies from domestic religious groups which, in turn, along with the Madres activated international human rights organizations, like Human Rights Watch and Amnesty International. Documenting violations of human rights, local groups provided information to the Organization of American States, the US State Department, and even to Pope John Paul II. This led to US economic sanctions and an official OAS investigation and report in 1979 that is generally regarded as checking the Argentine government's worst violations of human rights. The regime could no longer assume that it could act with impunity or without incurring international condemnation.[73] In the case of resistance to Argentina's dirty war, the TAN that worked in tandem with domestic NGOs and the Madres movement included TANGOs (e.g., Amnesty International), religious institutions, intergovernmental organizations (OAS), and units of other states (US State Department).

The complex process of resistance in Argentina illustrates what Margaret Keck and Kathryn Sikkink in their groundbreaking work, *Activists*

72. Lederach and Appleby, "Strategic Peacebuilding," 26–27. For examples of religious organizations working in tandem with governments and other NGOs on peacebuilding efforts, see ibid., 27–33.

73. Thalhammer et al, *Courageous Resistance*, 101–9.

Beyond Borders: Advocacy Networks in International Politics, call the "boomerang effect."[74]

Figure 6.1

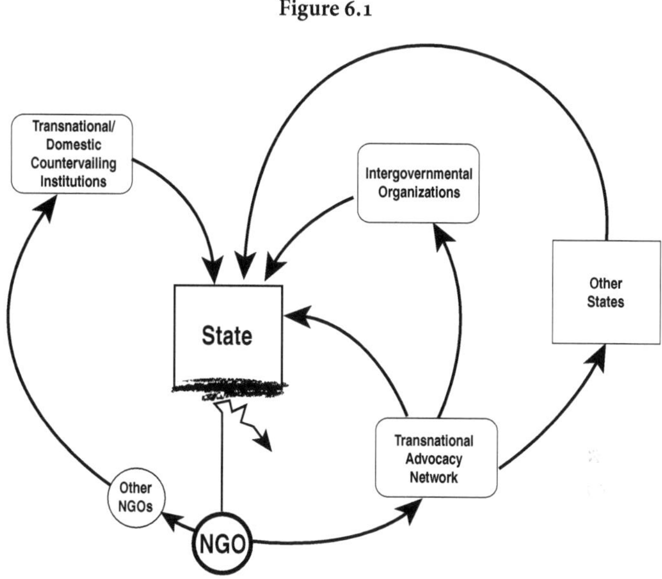

The "boomerang effect," as this figure illustrates, represents *one* way in which a TAN can leverage social change. In this case a domestic NGO is blocked in its efforts to change its own government's policies or practices. As we saw in chapter 5, TANs employ a multipronged politics. Information exchange through a TAN leads other NGOs to pressure their governments and intergovernmental organizations to, in turn, pressure the recalcitrant state to change. Information exchange is most effective when it is incorporated in symbolic frameworks, stories, and iconic examples that reshape the moral landscape. Along with leverage politics TANs also monitor and hold states accountable to their formal commitments to international law and international norms. Keck and Sikkink argue that the intricate interactions in the Argentine case illustrate this multipronged politics. A domestic social movement, the Madres, engaged in symbolic acts of resistance while domestic NGOs documented disappearances. International groups, using the information gathered, shone a spotlight on Argentina leveraging space for their domestic counterparts to act. They also placed the domestic symbolic politics on an international stage. The combined pressures led the military

74. Figure 6.1 is adapted in modified form from Keck and Sikkink, *Activists Beyond Borders*, 13.

junta to sharply curtail the number of disappearances after 1978.[75] To Keck and Sikknik's analysis I have added that domestic (e.g., the NAACP) and transnational countervailing institutions (e.g., US universities that engaged in divestiture as a protest against apartheid South Africa) may help to overcome the blockage (see figure 6.1).

All well and good, you may say, but what do such examples have to contribute to the dismantling of empire? I offer three examples of civil society actors working in tandem with sympathetic governments and intergovernmental agencies to challenge the United States' sovereign control over how it conducts military operations. In 1992, six NGOs met to form an International Campaign to Ban Landmines (ICBL). Each of the initial NGOs had been involved in clearing mines and aiding victims and saw this weapon as intrinsically evil because of its indiscriminate killing and maiming of civilians. This very focused goal of eliminating a weapon with over two hundred million in stockpiles and widely used was dismissed at the time as hopelessly utopian.[76] By framing the issue in terms of human costs, graphically portraying the harm done to civilians years after the end of conflict, and employing the advocacy of celebrities like Nelson Mandela and Princess Diana, the ICBL was able to shape the moral climate around the issue.[77] As the movement grew, the International Committee of the Red Cross (ICRC) lent its considerable prestige to the cause.[78]

The collaboration that evolved between the ICBL and the ICRC expanded to include more than a thousand NGOs, UN agencies, and key nations that assumed leadership after having unilaterally renounced their own production and use of landmines. The lead countries included Canada, Norway, Austria, and South Africa. Canada hosted what became known as the Ottawa Process that led to signing of the treaty by 122 nations in December 1997 to ban the production, stockpiling, and transfer of landmines.

75. With Argentina's return to democracy, the top leaders in the junta were tried for human rights violations in 1985. Ibid., 16–17, 21–22, 107–9. Numerous examples of the politics of TANs range from the human rights challenge to the military junta in Chile after the 1973 coup, and the network connections with Western religions of Eastern European human rights activists calling their governments to account for their treaty obligations under the Helsinki Final Act of 1975, to international campaigns for women's rights, TANGOs' pressures on the World Bank to alter its policies on development, and the Jubilee campaign to cancel the debt of Third World countries. See Khagram et al., *Restructuring World Politics*.

76. Williams and Goose, "Citizen Diplomacy and the Ottawa Process," 181–82, 196n1.

77. Ahmed and Potter, *NGOs in International Politics*, 159–60; Hubert, "Landmine Ban."

78. Mekata, "Transnational Peace Activism," 194–95

The treaty came into force in March 1999. Even nations like the United States, which have not become a party, have abandoned the use, production, and trading of this weapon. The possibility of being singled out for violating a now overwhelmingly endorsed international norm and the shame that would entail has led all but a very few nations to a de facto acceptance of the ban.[79]

Two things were new in this process. Of first importance was the involvement of TANGOs in every stage of the process including negotiations to draft the treaty, bringing pressure on states to sign the treaty, and the creation of mechanisms to monitor state parties' adherence to the treaty's provisions. Second, the willingness of small and medium-sized countries to lead the process in the face of stiff opposition from the large countries, including the United States, Russia, and China, was a critical breakthrough.[80] "Never before," declared Senator Patrick Leahy, who himself participated in the process, "have representatives from civil society collaborated with governments so closely and so effectively to produce a treaty to outlaw a weapon."[81] While some countries saw such nontraditional forms of diplomacy as unacceptable and others held that the Ottawa Process was a unique case and not replicable, the rapidity of the change inspired others to similar collaborations.

Following close on the heels of the landmine ban campaign, the UN process to create an International Criminal Court (ICC) incorporated a number of elements from the Ottawa Process. These included: (a) NGOs providing expert advice on international law, (b) inclusion of NGO representatives on several government delegations, and (c) an intensive campaign by over two thousand NGOs to secure ratification of the treaty. The ICC provides the possibility for legal recourse against regimes and their leaders that commit crimes against humanity. Throughout this process "the United

79. Herby and Lawand, "Unacceptable Behavior," 201–4, 209–11. As of July 2013, 161 nations had become party to the treaty. For updated information, see www.ICBL.org.

80. Given our own tunnel vision of America's hegemonic role, American public opinion is scarcely aware of, let alone credits, the role in peacemaking of the "middle powers." There is a long history of their efforts to abolish nuclear weapons including whole regions (beginning with the Treaty of Tlatelolco in 1967 among Latin American states) declaring themselves nuclear weapons free zones. In the Latin American breakthrough case there was intense involvement of peace and human rights NGOs contributing to the process. See Boulding, *Cultures of Peace*, 238–44.

81. Senator Patrick Leahy as cited in Ahmed and Potter, *NGOs in International Politics*, 161.

States exhibited fevered opposition to the ICC and aggressively sought to undermine it."[82]

Another demonstration that the Ottawa Process was replicable came with the development of a convention to prohibit the use or stockpiling of cluster munitions. The campaign was launched in November 2003 by some of the groups that had formed the ICBL. Soon they were joined by 350 NGOs in ninety countries. This TAN connected with like-minded nations, this time led by Norway, which launched the Oslo Process in February 2007 leading to the signing of the Convention in May 2008. The grounding for the campaign was international humanitarian law protecting civilians in times of war. As with landmines, unexploded cluster munitions level indiscriminate harm long after the conflict has ended. One hundred twelve countries have become party to the Convention which came into force in August 2010. Under the Convention, states—especially states that have used cluster munitions on the territory of a different country—are obligated to clear unexploded cluster munitions in affected countries. By the third anniversary of the Convention coming into force, states parties had destroyed 71 percent of their stockpiles.[83]

In a new twist of how civil society can be a force for global change, domestic NGOs in Switzerland have brought pressure on major Swiss banks to divest their holdings in companies that produce cluster bombs. Credit Suisse is one of the banks that have adopted this divestment policy. Similarly, Amnesty International UK targeted British banks. In May 2012, it was revealed that a number of the largest banks, including Lloyds Banking Group and the Royal Bank of Scotland, had joined the divestment movement. This movement to divest has become an international movement. As of July 2013, eight states parties had passed legislation to ban investments in cluster munitions producers by financial institutions in their country. Twenty-three states interpret their signing of the Convention as prohibiting investment although they have not passed legislation to that effect. An annual report published by several NGOs, including IKV Pax Christi (Netherlands), includes a "Hall of Shame" which lists financial institutions with the greatest investments in firms that produce cluster munitions. Of the top five, four are US investment banking service providers (Citigroup, JPMorgan Chase, Bank of America, and Goldman Sachs). By contrast, the

82. Williams and Goose, "Citizen Diplomacy," 190–91; Williams, "New Approaches in a Changing World," 289.

83. Landmine and Cluster Munitions Monitor, "Cluster Munitions Monitor, 2013," n.p.

report lists twenty-seven financial institutions in its "Hall of Fame" for having explicitly divested their holdings in cluster munitions manufacturers.[84]

Again, the United States is alone among its Western European allies, including the United Kingdom, and its North American neighbors not only in refusing to sign but in actively opposing the Convention. In November 2011, the United States along with Russia, China, India, and Israel sought to undermine the Convention by a proposal that would regulate but not ban these weapons. The proposal failed when fifty countries, led by Norway, Mexico, and Austria, along with the ICRC and other TANGOs, refused to cave into US pressure.[85] Here, too, middle-sized states asserted leadership in resisting blatant attempts by large states to undermine what had become an international norm.

Mere pinpricks in the armor of the empire? Maybe, but the length that the United States was willing to go in its attempt to subvert the Convention on Cluster Munitions tells a different story. Nations, argue Peter Herby and Kathleen Lawand, "need to be seen and accepted as members in good standing of the international community." When particular weapons or practices of warfare have been stigmatized in the public consciousness, non-compliant states risk being shamed in the face of the international community. That medium- and small-sized nations are no longer intimidated by US resistance in case after case of expansions to international law indicates that the United States is not considered, if it ever was, a *benign* hegemon.[86] More importantly, these nations pushing forward a just peacekeeping agenda demonstrate that the United States is not even the *hegemon* that some would believe. If, moreover, it is increasingly seen as an "outlier" nation, the will to resist among other nations will only grow stronger. Shakespeare's Richard II laments his own mortality but also the collapse of the illusion of a monarch's fearsome power. Death to both "comes at last and with a little pin bores through his castle wall."[87] When it comes to imperial pretensions, pinpricks matter.

84. See "New Credit Suisse Policy"; "UK Banks Blacklist Cluster Bomb Producers"; and "Growing Group of Countries Speaking Out."

85. Miles, "US Defeated in Bid on Cluster Bomb Accord."

86. Herby and Lawand, "Unacceptable Behavior," 200, 202, 209–10.

87. Shakespeare, *Richard II*, act 3, scene 2. I am grateful to James Block for this reference. A particularly egregious example of US resistance was its opposition during the George W. Bush administration to the UN's attempt to regulate the *illicit* trade of small arms. Green and Stassen, "Reduce Offensive Weapons," 188. But US opposition to attempts to regulate the international trade in arms continued with the Obama administration. After six years of work, a monthlong UN conference in July 2012 sought to negotiate a treaty that would prevent the sale of arms when there is a substantial risk that they would be used in committing human right violations. The draft was strongly

Shamima Ahmed and David Potter succinctly describe how TANGOs and TANs have become powerful actors on the international scene: by acting *as if* international norms of humane behavior exist, these advocacy organizations have made impressive gains in actually embedding these norms in international law. Just as importantly, the success of these early endeavors depended on a variety of strategies all of which transform our understanding of how new international norms are created[88] Several factors that led to the success of the ICBL, the formation of the ICC and the Convention on Cluster Munitions could be incorporated into other domestic and international coalitions to rein in American militarism.

- Focus on clear, limited objectives. (In 1956, cynics might well have laughed off focusing on seating arrangements on Montgomery buses as a mere pinprick on Jim Crow's armor.)
- Graphically portray the human costs of war and the weapons of war.
- Create a loose coalition clearly focused on the objective but open to a variety of tactics that fit with individual TANGOs' missions.
- Circulate information rapidly and extensively within the TAN, including expert advice from senior military experts.
- Above all, be willing to form new partnerships with countries, the UN, and international agencies that are willing to modify traditional forms of diplomacy to include TANGOs.
- Follow through to gain broad support for the objectives. Isolate the resistors.[89]

---

supported by US allies including the foreign ministers of the United Kingdom, France, and Germany. Although they, too, are major arms sellers, these countries promoted the draft of the treaty. In the course of the debate, the draft of the treaty was considerably weakened in an effort to gain consensus. When the draft was brought before the UN General Assembly, the United States reversed its initial opposition and voted in favor of the treaty. However, the NRA has led opposition to the ratification of the treaty and fifty senators have come out in opposition to it. Given this opposition, the real question is whether the United States will blindly forge ahead alienating its closest allies and neighbors or find a way to modify its fiercely defended sovereignty in order to build stronger international coalitions supporting disarmament and peace. See MacFarquhar, "U.N. Treaty Is First."

88. Ahmed and Potter, *NGOs in International Politics*, 15.

89. Herby and Lawand, "Unacceptable Behavior," 201–3; Williams and Goose, "Civilian Diplomacy," 182–88. See also Cluster Munition Coalition, "Model for Making Change Globally," http://www.stopclustermunitions.org/the-solution/change-globaly. Some have suggested that TANGOs and TANs play the crucial role in getting an issue placed on the international agenda, but the support of like-minded governments is crucial in bringing the process to a successful conclusion. There were several procedural factors that led to success in the ICBL case especially. First, the processes did

The analogy to the Montgomery bus boycott is worth reflection. No one can predict when a campaign focused on a clearly understood, symbolically potent objective will spark a conflagration. The American peace movement has largely focused on mega-goals like ending the wars in Iraq and Afghanistan by confronting the government in fits and starts. Perhaps such efforts ought to be conducted in tandem with intensive efforts pursued through transnational coalitions on specific objectives like ending the use of drones or sharply curtailing the international trade in small arms which might include campaigns on the part of religious institutions and universities to divest holdings in and to boycott patronizing the corporations that produce them. Such efforts will require alliances across the spectrum from the radical positions of the prophet and the bodhisattva to just war advocates.

In the 1980s the Plowshares Movement, as the cutting edge of the Nuclear Freeze movement, drew attention to the escalating threat of nuclear war. The Nuclear Freeze movement did not succeed in eliminating nuclear weapons It did lead Congress to cut off funding for "Star Wars" tests in violation of the Anti-Ballistic Missile treaty and to curtail new nuclear weapons programs, and, finally in 1992, to halt underground nuclear testing.[90] These were by no means merely symbolic victories. Call it the Lilliputian strategy—checking the rogue power of the imperial giant one rope at a time. New circumstances will require new forms of symbolic resistance but also new TANs that will organize around new objectives.

ANOTHER WORLD IS POSSIBLE

The previous section, which emphasizes transnational linkages, should not be read as downplaying the importance of organized resistance at the domestic level. It does recognize the sober truth that even the full range of engaged action at the domestic level—from cutting edge movements like Plowshares to communities that educate the young in cultures of peace, to all sorts of domestic advocacy networks—has barely dented the armor of imperial rule and American militarism. Dismantling the empire will require help from all corners of the globe.

---

not seek to achieve total consensus with the inevitable watering down of proposals. Instead, stringent terms acceptable to a strong majority were adopted by vote. Also in the cases of the Landmine treaty and the ICC formation, negotiations were not held by the government representatives behind closed doors. NGOs had direct access to the negotiating process. See, inter alia, Hubert, "Landmine Ban," 41–44.

90. Stassen, "Take Independent Initiatives," 60.

Dismantling is a long-term process. One can dismantle a machine (e.g., the military industrial complex), but transforming a matrix is an even longer-term proposition. It is important at this point to recall John Dominic Crossan's disturbing thesis that "empire is the normalcy of civilization's violence." To take on "empire-as-such," in reality, is to take on civilization as humans have lived it for at least six thousand years.[91] Mulling over this thesis, my inclination is to beat a strategic retreat: it is more than enough of a challenge to dismantle the American military empire one piece at a time. Transforming the matrix (in Crossan's terms, the normalcy of civilization's violence) seems a hopelessly utopian task. However, the precise strengths of the prophet's and the bodhisattva's practices in contrast to the just peacemaking, human security, and just war positions on our spectrum of approaches to imperial violence is to challenge the normalcy of civilization's violence. If it takes the next six hundred years (assuming that our species survives that long) to alter the matrix, Berrigan and Thich Nhat Hanh have each shown that it is possible to sustain such practices over a long lifetime.

Those who perform prophetic witness as well as those who pursue a pragmatic, long-term strategy of just peacemaking will need spiritual sustenance in order to "be peace." Recall Thich Nhat Hanh's insistence that preventing the *next* war requires transforming the culture of militarism. That matrix is both within us and around us. It is a delusion to think that the "new American militarism" has not invaded our psyches, colonized our minds.

> When we protest against a war, we may assume that we are a peaceful person . . . but this might not be the case. If we look deeply, we will observe that the roots of war are in the unmindful ways we have been living. We have not sown enough seeds of peace and understanding in ourselves and others, therefore, we are co-responsible. . . . To prevent war, to prevent the next crisis we must begin right now. . . . If we and our children practice ahimsa in our daily lives . . . , we will begin to establish real peace and, in that way we may be able to prevent the next war.[92]

Creating a culture of peace requires a spiritual practice and the cultivation of the virtue of ahimsa, the virtue of non-harming. In chapter 4 we looked at Gandhi's famous Salt March as a symbolic act of resistance with immense visceral power and as the epitome of *satyagraha*. Yet, Gandhi went further. His praxis of *satyagraha* was combined with an emphasis on *swaraj* which he translated as "self-rule." We forget the many years he spent building ashrams as training camps in nonviolence and living in one,

91. Crossan, *God and Empire*, 30.

92. Nhat Hanah, "Ahimsa," 66, 71.

spending hours each day spinning thread for homemade cloth in defiance of British monopoly on cloth production. Gandhi, like Thich Nhat Hanh, believed that inner transformation, in and through community-building, was necessary for outer transformation. Here, too, Gandhi created viscerally symbolic acts but focused on personal transformation. Emptying one's own chamber pot each morning rather than consigning that unpleasant task to untouchables became a powerful symbol of personal transformation directly challenging India's caste system. Where most members of India's independent Congress party sought first to gain power in order to promote social change, Gandhi reversed this order of business. He wanted Congress to address India's endemic social ills immediately and directly, completely ignoring British imperial domination. What Gandhi called his "constructive program," while rooted in powerful symbolic acts, required nothing less than a transformation of the place of women and untouchables in public life, a healing of pervasive conflict between Hindus and Muslims, addressing the issue of mass poverty, and disentangling Indian society from the tentacles of Westernization.[93] At the risk of oversimplification, we might say that *swaraj* was focused on the transformation of the Indian *matrix*, whereas *satyagraha* was designed to dismantle the British empire. Gandhi's synthesis, combining *satyagraha* and *swaraj*, grounds my conviction that the prophet's symbolic acts of resistance and the bodhisattva's community-building play an essential role in our struggle to transform the imperial *matrix*, as well. However, we should be clear that transforming a matrix is a multigenerational task. India, a country where interreligious violence is all too common and a nuclear power that has fought four wars with neighboring Pakistan, is far from being transformed.

To create a culture of peace we also desperately need multiple visions of what a post-hegemonic, peaceful United States would be like. Earlier in the chapter we examined what Bacevich calls the new aesthetic of war, war as spectacle. To counter this illusion of surgical, bloodless, victimless warfare, we need to see the true face of war but we also need empirically grounded visions of peace, visions of times and places where hope and history rhymed.

Throughout the preceding chapters I have stressed the role of the moral imagination and of forming communities with an edge if we are to sustain our efforts at just peacemaking. John Paul Lederach, who has spent decades resolving conflicts in some of the world's most troubled places, spells out exactly the type of imagination that is needed:

93. Schell, *Unconquerable World*, 138–42. For a clear summary of Gandhi's praxis, see Ackerman and Duvall, *Force More Powerful*, 61–111.

> Transcending violence is forged by the capacity to generate, mobilize, and build the moral imagination. The kind of imagination to which I refer . . . requires the capacity to imagine ourselves in a web of relationships that includes our enemies; the ability to sustain a paradoxical curiosity that embraces complexity without reliance on a dualistic polarity; the fundamental belief in and pursuit of the creative act; and the acceptance of the inherent risk of stepping into the mystery of the unknown that lies beyond the far too familiar landscape of violence.[94]

Such an imagination has nothing to do with flights of fancy. It stays rooted in the concrete realities and the power dynamics of conflict situations while it transcends "structurally determined dead ends." As such, imagination only emerges in concrete human acts. Imagination unfolds. It takes place in a community. The community's edge, its icebreaker, is its imagination. Not only does it proclaim that (in the phrase invented by the Zapatistas) "another world is possible," it opens a path to that world where the realism *du jour* says there is none.[95]

Buddhists across Asia have offered alternative visions by inventing symbolic acts of reconciliation in the very midst of violent conflicts. Think of A. T. Ariyaratne's Sarvodaya movement in Sri Lanka holding mass meditations that brought together hundreds of thousands of people from across religious and ethnic divisions as a witness for peace during that country's decades long civil war. Or remember the Cambodian monk Maha Ghosananda, who led peace marchers across Cambodia's war torn landscape creating reconciliation in the aftermath of the Khmer Rouge's genocidal rule. Or on a smaller scale think of the numerous cases during the war in Vietnam when monks and nuns, as well as Thich Nhat Hanh's students, crossed the battle lines between the North and the South Vietnamese soldiers in order to rescue villagers or, in one case during the Tet offensive, to protect eleven thousand refugees crammed into a Saigon university campus.[96]

Closer to home, two very specific examples come to mind of the moral imagination exercised by communities with an edge breaking the ice jam of everyday politics. The first example comes from my colleague, and nonviolent activist, Ken Butigan. It focuses not on the empire's war making power but on its increasing repression of its own people. San Francisco, perhaps to create what Martin Luther King Jr. called negative peace—order without

94. Lederach, *Moral Imagination*, 5.

95. Ibid., 26–27, 38–39.

96. Chan Kong, *Learning Love*, 110–14; On Sarvodaya, see Bond, "Sarvodaya Shramadana's Quest for Peace." On Ghosananda, see Weiner, "Maha Ghosananda."

justice—passed an ordinance that made it a crime to distribute food to the homeless in any public space. Butigan and a coalition of religious activists of all stripes, decided not to break the law by passing out peanut butter and jelly sandwiches but by creating a banquet in a public square to which all the homeless would be invited. The feast was served on tables with tablecloths, good china, and silverware. The powers that be were unwilling to crash and break up the party. Instead, they did the right thing and repealed the ordinance. As discussed earlier, Jesus practiced "open commensality," table fellowship that transgressed social barriers. He thereby created communities that not only embodied the reign of God but communities with an edge that unmasked the empire's violent normalcy. Ken Butigan's group in San Francisco went and did likewise. In the bodhisattva's vision of peace, the light shed by such actions reverberates through the whole of Indra's Net.

The second example concerns the creation of a community with an edge in defiance of the state's methods of corralling its citizens' identity. Militarization of the US-Mexico border, with its hundreds of miles of walls, its electronic sensors, and use of drone technology, is a sign of the new American militarism applied to the "protection" of fortress America in lieu of a bilateral treatment of the issue of migration. But such militarization also and inevitably serves to redefine who "we" are who are gathered behind the walls. Each Advent several hundred people gather to reenact the traditional Mexican Catholic ritual of Posada. Posada remembers the travail of Joseph and pregnant Mary searching in vain for shelter. But what makes "Posada sin Fronteras" unique is that the participants are gathered on both sides of the border. They are simultaneously denouncing the brutality of the US border policies that condemn hundreds of migrants to death in an unforgiving desert and proclaiming that God's love knows no boundaries. Sociologist Pierrette Hondagneu-Sotelo argues that Posada sin Fronteras offers "a counterhegemonic vision." It also redefines who "we" are. Those who perform the ritual are well aware that the militarization of the border has rapidly increased since September 11, 2001. Yet one participant still believes "that every time we come together, the wall comes down slightly. And I believe that one day, it will come down completely."[97] Hope says: Pinpricks can bore through border walls as well as castle walls.

97. Hondagneu-Sotelo, *God's Heart*, 133–35, 191–92. Taking students to the US-Mexico border for many years, I have witnessed numerous events where the mental walls separating ordinary Americans from Mexican and Central American migrants collapse and a community with an edge blooms if only for an evening. One such event occurred at a community center for migrants run by a Catholic parish in Altar, Sonora, where we shared a meal with migrants from Central America and southern Mexico. Some of the migrants were preparing to cross through the desert; others were set to try for a second or third time; still others, deported and defeated, were trying to earn

Such actions seem very small, very insignificant. So did that of Rosa Parks or that of the young vendor in Tunisia who in setting himself on fire lit a conflagration across the Arab world. Such actions give us hope. Hope with an edge. As we saw in the opening of this chapter, activist and writer, Rebecca Solnit, lays it on the line; she tells us just what sort of hope is necessary in a dark time—an ax which we wield with determination. To awaken from Stephen Daedalus' nightmare and find oneself in the dark is an austere form of hope. Embrace the "dark night of resistance," Daniel Berrigan says. Actions like those led by Ken Butigan or the "counterhegemonic" ritual of Posadas sin Fronteras are a special form of praxis, what Solnit calls the "politics of prefiguration . . . , the idea that if you embody what you aspire to, you have already succeeded. That is to say, if your activism is already democratic, peaceful, creative, then in one small corner of the world these things have triumphed."[98] Potent well beyond their immediate effects, they give us glimpses of the dawn, a time when the tidal wave of justice will rise once more.

---

money to return home. Each had a painful story to tell. We struggled with the barriers of language and our own incapacity to share such desperation. Suddenly one of the students pulled out a deck of cards and taught the other students and migrants alike a new card game. Soon suffering was put aside for an evening, and a laughter that knows no boundaries bound us together.

98. Solnit, *Hope in the Dark*, 86–87.

7

A PLANET ON FIRE

Climate Change, Environmental Justice, and Ecological Ethics

Mountains and waters right now are the actualization of the ancient Buddha way. Each abiding in its phenomenal expression realizes completeness. Because mountains and waters have been active since before the Empty Eon they are alive at this moment. Because they have been the self since before form arose they are emancipation-realization.[1]

—Eihei Dogen, "Mountains and Waters Sutra"

then showed me he
in right hand held
everything that is

the hand was a woman's
creation   all lusty
a meek bird's egg

nesting there   waiting
her word   and I heard it

1. Dogen, "Mountains and Waters Sutra," 97.

new born *I make you*
nestling *I love you*
homing *I keep you*[2]

—DANIEL BERRIGAN, "VISION (AFTER JULIANA OF NORWICH)"

THIS WONDERFUL SAYING OF the thirteenth-century Zen master Dogen calls us to mindful awareness of mountains and waters as ancient manifestations of Buddha reality. The universe as a whole and in each of its phenomena is the Dharmakaya, the illumination of the Buddha Way. In Dogen's sutra we can see the full flowering of the Mahayana tradition: Even so-called non-sentient beings have a Buddha Nature. Mountains and waters are ancient Buddhas. However, we should not assume that mindful awareness is a simple task, accomplished by a brief saunter in the woods that makes us feel "connected." What Dogen proposes is an arduous practice of overcoming ingrained perceptions, mental and emotional frameworks and dualistic interpretations of reality, not a fuzzy warm identification with non-human sentient beings.

> Green mountains master walking and eastern mountains master traveling on water. Accordingly, these activities are mountain's practice. . . . Don't slander by saying a green mountain cannot walk and an eastern mountain cannot travel on water. When your understanding is shallow, you doubt the phrase, "Green mountains are walking." When your learning is immature, you are shocked by the words "flowing mountains." Without fully understanding even the words, "flowing waters," you drown in small views and narrow understanding.[3]

Dogen is famous for declaring that this arduous practice *is* enlightenment. Dogen will be my guide in what follows.

The prophet is all too often transfixed by human culpability in corrupting not merely social reality but the very wellsprings of life. All the more wonderful when Daniel Berrigan gives breath to his lyrical imagination. In his striking image, the created universe is a fragile egg but cupped, warmed in the Creator's hands. One can rest there, be hatched there and fledgling fly. We are called to honor the sustaining Love and to beware of damaging the fragile egg or the fledgling bird.

2. Berrigan, "Vision (after Juliana of Norwich)," 220.
3. Dogen, "Mountains and Waters Sutra," 98–99.

THE SCIENCE OF CLIMATE CHANGE

"Our grandchildren are in for a rough ride." James Hansen is a grandfather. He is also America's leading climate scientist. In 1978 he was the scientist in charge of an experiment aboard a Pioneer mission designed to investigate Venus's atmosphere. Before the mission arrived, Hansen resigned, convinced that earth's climate was undergoing a dangerous change and studying those changes should be his priority. He has been sounding the alarm about the climate emergency since 1981.[4]

Hansen's moral commitment came from two sources. As a NASA scientist, he took to heart the first line of NASA's stated mission, "To understand and protect our home planet." Hansen's journey took him from the comfortable confines of scientific conferences to testimony before Congress and the president's cabinet. As years and decades passed, while our elected leaders fiddled, Hansen found himself having to create a new discourse grounded in the technicalities of climate "forcings" but condensed and reshaped to reach a broader public. His inspiration was his grandchildren—the second source of his moral commitment. He did not want them to say one day, "Opa understood what was happening, but he did not make it clear." Making it clear entailed mounting public platforms and it also meant that as a NASA scientist he would suffer clumsy attempts at censorship emanating from the White House during the Bush administration.[5]

The prophet's suit ill fits this scientist. You can feel him steeling himself to keep from running back to his lab. But you also see firsthand the scientist doggedly working, revising, correcting his predictions in light of new data. In 2000, he published a paper that argued that the safe limits of carbon dioxide in the atmosphere would be 450 parts per million (ppm). This conclusion resulted in an assumption that it would take centuries for earth's ice sheets to melt changing sea levels so slowly that humans and other species could adapt. Stable sea levels, Hansen argues, have been critical to human civilization providing plentiful marine food supply and allowing grain production in estuaries and flood plains. By 2005, paleoclimate data and data on the physics of ice melting made it clear that 450 ppm was a dangerously high estimate, and Hansen recalibrated the upper limit to 350 ppm.[6]

We live in a biosphere in which events are interwoven. As temperatures raise, the polar ice caps, the Greenland ice sheet, and the Himalayan glaciers melt. As they melt, the "albedo effect" is lessened: Ice and snow

4. Hansen, *Storms of My Grandchildren*, xiv–xv, 250.

5. Ibid., xii, 124–34.

6. Ibid., 140–44, 164–66.

reflect the heat of the sun back into space. Darker land and ocean absorb more heat creating more melting. A process that was thought to take millennia now is seen occurring within centuries. The melt area of the Greenland ice sheet has doubled in the last forty years. Were meltdown to continue to accelerate, sea levels would rise and coastal cities across the globe would be threatened—imagine Hurricane Sandy's impact on Manhattan and New Jersey or Hurricane Katrina's impact on New Orleans as a frequently recurring condition. More importantly, the fertile deltas key to global food production would be wiped out. Multiple feedback loops are at work. Hotter temperatures in the atmosphere also mean that more water vapor can be held, sucked up from the earth causing drought in one area and torrential downpours in another. Melting of the permafrost in the polar regions will release methane, a potent greenhouse gas. Each of these feedback loops amplifies the impact of global warming. At some point they become a runaway train which humans will not be able to control.[7]

At times it seems as if Hansen is a lonely Jeremiah challenging the Washington establishment in vain. But he is hardly alone. The Intergovernmental Panel on Climate Change, which has synthesized the work of two thousand scientists, has been issuing warnings since its first report in 1990. Its fourth report came in 2007.[8] Embodying the scientific consensus, the report is a conservative document. Its predictions of heat waves, desertification, floods, agricultural collapse, acidifying oceans, and their negative impact on marine life sound apocalyptic, but the actual rate of ice melting at the polar caps, for example, has superseded the IPCC's conservative estimates. Less noted than melting at the poles is what is happening to the Hindu Kush-Himalaya (HKH) Ice Sheet, which some have called "the Third Pole." The HKH is melting at a rate of 7 percent per year. "Himalayan glaciers, John Stanley argues, are receding faster than in any other part of the world."[9] Almost half of the human population from Pakistan and India to China and Vietnam depend upon the HKH ice sheet, which feeds into Asia's great rivers: the Indus, the Ganges, the Yellow, the Yangtze, and the Mekong. The farmlands of Asia's peoples depend upon the steady flow of water from the HKH.

Scientists like James Hansen have been joined by activists like Bill McKibben, founder of 350.org. In an article in *Rolling Stone*, McKibben pointed to the "terrifying new math" of global warming. Three numbers tell

7. Ibid., 42–43, 82–86, 256–58.

8. For IPCC's 4th Assessment, see http://ipcc.ch/publications_and_data/publications_ipcc_fourth_assessment_report_synthesis_report.htm.

9. Stanley, "Global Warming Science," 6, 44–45, 47–51. Stanley offers the clearest and most concise analysis of the science of climate change that I have come across.

us where we stand. Two degrees Celsius is the number accepted by virtually all scientists, and even the world leaders at Copenhagen, that global temperatures can rise in this century without the grave risk of tipping us over into a hostile climate regime.[10] Five hundred and sixty-five gigatons is the amount of carbon that can be released to the atmosphere by mid-century and stay on the safe side of two degrees Celsius. In 2011, we released about 31.6 gigatons and the amount is growing by 3 percent annually. Do the math, McKibben says. A final, truly terrifying number is 2,795 gigatons, which is the amount of carbon that would be released into the atmosphere if all *known* fossil fuel reserves were burned. And yet Exxon alone is spending thirty-seven billion dollars per year to find *new* reserves. Do we trust fossil fuel industries to leave untapped their twenty trillion dollars worth of assets?[11]

"We're hard at work," McKibben declares, "transforming [the planet we've known]—hard at work sabotaging its biology, draining its diversity, affecting every other kind of life that we were born into this planet with. *We're running Genesis backwards, de-creating*." This new, remade planet needs a new name, McKibben says. He calls it *Eaarth*. No longer can we say that our grandchildren are in for a rough ride. It has already begun. One example is the decline in the production of grains of about forty million tons a year, due to heat and drought. As a result, forty million more people were at risk for hunger in 2008.[12]

To add further detail to the climate change picture is not to my purpose here. The science is only uncertain about the rapidity and extent of change, not the fact of it. McKibben warns about creating apocalyptic scenarios that precipitate a leap from denials to despair, short circuiting action. Doomsaying leaves "no real room for creative thinking." We no longer can prevent climate change, but we can mitigate it; we can adapt. "Like someone lost in the woods, we need to . . . sit down, see what's in our pockets that might be of use, and start figuring out what steps to take."[13] One of these steps is a call for direct action by Hansen. He, along with McKibben and longtime civil rights activist Julian Bond, committed civil disobedience in February 2013 in front of the White House opposing any extension of the Keystone pipeline bringing more dirty ore from the Canadian tar sands to the United

10. Global average temperatures between 1800 and 2000 have already risen by 0.7 degrees Celsius, cutting into the margin separating the planet from disaster. Hansen, *Storms of My Grandchildren*, 142–43.

11. McKibben. "Global Warning's Terrifying New Math."

12. McKibben, *Eaarth*, 2, 6, 24–25; italics added.

13. Ibid., 99.

States.[14] Another step is modeled on the student movement that was part of the anti-apartheid campaign in the '80s and early '90s which pressured US universities to divest their holdings in companies that did business in South Africa. Now McKibben's NGO, 350.org, is organizing students to pressure their universities to divest their endowment holdings in fossil fuel industries.[15]

CLIMATE CHAOS

"My grandfather, father and I have worked these lands. But times have changed," comments a Mexican farmer. "The rain is coming later now, so that we produce less. The only solution is to go away, at least for a while [to the United States]." In Egypt's fertile Nile delta, peasant sharecroppers are squeezed between desertification and rising sea levels which increase ground water salinity. In the Maldives archipelago, considered the lowest lying country in the world, entire islands are being abandoned as their populations are resettled in more defensible islands.[16] Drought in Afghanistan affects farmers' choice of which crops to plant. Poppy requires one-sixth the water of wheat crops. Drought in the Nordeste of Brazil creates a large population of internally displaced subsistence farmers who flock to the slums surrounding the major cities. Finally, in northwest Kenya, Ekaru Loruman, a pastoralist from the Turkana tribe, lies dead, shot by someone from a neighboring tribe. Desertification had forced the Turkana south from their normal grazing range into an area close to their traditional enemies, the Pokot.[17]

What do these stories have in common? They are all examples of people already being pushed, squeezed, and relocated by factors directly associated with climate change. Reflecting on current movements of people in Africa, Robert Ford, a researcher at the National University of Rwanda observes: "In many parts of Africa, people living on the margin seem to quickly pick up on signals that indicate whether on balance life is better by going to the city or returning to the land. That this much ferment is happening now, before climate change really hits, tells one that we had better get prepared."[18]

How many people are likely to be displaced by climate change? While estimates differ greatly, the International Organization for Migration, a

14. Eilperin and Mufson, "Activists Arrested at White House."

15. See www.350.org.

16. Warner et al., "In Search of Shelter," 7, 17, 19.

17. Parenti, *Tropic of Chaos*, 3–4, 106–9, 126–30, 159–61.

18. Warner et al, "In Search of Shelter," 10.

UN agency, estimates that two hundred million people will be displaced by 2050.[19] Ford's comment reveals a second factor that my four examples have in common: They are poor, either as individuals or, in the case of the Maldives, a poor nation. That means that they have contributed almost nothing to the increase of greenhouse gases. And yet they are on the front lines of exposure to the perils of climate change. As in the case of Ekaru Loruman, they are its early casualties.

Christian Parenti cautions us against simplistic models of causality. Climate change did not produce the ethnic rivalries and traditions of cattle raiding between the Turkana and the Pokot. Nor did it create the vast caches of small arms weapons in Africa. The Cold War proxy wars did that. Subsequently the structural adjustment policies of the International Monetary Fund and the World Bank hollowed out fragile states leaving them unable to perform critical functions like digging deep water holes in drought stricken regions. "Climate change now joins these crises, acting as an accelerant. . . . All across the planet extreme weather and water scarcity inflame and escalate existing social conflicts." Parenti cites one study that estimates that up to 2.7 billion people live in countries where climate change could ignite violent conflict. Climate change "unfolds as part of a matrix of causality."[20]

Parenti illustrates this matrix with the story of Jose Ramirez, a Michoacan fisherman whom he met on the south side of the Rio Grande waiting to cross into the United States. Ostensibly Ramirez lost his livelihood when a series of El Nino events led to a red tide algae bloom killing or driving off fish. But an increased incidence of El Nino events is correlated with increased surface sea temperature, which is produced by climate change. Moreover, the bloom itself was fed by agricultural runoff, which in turn was exacerbated by unregulated urban development, which reduced the mangrove swamps and wetlands, which would have purified the run off. That Ramirez was left to fend for himself had much to do with Mexico's unqualified adoption of neoliberal economics and the structural adjustment policies imposed by international lenders.[21]

Ramirez, facing the extreme perils of an undocumented migrant, could in a perverse way be considered "lucky." He had crossed before and worked in the United States until he was deported. He had his old job waiting for him if he could cross. Migration requires resources: money, contacts,

19. Ibid., 2. To put this figure in perspective, in 2011 there were 15.2 million refugees and 26.4 million internally displaced persons worldwide. IOM's figure is roughly five times those combined numbers. See "Helpful Facts & Figures," *RefugeesInternational.org*, http://www.refugeesinternational.org/get-involved/helpful-facts-%2526-figures.

20. Parenti, *Tropic of Chaos*, 4–5, 8–9, 25, 184; See also 46–48, 62–65, 67–68.

21. Ibid., 183–86.

support networks, the possibility of employment and, if it is to be "legal," much more. Lacking these resources, the most vulnerable will be buffeted not only by the effects of climate change but by political processes over which they have no control.[22]

What are the likely responses to such a mass migration? The Ramirez case leads Parenti to suggest that the increasingly militarized border between the United States and Mexico offers us "a text from which to read the future—or a version of it." The catastrophic convergence of climate change and other factors exacerbating the vulnerability of people in the Global South propelling them to move may be met by the Global North turning itself into an "armed life boat" equipped with drone surveillance, infrared cameras, and National Guard helicopters. The "politics of the armed lifeboat" are playing out already not only in the form of a militarized border, but in anti-immigrant laws like Arizona's infamous SB1070, aggressive deportations by ICE, and current proposals in Congress to increase radically funding for border security.[23] As people move because of the added pressures of climate change, will they be met by xenophobic nations hiding behind their walls?

CLIMATE CHANGE AND MORAL CORRUPTION

One would think that faced with an unprecedented global emergency that a straightforward moral and practical response by peoples and nations acting in solidarity would by now be well underway. Not so, argues Stephen Gardiner. There are three factors connected with climate change that transform it into "a perfect moral storm." By "perfect" storm Gardiner means the confluence of several factors whose combined force threatens to undermine ethical reflection and derail action. By "moral storm" Gardiner means a high propensity to moral corruption. The *first* storm is that climate change is a global problem but one whose impact is asymmetrical. Rich nations are both much more responsible for the emission over time of greenhouse gases and less vulnerable to their impact on earth's climate. Rich nations have greater capacity to adapt to climate change.[24]

The *second* storm arises from the intergenerational character of climate change. Climate change is significantly "backloaded," that is, emissions in the present have their greatest impact on future generations. Because rich nations have benefitted greatly from the fossil fuel economy *and* the worst

22. Warner et al., "In Search of Shelter," iv.

23. Parenti, *Tropic of Chaos*, 187, 207–8, 219–20, 225–26.

24. Gardiner, *Perfect Moral Storm*, 6–8, 30–31.

effects of consequent climate change will *not* occur in the present but in the future, the present generation has less of an incentive to act decisively to transform its economy.[25] What results is a high propensity for "intergenerational buck passing."

The *third* storm, Gardiner argues, is caused by a lack of robust ethical theories in areas such as international justice and our moral obligations toward future human generations and nonhuman species. Cost-benefit analyses, for example, which predominate in political debates, are ill-equipped to deal with future contingencies, especially when intergenerational buck-passing may have a multiplier effect on the severity of the problem.[26]

These three storms are exacerbated because climate change while a global phenomenon is brought about by a vast number of dispersed agents with its effects distributed over centuries. If we assume that governments have the duty to address the issue, there are no global institutions that hold them accountable. This has led to a series of conventions agreed to by most nations that have been ignored in practice. As in Garrett Hardin's "tragedy of the commons," each nation has an incentive to do nothing while presuming and presupposing that all others will live up to their agreements. All of these factors create a situation of vulnerability to moral corruption for those of us who participate in and benefit from a highly developed and excessively polluting economy. The threat posed by this perfect storm targets our ways of thinking and talking about climate change. The record of public debate over the last two decades is replete with rationalizations, self-serving arguments, and inflations of scientific uncertainty into denials of climate change which sap our resolve to act. Specious argumentation leads to procrastination which then becomes a crime that we, the current generation of citizens of affluent nations, can get away with—except for the loss of our moral compass. "In the perfect moral storm, the threat is acute, even potentially fatal, because of the severe nature of some of the asymmetries of power and because those who are damaged by them—the poor, future generations, animals, and the rest of nature—are poorly placed to defend themselves against it."[27] Who then speaks on behalf of the voiceless? Not our current governments, not the fossil fuel industry which finances the climate change deniers.[28] At the end of his argument, Gardiner sounds a pessimistic note by quoting Socrates: "It is a difficult thing, . . . and one that merits much praise, to live your whole life justly when you've found yourself

25. Ibid., 32–35.

26. Ibid., 39–42.

27. Ibid., 24–29, 301–2, 304–5, 307.

28. Parenti, *Tropic of Chaos*, 230–31.

having ample freedom to do what is unjust. Few are those to be like that" (Gorgias 526a).[29]

Gardiner's brief against moral corruption bears clear resemblance to J. M. Coetzee's analysis of moral devolution through the image of scales forming over our eyes. Laser surgery, I have argued, requires more than a philosophical bent; it calls for prophets. Today, more than ever, we need the prophetic voice to cut through the rhetoric of obfuscation, to restore moral sanity, and to proclaim that our earth need not be held forever in fossil fuel's death grip.

THE PROPHET'S THEOCENTRIC LOVE OF CREATION

Daniel Berrigan offers no sustained reflection on ecological issues. There are, however, in his commentaries on the prophets frequent passing glances. Eagle sharp, they grasp the heart. So, in Berrigan's poetic riff on Jeremiah 8:4–7, storks, turtledoves, and thrushes migrate with the seasons, mindful of nature's flux. Heedless humans ignore God's will written in the land. In Israel's world they create a desert and call it peace. The consequences affect the innocent, the lowly, and children yet to be born. Berrigan conveys the prophets' verdict in an arresting image:

> Afield, in the dust
> a doe gives birth
> atremble, wanders away
> disconsolate
> her faun's first breath
> its last.[30]

In the disconsolate doe we find an image of the earth's mourning and an echo of the prophet's grief. Berrigan comments: "No greater lover of creation than Jeremiah, no more bitter mourner for its despoiling . . . . Where once creation flourished a wasteland stretches to the horizon . . . . Beings that flew and moved free and sang and bellowed, barked and screeched and roared . . . —entire species have been made to disappear. The oracle is of today, of ourselves."[31]

The prophet's theocentric imagination envisions not, as is often assumed, a purely bilateral covenant but repeatedly a triangular covenant that includes all creation as well as God and humans. The prophet's theocentric

29. Socrates, as cited in Gardiner, *Perfect Moral Storm*, 439.

30. Berrigan, *Jeremiah*, 46, 68.

31. Ibid., 49.

imagination operates within "a relational matrix" that includes God, humans, and the land interpreted as including all of the nonhuman creation; a change in any angle of a triangular relationship affects the other angles.[32] Within this encompassing matrix, justice is not just a human value but "part of the very fabric of the created order."[33]

Berrigan sees a linkage between contempt for God and for creation, a deadly interweaving that he calls "atheism in practice."[34] From the Hebrew prophets we can distill a composite pattern. Those in power *commandeer* Yahweh's gift of the land, *dispossessing* the vulnerable. Exploitation of people and land are inextricably intertwined, so the land is *despoiled*. Then the rich and poor alike are *displaced*. For the early as well as the later prophets there is, nevertheless, the hope of *restoration* of both the land and the people. Lest we think that the land is merely a passive recipient of human use and abuse or a passive instrument of divine reward and punishment, Hillary Marlow emphasizes passages that occur in nine different texts (in Isaiah, Jeremiah, Hosea, Joel, and Amos) articulated across a large span of time where the Hebrew verb conveys the double meaning of "to mourn" and "to dry up." Such passages indicate, Marlow continues, "that the non-human creation is somehow involved in YHWH's theophany, not as a passive victim, but actively responding to God's call for action."[35] Quoting Katherine Hayes, she continues, "The earth mourns for its own death as well as the nation's and experiences both mourning and dying in the act of drying up."[36] The integrity and well-being of the land is seen as valuable in its own right. Its death matters in God's eyes and not just to the humans who depend upon it. As Yahweh's creation it is not to be treated as a commodity.[37]

While the earth mourns, among humans, Berrigan says, "a bleak fatalism prevails." There is a reason for this failure to wake up and act. "Along with the ferocious plundering of the resources of the planet, our spiritual resources . . . all but vanish." Not only are we unable to imagine a postindustrial society that lives gently on this small planet but we cannot imagine

32. Ibid., 29; Berrigan, *Isaiah*, 51. For an extensive treatment of this theme in the eighth-century BCE prophets, see Marlow, *Biblical Prophets*. For a review of what is called "ecological hermeneutics" as an approach to the Jewish and Christian scriptures, see ibid., ch. 3.

33. Doran. "Environmental Curses and Blessings," 294.

34. Berrigan, *Jeremiah*, 27–28; Berrigan, *Isaiah*, 52.

35. Marlow, *Biblical Prophets*, 134–35, see also 190, 201; for Berrigan's treatment of this theme, see *Jeremiah*, 67–68.

36. Hayes, as cited in Marlow, *Biblical Prophets*, 136.

37. Marlow, *Biblical Prophets*, 265.

ourselves as the kinds of persons who would reinvent our world. "We stand benighted amid the ruin of creation."[38]

And yet. And yet. Berrigan draws upon the Hebrew prophets' hopes for restoration of the land as well as the people. I find it interesting that Berrigan devotes only a few sentences to Isaiah's (11:1–10) idyllic view of a restored creation, a world absent of tooth and claw where lions and oxen feed on straw. That vision, he intimates, is "beyond words."[39] Rather, Berrigan draws more extensively and most intimately upon Jeremiah's act of hope against hope. Commanded by God, Jeremiah purchases a field in territory occupied by an invading army, while Jerusalem itself is under siege. It "is as though," Berrigan comments, "a divine husbandman were planting healing realities in minds blinded and polluted by the smoke of battle."[40] In Rebecca Solnit's terms, Jeremiah offers us the "politics of prefigurement."

THE BODHISATTVA EARTH HOLDER

Comments about caring for the earth as caring for our larger body weave their way through many of Thich Nhat Hanh's writings. Of course, the teaching of interdependence (pratitya samutpada or dependent co-arising) or, as Thich Nhat Hanh prefers, the concept of interbeing, plays a prominent part in these works. However, contrary to more superficial Buddhist treatments of ecological issues, the notion of interdependence is solidly rooted in the concepts of emptiness, impermanence, and the non-self. It is amplified by reflections on thusness or suchness and the *Dharmakaya*, the universe in each and every atom revealing the Buddha reality. More to the point, Thich Nhat Hanh insists that these are not ideas but practices.[41]

We are, the opening of *The World We Have: A Buddhist Approach to Peace and Ecology* suggests, like sleepwalkers caught in a dream, the unsustainable American dream. We need a collective awakening. A new dream is ready-to-hand, revealed in every atom of the world we have. We need not be trapped in despair. Instead of just blaming corporations and governments, we can organize ourselves; we can act. As a model for action, Thich Nhat Hanh introduces another bodhisattva from the Lotus Sutra, Dharanimdhara, Earth Holder. She creates a space for us to live in; builds bridges to connect us with others and furthers communication among species. Earth Holder lacks a chapter of her own in the *Lotus Sutra*, so Thich

38. Berrigan, *Jeremiah*, 100; Berrigan, *Isaiah*, 52.

39. Berrigan, *Isaiah*, 43–44.

40. Berrigan, *Jeremiah*, 136–37, 140.

41. Nhat Hanh, "Sun My Heart," 129, 131; Nhat Hanh, *World We Have*, 65.

Nhat Hanh calls us to write a new chapter through our actions that will detail the myriad ways that we have protected the earth.[42]

How do we begin? As with the Buddha, we begin with the First Noble Truth. There is suffering. However, Thich Nhat Hanh explains that in a world of constant change, suffering too changes. Each age expresses distinctive forms of suffering, so each age must evolve new practices for transforming dukkha. What is the new form of dukkha? Thich Nhat Hanh answers this question by recounting a gruesome tale ascribed to the Buddha of a mother and father crossing a vast desert who survive by eating the flesh of the young son they have killed. Our dukkha begins with what and how we eat. Thich Nhat Hanh makes the connection between our meat rich and unhealthy diet, monoculture agriculture with its heavy reliance on chemical fertilizers and pesticides, livestock's contribution to greenhouse gases and water pollution, violence toward other species, and world hunger.[43]

The dictum "We are what we consume" applies to more than what we put in our bodies. We consume toxic sensory impressions especially through mass media and advertisements that, in turn, fuel endless craving. "The poisoning of our ecosystem, the exploding of bombs, the violence in our neighborhoods and in society, the pressures of time, noise and pollution—all of these have been created by the course of our economic growth and they are all sources of mental illness." Interdependence here is not a Hallmark card vision of oneness. It is the recognition that the collective dukkha, our addiction to a toxic way of living, is shared at both conscious and unconscious levels by all of us.[44] There is no easy path to a genuine affirmation of interdependence. We can say "the sun, my heart," but that does little to restore our polluted consciousness. The journey to realize what interdependence means entails the practice of impermanence. We recognize that everything changes and eventually dies. We die and so does our civilization. Only by embracing our fears can we overcome our addiction to tranquilizing consumption and if we cannot curb overconsumption our civilization will die sooner rather than later.

Impermanence and emptiness go hand in hand. To develop a truly *deep* ecology, Thich Nhat Hanh points us to the Diamond Sutra. He recasts the disciple Subhuti's opening question to the Buddha to read: "If I want to

42. Nhat Hanh, *World We Have*, 1–4, 8–9.

43. Ibid., 17–18, 23–25.

44. Ibid., 27–32, 40. The critique of consumer society and consumer addiction especially in view of its ecological impact is commonplace among engaged Buddhists. Consumerism is a collective form of the poison of greed which is fostered by the advertising industry which creates a collective form of delusion. See, inter alia, Loy, *Money, Sex, War, Karma*.

use my whole being to protect life what methods and principles should I use?" The Buddha's response is succinct. We must act to liberate all beings but realize that when the liberation of all has been accomplished no *beings* have been liberated. Why? Because the very way we have conceptualized this process indicates that we "are still caught in the idea of a self, a person, a living being, or a life span." These four concepts are hindrances to apprehending reality. Each of these deluded ideas discriminates. When we examine the self, as we have discussed repeatedly, we see non-self elements; examining the concept of a human person, we see nonhuman elements; studying life, we acknowledge nonliving elements. Finally we recognize that the idea of a life span—fixed in dates that can be chiseled onto our tombstone—only anchors the delusion of a separate self.[45] Thich Nhat Hanh says we are not to let go of these four concepts, rather we are to *throw* them away. The profoundly decentering teachings of emptiness and the anatman are key to a genuinely ecological understanding. As Dogen puts it, "To study the self is to forget the self. To forget the self is to be actualized by myriad things."[46] Forgetting the self is key for both Dogen and Thich Nhat Hanh but it does not lead to a fuzzy notion of oneness.

Thich Nhat Hanh draws upon the Avatamsaka Sutra to uncover the profoundly positive import of throwing away not only these four concepts but other pairs, like one/many, and inside/outside, that trap us, as well. "In every speck of dust I see innumerable Buddha worlds," this sutra says, "in each of these worlds countless Buddhas . . . their precious auras shining." These worlds interpenetrate.[47] Like grey-bearded Walt Whitman, we, too, contain multitudes. Contained and container, to be sure, are frameworks to be discarded. We think of disparate entities—stars, trees, persons—when all phenomena come to be and pass away within a dynamic fabric of interwoven events.

Reality, freed from all conceptualization, is called "suchness." "You and I, a caterpillar, all arise from suchness, all abide in suchness. . . . One can never leave suchness."[48] Breaking the frameworks that divide us into sepa-

45. Nhat Hanh, *World We Have*, 70–74.

46. Nhat Hanh, *Sun My Heart*, 60–63; Dogen, "Actualizing the Fundamental Point," 70. Against those who see Buddhist ecological thinkers as misusing the early Buddhist concept of dependent co-arising, Nhat Hanh's understanding, like Dogen's, is marked by the three "Dharma Seals" of impermanence, anatman, and emancipation-realization. See Nhat Hanh, *Heart of Buddha's Teaching*, ch. 18.

47. Nhat Hanh, *World We Have*, 60–63.

48. Nhat Hanh, *Sun My Heart*, 89–90. This positive valuation of the suchness of ordinary beings stands in clear contrast to early Buddhist understandings of nature as samsara, the realm of dukkha. Nevertheless, it is not, as Nhat Hanh clearly shows through his interpretation of the Avatamsaka Sutra, an invention of modernity and it

rate entities, acknowledging the suchness of all phenomena, gives rise to a clear ethos underlying Thich Nhat Hanh's approach to an ecological ethics.

> We humans think we are smart but an orchid, for example, knows how to produce noble, symmetrical flowers, and a snail knows how to make a beautiful, well-proportioned shell. . . . We should bow deeply before the orchid and the snail and join our palms reverently before the monarch butterfly and the magnolia tree. The feeling of respect for all species will help us recognize the noblest nature in ourselves.[49]

The kind of ecology that Thich Nhat Hanh promotes is not only a healthy biosphere but a healthy individual and collective consciousness free from toxic, violent, and entrapping images, free from the colonization of our minds by TV, movies, and the Internet.[50] To foster this form of "universal ecology," *The World We Have* closes with a rich set of spiritual practices that begin with "Earth Gathas." These short sayings function as mindfulness bells punctuating our day. Taking our first step of the day, we recite, "Walking on the Earth / is a miracle. Each mindful step / reveals the wondrous Dharmakaya." From that first step we go on to wash our hands, serve food, water the garden, and recycle, each action prefaced by a gatha to awaken us to the world around us. In addition to the gathas, there are breathing and relaxation exercises and a ritual of Touching the Earth in order "to return to the Earth, to our roots, to our ancestors . . . to let go of the idea that we are separate and to remind us that we are part of Earth and part of life." Finally, we are offered an "Earth Peace Treaty Commitment Sheet" with over fifty possible actions from which we can choose those that we will pledge to perform to reduce our impact on the environment.[51]

VIRTUE IN EXTREMIS

Chapter 3 examined the kind of virtue that is called for in extreme circumstances. Articulating that type of virtue but, more to the point, acting virtuously in that manner, Daniel Berrigan was preoccupied with America's endless wars. Only in passing, as we have just seen, did he draw the toxic connection between militarism and the ruthless exploitation of the earth. The laser intensity of the prophet's vision missed something dreadful

---

also can be clearly seen in the Dogen quotation that opened this chapter.

49. Nhat Hanh, "Sun My Heart," 130.

50. Nhat Hanh, *World We Have*, 74, 84–85.

51. Ibid., 105–40.

looming on its periphery. I make no moral judgment here. Berrigan's preoccupations were mine as well. The birth of my grandchildren and the inspiration of a son who studied environmental science in college and has become a science journalist have belatedly wakened me to the climate emergency. For those who saw the ecological signs of the times much earlier, there were key secular prophets, paragons of courage who also expressed a bodhisattva's love for all sentient beings: Rachel Carson, Aldo Leopold, and Arne Naess, among others. For me, however, it was certain Buddhists who had assumed a prophetic voice, who set me on a different path, preeminently Joanna Macy and Gary Snyder.

Early in the 1980s, Macy saw and wrote about three interconnected perils: "the threat of nuclear war," "the progressive destruction of our life-support system," and "the growing misery of half the planet's people." Together, she suggested, these threats engender a form of collective despair, despair over the ominous possibility that humans by their own hands would bring about the death of their own species. Drawing upon the work of psychologist Robert J. Lifton, Macy saw our repressed despair producing a "psychic numbing."[52]

True to her Buddhist commitment, Macy developed a spiritual practice that took the form of "Despair and Empowerment" training workshops. Through a series of exercises, she takes groups through the experience of touching, acknowledging, and embracing our collective despair. As we saw with the prophet's response to empire in chapter 6, grief is the work of coming back to life, like the pain which accompanies a numb limb starting to feel again. Embracing our pain leads to a second stage of practices that Macy calls "The Turning." "Here, the collective nature of our pain for our world is recognized as evidence of our interexistence, revealing the larger transpersonal context or matrix of our lives." A final stage involves exercises that demonstrate how our felt-connection with others can lead to personal empowerment. "In this kind of power we do not rely on ourselves alone, but on the web in which we take being."[53] More than three decades ago, Macy was laying the groundwork for and creating practices to support a virtuous life that can flourish even under the shadow of a potential global catastrophe.

Taigen Dan Leighton modifies an old Zen koan that we should act as if our heads are on fire but also as if we have all the time in the world. Now, Leighton says, it is our planet whose head is on fire. This note of urgency is conveyed in the title of the collection in which Leighton's article appears,

52. Macy, *Despair and Personal Empowerment*, 1–3, 13.

53. Ibid., 69, 132.

A Buddhist Response to the Climate Emergency.[54] Not climate change, mind you, but a true emergency. One who speaks with her head on fire assumes a prophetic voice—think of Isaiah with the burning coal pressed to his lips. Or the description of Berrigan and Thich Nhat Hanh that I offered in the Introduction: "present tense afire."

And yet, Thich Nhat Hanh calls us to be the one calm person in a small boat on a stormy sea. Gary Snyder, another prophet-bodhisattva, urges us—in this time of emergency—to re-inhabit the planet place by place, that is, to commit ourselves to where we actually are as if we were engaged with it and its wellbeing for many generations to come.[55] Both the prophet, with head on fire, and the bodhisattva, calmly standing in a tossing and turning boat, offer schooling in a virtuous life for an endangered planet.

DEEP ECOLOGY

Buddhism has for some time been treated as the quintessentially green religion. In contrast to Western religious traditions, it is viewed as non-anthropocentric. Mahayana Buddhism especially sees all sentient beings as having a Buddha Nature and extends sentience to include all of reality. Buddhism has also been characterized as genuinely open to the findings of science. Because Arne Naess drew on Mahayana Buddhist teachings in developing his understanding of what he named "deep ecology," Buddhism has particularly been associated with the movement that Naess started.[56]

Naess invented the term deep ecology and contrasted it with shallow ecology which focuses on the conservation of natural "resources" for human purposes and which accepts the basic institutions of an industrial and technological society. Deep ecologists affirm some version of holism which sees all beings as intrinsically related; we exist in a web of relations rather than as isolated beings. An ecological consciousness is seen as fundamentally divergent from the dominant worldview of modern industrial society which views humans apart from and superior to the rest of nature.[57] Naess crystallized this theory around an eight point platform:

54. Leighton, "Planet Has Its Head on Fire," 192.

55. Snyder, *Place in Space*, 246–47.

56. See Naess, "Deep Ecology Movement, 271. The assumption that Buddhism is a green religion owes something to a famous article by Lynn White in which he set Buddhism in contrast to Christianity which he argued was at the roots of our destructive approach to the dominance of nature. "Historic Roots of Our Ecologic Crisis," 1203–7.

57. Devall and Sessions, *Deep Ecology*, 65.

- Both human and nonhuman life have intrinsic value apart from any utilitarian value of nonhuman life.
- Biodiversity is a value in itself.
- Humans have no right to reduce the diversity of life except to meet vital needs.
- The flourishing of nonhuman life requires a reduction in the human population.
- Human interference with the nonhuman world is excessive.
- Policies regarding the basic economic and technological structure of society must be changed in light of the above.
- An ideological change to value quality of life rather than the accumulation of material goods is necessary.
- We have an obligation to implement these principles.[58]

The first proposition of the platform has been taken to imply some sort of biocentric equality and the right of all living organisms to "self-realization." This implication has been subjected to considerable debate. Does a tuberculosis bacillus have the same right to exist as the human being infected by it? If not, what do we mean by the intrinsic value of all sentient beings?[59]

We have just seen that Thich Nhat Hanh sees the Diamond Sutra (and certainly the Avatamsaka Sutra) as a basis for a truly deep ecological consciousness. Virtually all engaged Buddhists point to the concept of dependent co-arising (*pratitya samutpada*) as a key element in their ecological consciousness. However, we must be clear that any religiously based ecological consciousness is a hybrid. Scholars point out that in early Buddhism the concept of dependent co-arising was not intended as a descriptive ontology.[60] Instead it was a skillful means (*upaya*) for liberating oneself from suffering (*dukkha*). The realm of causes and conditions is *samsara* where we are wracked on the wheel of suffering. Joanna Macy agrees: "This doctrine . . . arose out of religious and ethical concerns, as a fruit of a quest for emancipation."[61]

58. Naess, "Deep Ecology Movement," 264–68.

59. Palmer, "Overview of Environmental Ethics," 23, 29–31.

60. Harris, "Buddhism and the Discourse of Environmental Concern," 388; see also Eckel, "Buddhist Philosophy of Nature," 327. In my estimation the most balanced and nuanced analysis of the development and permutations of the concept of dependent co-arising over the long course of the Buddhist tradition is McMahan, *Making of Buddhist Modernism*, ch. 6.

61. Macy, *Mutual Causality*, 26–27, 34–35, 37.

In her early work on this issue, *Mutual Causality in Buddhism and General Systems Theory*, Macy also distinguishes the two poles of her investigation—reflected in the title of her book—as different in method and purpose. Buddhist concepts are guiding means for dealing with existential issues of suffering and liberation. System theory seeks to understand the causal principles underlying many types of phenomena.

> A system is less a thing than a pattern. It is a pattern of events, its existence and character deriving less from the nature of its components than from their organization. As such it consists of a dynamic flow of interactions. . . . The organized whole found in nature . . . is not only a system but an *open* system. It maintains and organizes itself by exchanging matter, energy, and information with its environment. These flow through the system and are transformed by it. These exchanges and transformations are the system's life and continuity, for no component of the system is permanent.[62]

Macy suggests that the juxtaposition of systems theory to the Buddhist understanding of dependent co-arising can uncover the mutual causality inherent in, among other things, our moral life. "Systems concepts provide explanations and analogies which can illuminate Buddhist ideas that are less accessible from a linear causal point of view."[63] They challenge the frameworks that we implicitly draw upon to interpret Buddhist teachings. Juxtaposing Buddhist understandings of mutual causality with general systems theory adds an essential ingredient to any ecological ethics which in the pre-scientific era of twenty-six thousand years ago was not culturally available, namely the idea of a living "open system." The purpose for such an appropriation, however, remains transformative.

From this creative extrapolation of an ancient Buddhist concept, John Holder draws two modest but critical conclusions that seem to be incontrovertible. First, human live in continuity with the natural world and are subject to the same causes and conditions as any other natural phenomena. Second, when the teaching of dependent co arising is applied as means for spiritual transformation, it has a "decentering effect that identifies human concern with a concern for the suffering of all sentient beings," a process that has deep ethical significance.[64]

In Thich Nhat Hanh's case and in that of many other engaged Buddhists, as we have just seen, the notion of dependent co arisisng is spliced

62. Ibid., 72–73.

63. Ibid., 1–2.

64. Holder, "Suffering Nature, 116.

with the ideas of Buddha Nature, suchness, emptiness, and the interpenetration of all beings that came to full expression in the Avatamsaka Sutra. Steve Odin argues that this Chinese vision shares with deep ecologists a rejection of "object ontology." As ecologist J. Baird Callicott puts it, "Living natural objects should be regarded as ontologically subordinate to 'events' . . . or 'field patterns.' . . . In the worldview of ecology . . . organisms in nature are a 'local perturbation' in an energy flux."[65] So it is clear that the bases for a Buddhist ecological ethic developed over not just centuries but millennia. The latest hybrid, fusing Buddhist concepts with contemporary theories like system theory, is a new chapter in the reinvention of Buddhism.

CHALLENGES TO DEEP ECOLOGY (AND A BUDDHIST ECOLOGICAL ETHICS)

Bron Taylor has developed a number of criticisms of the deep ecology philosophy that, arguably, can apply to a Buddhist ecological ethics as well. First, Taylor sees deep ecology's appropriation of non-Western religious traditions as a "reverse orientalism" that views these conflated traditions as purely positive in thought and practice over against Western consciousness seen as uniformly alienated from nature. Second, deep ecologists create a series of dichotomies (biocentric versus anthropocentric, intuition versus reason, decentralization versus centralization) in their comparisons of an alternative ecological consciousness and "Western" consciousness. Third, suggesting that the jury is still out on the contribution of Eastern religious traditions to ecological activism, Taylor argues that the Buddhist view of nature along with other Eastern traditions is "highly abstract and idealized" and leaves little room for efficacious and strategic human action in conserving nature.[66] Jerry Stark adds to this criticism that deep ecologists eschew rational discourse to provide specific ethical guidelines in favor of intuition.[67] What are we to do about the tuberculosis bacillus and how do we justify to others our actions or inaction?

Whatever the merits of these criticisms of deep ecologists, several points should be made in defense of a Buddhist ecological ethics. First, engaged Buddhists are virtually uniform in eschewing any form of religious triumphalism. Buddhism, Thai activist Sulak Sivaraksa argues, does not presume that the world would be better off if we all became Buddhists.

65. Callicott, as cited in Odin, "Japanese Concept of Nature," 93.

66. Taylor, "Deep Ecology," 220–24, 235n47. See also Harris, "Buddhism and the Discourse of Environmental Concern," 388.

67. Stark, "Postmodern Environmentalism," 269–70.

We need instead "buddhism with a small b," a willingness to act on Buddhist principles without seeking to convert others to a single path.[68] Second, the creation of dichotomies between "Eastern" and "Western" forms of consciousness reflects dualistic understandings that are clearly forms of delusion. Stereotypical generalizations are not what a mindful practice will generate. As we will soon discuss, the crisis of climate change renders any dualistic "either/or" between a biocentric versus an anthropocentric approach as counterproductive. Earlier we discussed the Mindfulness Trainings that calls upon us to take firm ethical stances but without engaging in polarized debates or actions. Buddhist ethics are not anthropocentric or biocentric. In Indra's Net each reality as thoroughly permeated incarnates the whole cosmos. Yet, as empty of own-being, it is not reified. The Net is impermanent, constantly changing with all actions by all beings shimmering through every node of the Net. Those who work to mitigate the human impact of climate change, e.g., by helping people living in fertile deltas to cope with rising sea levels, and those who work to protect biodiversity in local ecosystems are not two.

Third, Taylor's contention that the Buddhist view of nature is highly idealized and, therefore, of little value for strategic action misses the point of the Buddhist understanding of Buddha Nature and Indra's Net. These teachings ground the person as a moral agent who takes on, as the Dalai Lama puts it, a universal responsibility. They open up a moral horizon by placing us and our actions within a field of interdependent relations and they affirm our capacity to liberate ourselves. True, such visions have more to do with wisdom (*prajna*) than reason, but some such vision is necessary for moral agency to make any sense at all. Visions must be enacted and actions in accord with vision follow a general ethos. In the Buddhist case, that ethos is the practice of compassion and non-harming (*ahimsa*). Again, the emphasis is on practice. Nonviolence is never perfect. It exists along a spectrum with violence. Practicing *ahimsa* means moving closer to the nonviolent pole.[69]

Practice as the backbone of moral action has several advantages over the abstract, rational development of ethical guidelines that Taylor and Stark see deep ecology as lacking.

- Because a practice takes practice it involves a long-term commitment, steady work on a particular problem and particular approach over time. Learning and a clearer sense of direction arise through engagement in action.

68. Sivaraksa, "Buddhism with a Small 'b,'" 117–24.
69. Nhat Hanh, *Calming Mind*, 36–37.

- A practice involves self-transformation as well as action upon the world. Through practice one becomes a virtuous self who acts consistently to lessen the amount of suffering in the world.
- A practice, at least as Buddhists conceive of it, requires mindful concentration in the very midst of practice. This is a much broader understanding of how the mind works to develop a sense of direction than a rational process of decision-making.
- Any practice involves the development of basic skills over time. One becomes capable of acting spontaneously but in a structured fashion. Practice overcomes the separation of rational reflection and decision making, on the one hand, and daily action on the other.

THE PRACTICE OF THE WILD

Gary Snyder, Beat poet, Buddhist practitioner, rural laborer, more than most Buddhists has both elaborated the Buddhist virtue ethic as "the practice of the wild" and tied it to bioregionalism as a specific environmental strategy. In common parlance, the wild gets defined by what it is not, "not tame, not cultivated, not civilized, not subordinate, not restrained." "Turn it the other way," Snyder insists. The wild is free, self-propagating, independent, self-authenticating. But it is especially "wild systems"—an oxymoron for most of us—that attract Snyder's attention. The wild is, above all, self-organizing with its own "long-range strategies." It is the "ordering of impermanence." To think of the wild as other and as somewhere else is to miss the point. The wild surrounds us: "Exquisite complex beings in their energy webs inhabiting the fertile corners of the urban world in accord with the rules of wild systems, the visible hardy stalks and stems of vacant lots and railroads, the persistent raccoon squads, bacteria in the loam and in our yogurt."[70]

What then does it mean to *practice* the wild? Snyder suggests a metaphor for a life lived in the grain of things. "One of the first practices that I learned is that when you're working with another person on a two-person crosscut saw, you never push, you only pull; my father taught me that when I was eight."[71] Above all, the practice of the wild entails finding a place and learning from it. Snyder's bioregionalist ethic begins with not one but two categorical imperatives: "First, don't move and second, find out what that

70. Snyder, *Practice of the Wild*, 5, 8–11, 15, 90, 181. For a fuller presentation of Snyder's position, see Strain, "Pacific Buddha's Wild Practice," 143–67.

71. Snyder, *Real Work*, 134–35.

teaches you."[72] With his move by 1970 to the Sierra Nevada, Snyder took up the challenge of these imperatives. They call us, he said,

> to see our country in terms of its landforms, plant life, weather patterns, and seasonal changes—its whole natural history before the net of political jurisdiction was cast over it. People are challenged to become "reinhabitory"—that is, to become people who are learning to live and think "as if" they were totally engaged with their place for the long future. This doesn't mean some return to a primitive lifestyle or utopian provincialism; it simply implies an engagement with community and a search for the sustainable sophisticated mix of economic practices that would enable people to live regionally and yet learn from and contribute to a planetary society.[73]

72. Martin, "Coyote Mind," 170.

73. Gary Snyder, *Place in Space*, 246–47. Snyder himself adopted an early version of ecological theories which saw ecological systems, absent severe disturbances, as evolving to a mature "climax state." Even with disturbance, the thrust of the system was to reestablish equilibrium as a stretched rubber band will return to its former shape when an external force is removed. Snyder, *Real Work*, 173. One of the pioneers of ecological science, Eugene Odum, saw mature ecosystems as characterized by "overall homeostasis." Except in severe cases, once a disturbance was removed, the system, much like an organism, would return to its earlier equilibrium state. Heneghan, "Out of Kilter." J. Baird Callicott argues that this "balance of nature" paradigm has been replaced by the "flux of nature" paradigm and that Buddhist or any other ecological ethicists need to come to terms with the new science. Callicott, "New New (Buddhist?) Ecology," 175–76. Two changes in the way scientists are approaching the study of ecological systems are of key importance. First is the increasing emphasis on "social-ecological systems" (S-ES). This entails a recognition that (a) humans are embedded in the natural world, (b) the idea of wilderness as a place where humans do not interfere with natural processes is a fiction, if a necessary one, and (c) humans are, willy-nilly, stewards of creation. The question is not whether we manage the world around us but how well we manage it. Second, instead of talking about maintaining equilibrium in a climax state, scientists speak of ecosystem *resilience*. Resilience is the adaptive capacity to remain in a desirable stable state, for example, at the largest scale, the stable state of the past ten thousand years that was favorable to the development of agriculture and thereby the growth of civilizations. If disturbances are too great, an S-ES may be pushed over a threshold into a new state or regime in which feedback loops shift and the basic structure of the system is altered. Folke, "Resilience," 253–67; Walker and Salt, *Resilience Thinking*, xiii, 1, 32, 53–54, 112. The old ecological model with its concept of climax state provided a telos that guided ethical inquiry. The goal was to restore North American land to an allegedly pristine, pre-Columbian baseline. The new ecological model recognizes that humans have been altering their environment for millennia and open systems are constantly changing. In the new model, resilience "emphasizes non-linear dynamics, thresholds, uncertainty and surprise." For a history of the changes in the concept of ecology, see Worster, *Nature's Economy*.

Two Buddhist elements in Snyder's bioregionalist ethics are particularly relevant to our task. The first is its emphasis on community, the *sangha*, as necessary for any transformation. The second is the practice of mindful concentration, *samadhi*, refocused as the kind of attention to the detailed variations of climate and soil, to what will flourish and what will not in this place that "any true farmer" practices. Snyder speculates that *samadhi*, in fact, predates farmers. The stillness of hunters and the "field-sensing" of gatherers laid the foundation for zazen. Bioregionalists require the same multidimensional field sensing as their Neolithic forebears who memorized the landscape in all its details.[74] Mindful practices, in turn, create what Peter Hershock calls a liberating intimacy with ourselves and our environmental matrix. The practice of reinhabitation assumes that humans have a place, must find a place in the wild. Having a place means using its resources wisely; it entails a blurring of the lines of division separating wilderness preservation and natural resource management. In the Sierra Nevada, it means clearing undergrowth, conducting bioregional inventories, banding migrant song birds, and establishing the joint management of private and public lands.[75] It also entails collaboration and consensus building with neighbors, local industry and both local, state and federal government agencies.[76]

SLOW VIOLENCE AND ENVIRONMENTAL JUSTICE

Deep ecologists and Buddhists like Snyder do accentuate the importance of a transformation of consciousness and a decisive break with the mentality of the scientific industrial order. Yet Bron Taylor argues that people struggling with environmental degradation do not generally look outside their own tradition for resources but look within those traditions. There is ample evidence that a variety of religious and philosophical traditions are able to green themselves drawing on internal spiritual resources. More importantly, Taylor contests the idea that "consciousness change toward an ecocentric deep ecological spirituality is a precondition of 'radical environmental action.'" In studying grassroots activists in nonindustrialized countries, Taylor discovered that these activists eschew the polar opposition of biocentric and anthropocentric strategies and draw upon concepts of sustainable

74. Snyder, *Real Work*, 107–8, 141.

75. Snyder, *Place in Space*, 7, 79, 260–62.

76. On such collaborative movements in Northern California, see Lipschutz, *Global Environmental Governance*, ch. 4. Emma Marris discusses more fully the implications of the shift in ecological models for environmental activism in *Rambunctious Garden*.

development and environmental justice that some deep ecologists dismiss as too anthropocentric.[77]

In *Slow Violence and the Environmentalism of the Poor*, Rob Nixon traces the struggles of people in the Global South to defend their traditional ways of life against the rapacious forces of globalization and thereby shifts our focus to issues of environmental justice that are often overlooked by ecological activists from the Global North. Liberation theology added the phrase "structural violence" to our vocabulary of injustice. Faced with the reality of environmental injustice, Rob Nixon offers the phrase "slow violence." Like other forms of violence, slow violence kills, maims, destroys life. Whereas ordinary violence is explosive, immediate in time, visible in space, slow violence is dispersed, often untraceable. Its destructive force may continue for decades or even generations. The toxic impacts of a Chernobyl, a Bhopal, or a Fukushima show up generations later in genetic mutations and birth defects long after the triggering event has faded from memory. The dramatic concussion of violence takes place invisibly at the cellular level. More than three decades after the last American soldier left Vietnam, "Agent Orange continues to wreak havoc, as through biomagnification, dioxin builds up in the fatty tissues of pivotal foods like duck and fish" and passes "into the cooking pot" creating new generations of victims.[78]

Agent Orange's slow violence is mirrored in the radioactive poisoning, the ongoing legacy of the depleted uranium shells unleashed in Iraq during the two Gulf Wars. "Depleted uranium" is one of those military euphemisms that conceals lethality. The three hundred and forty tons of "depleted" uranium used in shells in the very brief first Gulf War retain 60 percent of uranium's natural radioactivity with a half-life of *4.51 billion years*. Nixon details the catastrophic impact of the radiation on soldiers who worked in field hospitals next to destroyed Iraqi tanks or assigned to detoxify US tanks. How many generations of Iraqi children who play hide and seek in these burned out tanks will be affected? The UN refers to depleted uranium shells as a "weapon of indiscriminate effect." Nixon adds a final chilling note: "Since 1991 depleted uranium ordinance has been deployed in Afghanistan, Bosnia, Kosovo, Kuwait, Serbia, Somalia and Chechnya and—in unprecedented quantities—during the 2003 war in Iraq."[79] It may seem possible now to assign responsibility for these long-term indiscriminate effects but who will connect the dots when a birth defect shows up several genera-

77. Taylor, "Deep Ecology," 223–25.

78. Nixon, *Slow Violence*, 2, 6–7, 8–11, 13–14.

79. Ibid., 201, 204–5, 209, 211, 218. The ongoing slow violence of war adds a new dimension to our discussion of militarism in chapter 6.

tions removed from exposure to toxic chemicals? In 2001, DOW Chemical bought out Union Carbide and simultaneously disclaimed responsibility for the Bhopal disaster; it "off loaded historical culpability." So even if dots are connected generations hence, from whom shall the victims seek redress?[80]

In what has been called the second race for Africa, major extraction industries enter into sweetheart deals with corrupt governments. They violate the environmental safeguards that they routinely follow in the Global North. Companies like Shell and Chevron offload the responsibility for the military repression that accompanies protest against the destruction of farm land, forests, and fisheries declaring that they cannot intervene in the internal affairs of a sovereign state.[81] Before his execution on trumped-up charges, Ken Saro-Wiwa, who led the Ogoni people in protesting the rape of their ancestral Nigerian homeland by transnational oil companies, put it succinctly on behalf of all indigenous minorities: "The Ogoni people were being killed all right, but in an unconventional way. . . . Environmental degradation has been a lethal weapon in the war against the indigenous Ogoni people."[82]

In many countries of the Global South, building dams has become *the* symbol of modernization. As Nixon puts it, "To erect a megadam was literally to concretize the postcolonial nation's modernity, prosperity and autonomy." For decades dam building was fostered by World Bank loans that quickly plunged nations into debt and into "structural adjustment policies" as conditions of emergency loans from the International Monetary Fund. These dams which provided electrical power to cities displaced rural peoples who had farmed the river flood plains for centuries. They became "development refugees." Because in many cases these peoples lacked legal title to their ancestral lands they were treated as "uninhabitants."[83]

Dr. Paul Farmer traces the convoluted trajectory of an actual case of slow violence instigated by dam building in Haiti. Violence began with the building of Haiti's largest dam to serve Port-au-Prince. Subsistence farmers were forced from arable bottom land up into a hard scrabble hilly terrain. This led, in turn, to conflicts over land and to significant decline in livelihoods. In one hard-pressed family, an attractive young woman named

80. Ibid., 63.

81. Ibid., 2, 106–7, 110–11.

82. Saro-Wiwa, as cited in Nixon, *Slow Violence*, 10–11. On Saro-Wiwa, see further ibid., 103–27.

83. Ibid., 161–64, 166–67. One estimate of the number of "developmental refugees" puts the number at between thirty and sixty million people. In a 1994 study, the World Bank admitted that of 192 dam projects it had funded only *one* involved adequate support for resettlement. Ibid., 152.

Acephie sought to aid her family by forming a liaison with a soldier, a man with a salary. He died from AIDS, leaving Acephie unknowingly infected. She worked for a time as a domestic until she was fired because she was pregnant. Returning home to her family, Acephie died of AIDS leaving an HIV-infected child and a parent so distressed by the loss of his daughter that he committed suicide.[84]

Slow violence kills but its trajectory is more of an entangled web. Who is morally responsible for Acephie's death? Acephie herself? The soldier who infected her? The engineers who designed the dam and supervised its construction? Corrupt Haitian government officials who found in the dam a personal boondoggle? The World Bank bureaucrat who approved the loan? As we pull on the threads of the entangled web, slow violence morphs into structural violence. It also carves out a distinctive role for the prophet. Prophets, I have repeatedly argued, peel back our eyes, perform laser surgery on our moral opaqueness. In the case of slow violence, this means beginning to see patterns in entangled webs that stretch across space and, especially, time.

Indian journalist Ramachandra Guha has covered the environmentalism of the poor extensively. Conflicts over dams, turning over of forests to timber industries, pollution of rivers "pit 'ecosystem people'—that is, those communities which depend very heavily on the natural resources of their own locality—against 'omnivores,' individuals and groups with the social power to capture, transform, and use natural resources from a much wider catchment area; sometimes, indeed, the whole world." Development in India, Guha maintains, can be seen as omnivores capturing natural resources at the expense of ecosystem people turning the latter into development refugees who in order to survive migrate to urban slums.[85]

Guha contrasts Western environmentalism focused on wilderness preservation with its primary commitment to maintaining biodiversity with the environmentalism of the poor which is to sustain village-based agrarian subsistence economies that have existed in relative harmony with their local ecosystem for centuries.[86] Wilderness preservation assumes that "*all* human intervention is bad for the retention of diversity." In Third World countries setting aside wildlife reserves has meant the uprooting of hundreds of thousands of ecosystem people, while millions have had their access to "common" lands restricted. Meanwhile, omnivores can drive or fly thousands of miles to enjoy the beauty of wilderness without assuming the

84. Farmer, *Pathologies of Power*, 31–35.

85. Guha and Martinez-Alier, "Environmentalism of the Poor," 304–5.

86. Guha, "Cross-Cultural Environmental Ethic," 433–34.

environmental and social costs of their pleasure trips. "The conservationist wants to 'protect the tiger or whale for posterity,' yet expects other people to make the sacrifice. . . . Few among these lovers of nature scrutinize their own lifestyle . . . and the ecological footprint their consumption patterns leave on the soil, forests and water, and air of lands other than their own."[87] Nixon puts the contrast bluntly: "the environmentalism of the poor is inseparable from distributive justice."[88]

Guha's point is *not* to dismiss one environmental ideology and practice in favor of another but to point to the ambiguity of each and, most especially, to critically analyze the utopian assumptions that undergird each. For example, the deep ecologists who favor the wilderness ideal seem to presume the radical reduction of a huge percentage of the human population while the Gandhian agrarian ideal romanticizes rural life. By looking at multiple environmental ideologies, Guha avoids "a Manichean struggle between one set of good ideas . . . and another set of evil ones." Rather than favoring any single environmental ideology, Guha suggests drawing key principles from each. Modernity which gave us scientific industrialism with its huge negative impact on the environment also bequeathed to us the value of equity. The wilderness ethic in rejecting the exploitative sway of scientific industrialism offers the core principle of diversity. Peasant cultures, so far, are the only ones that have proven to be sustainable over the very long term. Diversity, sustainability, and equity, Guha says, are the "building blocks" of a more adequate environmental ethics.[89]

SYMBOLIC ACTS OF RESISTANCE AGAINST SLOW VIOLENCE

Ecosystem peoples not only challenge Western environmental assumptions. Across the globe they have employed multiple symbolic acts of resistance. For example, in India ecosystem peoples have adopted Gandhian methods of nonviolent direct action including civil disobedience to preserve land held in common for centuries which while biodiverse also provided food, fodder, and fuel to villagers. State governments have increasingly turned over the commons to the timber industry. Industry in turn has clear cut forests and planted fast growing eucalyptus trees which neither provide for

87. Guha, "Paradox of Global Environmentalism," 368.

88. Nixon, *Slow Violence*, 149.

89. Guha, "Cross-Cultural Environmental Ethic," 432–33, 435–42. For a more extensive treatment of Guha's environmental ethics, drawn from an analysis of the Indian context, see Gadgil and Guha, *Ecology and Equity*.

biodiversity, nor meet the subsistence needs of villagers. In response, villagers have practiced "Pluck and Plant" *satyagraha*—pulling out the eucalyptus saplings and planting a diverse combination of native trees.[90]

In Thailand, Buddhist monks have invented a new ritual of "tree ordination" in order to protect forests held in common by villagers against devastating practices of deforestation promoted under the banner of exported-oriented "development." These rituals in which trees are wrapped in monastic robes combine Buddhist and animist practices to invoke the protection of "the good Buddha and the fierce Spirits." In the ritual context the monks have encouraged villagers to adopt a self-sufficient and sustainable livelihood that strictly controls the harvesting of trees and other forest gifts versus clear-cutting of forests to pursue cash-crop agriculture. The monks mediate between the villagers and environmental NGOs which provide knowledge of alternative practices. The monks do not generally emphasize Buddhist teachings which bear affinity with the deep ecology philosophy, rather they refer to Western models of development as permeated by the three poisons. Some monks have also adapted a folk ritual for long life to protect streams threatened by drought and pollution.[91] As with other movements in the Global South, these practices do not create a false duality between supporting the livelihood of villagers and protecting the environment.

Rob Nixon devotes a chapter in *Slow Violence* to the work of Nobel laureate Wangari Maathai and her Greenbelt Movement (GBM). GBM has become the most successful example of integrating Guha's three principles. It has employed one hundred thousand women and planted over thirty million trees in Kenya and a dozen other African countries. It is important to note the multiple levels on which GBM worked. First, it began as an effort to combat erosion which directly impacted women as the primary subsistence farmers. So, food security was directly at stake. But this pragmatic strategy

90. Guha and Martinez-Alier, "Environmentalism of the Poor," 300–304.

91. When these rituals were inaugurated in the late '80s, the monks were heavily criticized by powerful government, corporate and media sources and also by the Buddhist hierarchy. As the rituals gained widespread popularity, these power elites began to coopt the rituals. In 1996–97, the King called for the planting of fifty million trees in honor of the fiftieth anniversary of his reign. The meaning of the ritual then took on an added layer as the affirmation of Thai identity. The tree ordination rituals do not invoke Buddhist scriptures used in the ordination of monks but the monks view the rites as a way of propagating Buddhist teachings while resisting deforestation. See, inter alia, Darlington, "Good Buddha and Fierce Spirits," 169–85; Morrow, "Tree Ordination as Invented Tradition," 53–60; Tannenbaum, "Protest, Tree Ordination," 109–27.

also combated the shortages of firewood and fodder, and the damage to rivers and streams that exacerbated women's daily workload.[92]

Second, it became a symbolic act of civil disobedience as tree planting resisted the Kenyan government's illegal takeover of common lands and its promoting deforestation as "development." GBM adopted "a narrative of territorial theft" that linked Kenya's authoritarian government with the original takeover of land by the British colonial regime.[93] This discourse and the symbolic acts of resistance that expressed it, named both the historical and the contemporary actors who pulled the trigger of slow violence.

Third, Maathai and GBM cultivated linkages with other social movements, particularly those that struggled on behalf of women's rights. Maathai spoke out on political prisoners and advocated for forgiveness of Third World countries' debt. This practice of what Nixon calls "intersectional environmentalism" contrasts sharply with the colonial and post-colonial emphasis on a form of conservation that involves the removal of indigenous peoples coupled with the promotion of industrial agriculture.[94]

Finally, Maathai and GBM linked the local with the global by working closely with local women with their abundance of local knowledge as their organizers. Simultaneously, the symbolic resonance of tree planting gleaned international allies as well, including the UN. This gave GBM more leverage in resisting political repression.[95] Nixon summarizes this deep level on which GBM functioned:

> The theatre of the tree afforded the social movement a rich symbolic vocabulary that helped extend its civic reach. Maathai recast the simple gesture of digging a hole and putting a sapling in it as a way of "planting the seeds of peace." To plant trees was to metaphorically cultivate democratic change. . . . To plant a tree is an act of intergenerational optimism . . . an investment in a communal future the planter will not see. . . . To act in this manner was to secede ethically from Kenya's top-down culture of ruthless self-interest.[96]

What Wangari Maathai offers is a form of sustainability that synthesizes environmental and social justice and transcends the dichotomy

92. Nixon, *Slow Violence*, 129, 131, 133, 238–49.

93. Ibid., 129, 146, 140–41. The British had dispossessed women as the primary cultivators by vesting clan owned lands as private property held by males and fostering cash crop agriculture that disempowered women economically. Ibid., 140.

94. Ibid., 138–40.

95. Ibid., 141.

96. Ibid., 133–34.

between a biocentric and an anthropocentric orientation. Ecosystem people are drawn to political action and symbolic acts of resistance when their livelihood and their traditional ways of life are threatened.[97] Maintenance or restoration of biodiversity is seen as the traditional responsibility of those who have lived in a place sustainably for centuries. In many cases, as the example of Maathai demonstrates, the leaders of these movements are women whose burdens—collecting water, finding fuel, farming the land—increase dramatically from the encroachment of outside forces which claim legal ownership of the commons. Ecosystem peoples are asserting the *right* to control their own natural resources as essential to both the survival of their community and the integrity of their culture. "The assertion of this right," argues Heidi Hadsell, "must be preceded by the general realization among them that they do indeed have such moral and political rights."[98] This is no small achievement for peoples who have historically been exploited and subjugated. So, protection of the environment and its biodiversity occurs in tandem with a process of consciousness raising issuing in liberating acts of resistance. Across the globe these grassroots movements offer models of both environmental and social justice.

PRAGMATIC REFORMISM

Anthony Giddens takes a rigorously pragmatic approach to dealing with climate change. He argues that many green values, for example, a commitment to biocentric equality have nothing intrinsically to do with combating climate change except when protecting biological diversity is necessary to reduce carbon emissions. "Mystical reverence for nature" must be disavowed as a distraction from the pragmatic goal of addressing climate change. More to the point "green politics" tends to be suspicious of power and supportive of decentralization. To the contrary, Giddens insists, states must play the key role in planning ahead to adapt to climate change, in providing incentives to the economic sector to develop new technologies and efficiencies and to ordinary citizens to modify their behavior, in institutionalizing the Polluter-Pays Principle through some form of a carbon tax, and in shifting subsidies from the fossil fuel industry to new forms of renewable, clean energy. Touting decentralization is counterproductive to the effort to gain

97. Taylor, "Popular Ecological Resistance," 335, 339, 342–43.

98. Hadsell, "Profits, Parrots, and Peons," 75. An affirmation of this right clearly requires rethinking the whole notion of private property since "ecosystem people" depend on resources held in common. It would also mean expanding the meaning of Nussbaum's right to control one's environment. See chapter 5 above.

public support for each of these vital strategies.[99] Apart from state regulation, do we really expect the fossil fuel industries to keep the bulk of their twenty trillion dollars worth of assets in the ground? Moreover, apocalyptic discourse employed by some green activists, Giddens contends, will only increase fatalism. Instead, states must consistently emphasize the positive opportunities for business entrepreneurs and the improvement in quality of life for ordinary citizens that will come with a low carbon emission future. A form of "ecological modernization" involving partnerships among government, businesses, science, and environmental NGOs not some sort of conversion to a green philosophy, represents our best hope of mitigating and adapting to climate change.[100]

Giddens calls for a "radicalism of the centre" not built on an all-or-nothing consensus but on a *concordat*, a commitment of all political parties to firm principles, short term targets coupled with long-term planning, specific policies, plus a monitoring body. The government should become the model of environmentally effective practices. A concordat means that one political party will not seek to entice voters with the delusion that deep changes in the economy and personal behaviors are unnecessary. Giddens points to the United States as the prime example of the disaster that ensues when climate change politics becomes polarized. Yet Giddens admits that public support for major changes is "likely to wax and wane."[101]

James Martin-Schramm takes a mediating position that addresses the need for development in the Global South and the urgent need to combat climate change. He formalizes an "ethic of ecojustice" from his Christian standpoint. His four moral norms, however, could easily be affirmed from an engaged Buddhist standpoint. The norm of *sustainability* focuses on the integrity of creation, maintaining a healthy biosphere for future generations as well as the present generation. *Sufficiency* recognizes the right of all living beings to have their basic needs met. In terms of the present gross unequal distribution of basic goods, the norm of sufficiency requires that climate change not be addressed by abrogating the rights of development of poor people so that their basic needs can be met. Mitigating climate change impacts requires a clear distinction between "luxury emissions" of the well-to-do and the "survival emissions" of the poor. *Participation* as a moral norm demands that the interests of human and nonhuman forms of life be represented in decision making processes—a norm that is routinely violated in the outsized influence of fossil fuel lobbyists on US environmental policies.

99. Giddens, *Politics of Climate Change*, 52–55, 94–97.

100. Ibid., 72–73, 108–10, 114–15.

101. Ibid., 87–90, 116–19, 231.

Finally Martin-Schramm offers *solidarity* as the ethical response to the fact of interdependence, solidarity between rich and poor, between present and future generations, and between humans and nonhumans. This norm of solidarity entails taking historical responsibility for past emissions and acknowledging that different countries have varying capacity to address climate change. Historical responsibility reflects a common principle among environmental ethicists, namely, "the Polluter-Pays Principle," and existing capacity reflects the "Ability-to-Pay principle."[102]

Martin-Schramm takes a step beyond what most ethicists, including myself, are able to accomplish by moving boldly into the thicket of scientific, technical, economic, and political details in order to suggest policy changes consistent with these moral norms and guidelines. Some of these policy changes make common sense. For example, a carbon tax levied on all fossil fuels, redistributed to provide cost subsidies to the poor, to support the development of alternative renewable energy sources and public transportation would mean that greenhouse gas emissions would not be treated as "externalities." Other policy changes challenge the way power in the energy field is concentrated in huge corporations, for example, providing the technology to allow for a much more decentralized residential and community generation of electricity using renewable resources.[103] Good policy recommendations abound and the choice among sustainable options is well worth public debate. The real issue of the present policy recommendations is the lack of political will.

In terms of international climate policy, Martin-Schramm supports the "Greenhouse Development Rights Framework" created by the Stockholm Environmental Institute and Ecoequity that seeks to overcome the political divide between developed and developing countries in addressing climate change. This report calculates per capita greenhouse gas emissions by country since 1990, when awareness of climate change became widespread, to establish responsibility and the percentage of each country's population above a basic threshold ($7,500 purchasing parity) to establish capacity. A combined "Responsibility-Capacity Index" is offered as incorporating both the Polluter-Pays Principle and the basic right of poor peoples to development to reach a threshold of sufficiency. In such a framework the United States, for example, holds 33 percent of global responsibility to address climate

102. Ibid., Martin-Schramm, *Climate Justice*, 41–44, 128. Martin-Schramm's multiplicity of principles corresponds to Martha Nussbaum's view of the multiplicity of capabilities necessary for a life of dignity and of the importance of not sacrificing one capability in order to support another. Nussbaum's list of capabilities, however, needs revision to include as a primary capability inhabiting a healthy ecosystem.

103. Ibid., 105–10.

change. India, with 95 percent of its population still below the threshold would only have seven percent responsibility but that would change as a greater percentage of its population moved above the threshold.[104]

We are now in a position to chart a range of ethical approaches to address the environmental crises that we face.

Table 7.1

Prophet (Berrigan)	Environmental Justice (Maathai)	Pragmatic Reform (Giddens)	Practice of the Wild (Snyder)	Deep Ecology (Naess)	Bodhisattva (Thich Nhat Hanh)
Theocentric Triangular covenant Challenges moral corruption Stewardship Civil disobedience Divestiture Movement	Grassroots ecology Biocentric and anthropocentric Intersectional environmentalism Right to development Polluter Pays Principle Symbolic acts of resistance and restoration	Anthropocentric Accepts basic structures of society Consequentialist Critical role of the state in combatting climate change Radicalism of the centre TANGOS and TANS work with state and intergovernmental agencies	Biocentric The Wild as ordering of impermanence Biodiversity Decentralization and bioregionalism Reinhabitation as multigenerational practice	Biocentric equality Intrinsic value of humans and nonhumans Biodiversity Transformation of industrial society and growth economy Reduction of human population	Universe as Dharmakaya Emptiness Virtue ethics (ahimsa) Liberation of all sentient beings Interdependence and systems theory Critique of consumerism

As in chapter 6, I believe that a strong case can be made in favor of a pluralism of ethical approaches to the issue of climate change. Clearly there are distinctive strengths to each of the approaches in this chart. A prophetic

104. Ibid., 129–36.

voice is necessary to overcome Gardiner's perfect moral storm and to galvanize us into moral action. The bodhisattva's vision is surely utopian but it calls us to practice diligently and supports us for the long haul. It also can detoxify us of the poisons endemic to a culture of consumption. Deep ecologists provide a thoroughgoing critique of an industrial, technological society. For his part, Gary Snyder's practice of the wild takes a pragmatic approach to reinhabiting the planet one bioregion at a time. Voices from the Global South remind us that addressing climate change cannot preclude the right of development of poor peoples. James Martin-Schramm's several principles for ecojustice make us aware of the multiple goods that must be juggled in pursuing environmental justice. Anthony Gidden's pragmatic reformism reminds us that in the absence of international governing bodies, nation states must play a key role in immediately legislating policies to combat climate change.

It goes without saying that the dialectic among these ethical and political positions will also point out the weaknesses of each of these positions in isolation. Deep ecologists and Gary Snyder, for example, will question whether a nation state which is firmly in the grip of fossil fuel lobbyists can deal with the magnitude of the change that is needed. On the other hand, others, like Bron Taylor, will charge that the deep ecologists are naïve about power and have little besides local resistance to suggest in order to combat the globalizing economic forces that are placing our planet in jeopardy.[105] But Giddens and Martin-Schramm can be criticized for not addressing the crucial questions of moral motivation and, especially, political will. Anthony Giddens called for a concordat among political parties to avoid polarized debates and to create a common front in addressing the issue of climate change. Is a similar concordat at all possible among the different approaches to an ecological ethics and politics represented in this table?

WORKING THE LINKAGES

Gidden's analysis with its focus on the role of the state, fails to account for the roles that domestic environmental NGOs and the environmental TANs born with the emergence of a global civil society can play in promoting change. I offer four examples of what I have been calling "working the linkages" as a way of leveraging social transformation. The first we have already studied in this chapter Wangari Maathai and GBM practiced "intersectional environmentalism." They formed alliances with women's rights movements and movements against political repression in Kenya but they also formed

105. Taylor, "Deep Ecology," 227.

linkages with the UN and international funders which strengthened their position against the Kenyan government.

The next two examples focus on the role that environmental TANs played in the 1980s that led to major changes in the policies and practices of the World Bank regarding the social and environmental impact of their development loans. One key component of this process was the grassroots resistance of "ecosystem people" against the World Bank's funding of the Narmanda dam project that sought to create three thousand dams along the Narmanda River in India. This project would have displaced hundreds of thousands of Indians. Grassroots organizations were able to enlist the support of TANs that were working to change World Bank policies. The TANs in turn were able to garner the support of a US Congressional committee which then brought pressure to bear on the Bank.

A similar example of what Keck and Sikkink call the "boomerang effect" can be seen in the struggles of rubber tappers in Brazil seeking to preserve their livelihoods in the face of deforestation of the Amazonian rain forest. Chico Mendes, the leader of these workers until his assassination in 1988, was also able to forge an alliance with the TANs working to change the World Bank. Again, the leverage of the US Congress was employed. Most important for our discussion, Mendes was able to offer a model of sustainable development that brought about a rapprochement of the interests of the Global South and the Global North. "By linking environmental destruction to a concrete picture of how local populations lived in the forest," Keck and Sikkink conclude, "environmentalists were able to make the tropical forest issue real to an international public." It proved the importance of linking testimony from local people most affected by environmental degradation to changing mega-institutions like the World Bank.[106]

My final example focuses on the current beginning of a mass movement to pressure states to impose a range of policies to mitigate climate change. Led by well-institutionalized conservation organizations like the Sierra Club and upstarts like 350.org, the movement has developed an international reach. There is a transnational advocacy network with hundreds of partner organizations. The Sierra Club fosters local campaigns against dirty coal, and its student coalition is organizing college campuses. So far, dozens of colleges have pledged to end their use of coal to meet their energy needs.[107] On campuses, as well, 350.org pushes for divestiture of fossil fuel holdings. Given the multiple sources of greenhouse gases, and hence climate change, the environmental TANs lack the specific target of an ICBL or the

106. Keck and Sikkink, *Activists Beyond Borders*, 140–42.

107. See the Sierra Student Coalition online: http://ssc.org/campaigns.

goal of creating a strong protocol which was the goal at Kyoto a generation ago. At this late stage both the movement and the network seem more like Berrigan's newborn bird.

CONCLUSION

Throughout this chapter we have been reflecting on the Zen koan that calls us to act as if our heads are on fire but also as if we have ten thousand lives to liberate sentient beings. In an earlier era, Dr. Martin Luther King confronted us with "the fierce urgency of now." Now, we can say that it is the polar ice caps, the Greenland ice sheet, the Himalyan glaciers, to say nothing of the desertification of Africa, the deforestation of the Amazon, or sea levels swamping the Maldives that are confronting us. And yet, we do need the long-term practice of the wild of a Gary Snyder. We are not yet the people that we need to be in this present crisis. Joanna Macy offers us an exercise of the moral imagination that speaks to our dilemma. When I, in turn, have offered her lesson to students, the impact has been stunning. Imagine, Macy says, "that we have, in some way, chosen to be here at this . . . turning point. We have opted to be alive when the stakes are high, to test everything we have ever learned about interconnectedness, about courage—to test it now when Gaia is ailing and her children are ill." And then Macy adds that we imagine this scenario "so that we can wake up and assume the rights and responsibilities of planetary adulthood."[108] Waking up, we bow before mountains and waters, those ancient Buddhas, and we cradle creation, that fragile egg, then we act. "When you find your place where you are," Dogen adds, "practice occurs. . . . When you find our way at this moment, practice occurs."[109] No small feat; no more important task.

108. Macy, "Our Life as Gaia," 63–64.

109. Dogen, "Actualizing the Fundamental Point," 72.

Conclusion

CROSSING BOUNDARIES AND LIVING ON THE EDGE

Nhat Hanh: *There are things that the Buddha or Jesus said thousands of years ago; they may begin only now to have an effect. You cannot hastily say whether something is effective or not. . . . One Bodhisattva, described in the Lotus Sutra, is a traveler who does nothing except come to every person to say, "Well. I do not dare to take you lightly; I know that you are a Buddha and you have the capability of being a Buddha."*

Berrigan: *I think this hope is a kind of bridge of which the piers on both sides are reality rather than illusion. . . . It's really that one is trying to be faithful to an impetus which is already set in motion, an invitation . . . [that] expresses both the urgency of living where one is fully and really and consciously as possible; and carrying that with him so that nothing is lost as the movement goes forward.*[1]

—*The Raft Is Not the Shore*

One way to think about the process that we have been following in this book is modeled by Paul Knitter. *Without Buddha I Could Not Be a Christian*

1. Berrigan and Nhat Hanh, *Raft*, 25–26.

records his deeply honest, personal, and intellectual journey. Each of his main chapters focuses on a central Christian teaching or practice and has a tripartite structure. First, Knitter discusses his struggle with the teaching or practice, then he "passes over" to immerse himself in a related Buddhist teaching or practice. Finally, he "passes back" to reaffirm his commitment as a Christian but in a transformed way.[2] However, if we look at the previous chapters, the process in this exploration is more of a "passing back and forth" than a passing over and passing back. This is to say that *for me* neither the prophet nor the bodhisattva has primacy. They are both fellow travelers along a spiritual journey. I tell students that I first came to Buddhism seeking an antidote to what I saw as a damaging flaw within Christian liberation theology and praxis which I espoused. Specifically this was the tendency to engage in dualistic thinking and acting with an inevitable inclination to moral righteousness.[3] Moreover, I had been a part of the American peace movement that Thich Nhat Hanh found to be anything but peaceful. His insight rang true and this also troubled me. I turned to Buddhist teachings and practice as an antidote to my experience of prophetic Christianity as a diabetic takes a daily dose of insulin. As years passed, the bodhisattva path became more than an antidote. I found myself living and acting in the magnetic field created by the twin poles of the prophet and the bodhisattva. Each became part of my identity as a moral agent.

This last statement must be qualified. In earlier chapters, I have followed David Tracy in seeing Daniel Berrigan's writings on the prophets and Thich Nhat Hanh's many commentaries on Buddhist sutras as classics. "If the text is a genuinely classic one," I quoted Tracy as saying, "my present horizon of understanding should always be provoked, challenged, transformed."[4] Stated more simply, I cannot and do not claim to have met the challenge provoked by these texts. They remain disconcerting, decentering, and demanding. This is even more the case with the lives of Berrigan and Thich Nhat Hanh as classic embodiments of their respective moral types. In the introduction, I quoted David Clairmont as suggesting that what makes a *person* a classic is their moral struggle which, in the context of a limited life, must necessarily be incomplete. "Despite this incompleteness," Clairmont concludes, "such lives nonetheless point beyond themselves."[5] Clairmont's

2. Knitter, *Without Buddha*. Knitter follows in the footsteps of Notre Dame theologian, Reverend John Dunne, who first described passing over and coming back as "the spiritual adventure of our time." Ibid., 217.

3. I hasten to add that my experience of this flaw is by no means indicative of a universal trait in liberation theology.

4. Tracy, *Analogical Imagination*, 102.

5. Clairmont, "Persons as Religious Classics," 712–13.

definition has given me hope that finding my own way to move ahead is also a way of honoring these classic lives. I say moving *ahead* because in the deepest sense we cannot move *beyond* such classic persons and writings. They are always by our side pointing beyond themselves *and ourselves.*

The introduction also opened with two stories that involved transgressing borders and boundaries between religious traditions and between life and death. "Our religious identity," Knitter argues, like our cultural identity "is not purebred, it's hybrid. . . . We're constantly changing and we're changing through the hybridization process of interacting with others who often are very different from us."[6] But the purebred ideal is hard to shake. How often do others ask or, more painfully, do we ask ourselves: "How can you call yourself a Christian, if you . . . ?" Or: "How can you call yourself a Buddhist, if you . . . ?"

Transgressing borders is more than a metaphor for me. Since 1994, I have been taking students to the Arizona–Sonora, Mexico, borderlands. There we have met with migrants, workers in the Mexican maquiladora assembly plants, human rights activists, environmentalists, and many others, including Border Patrol. I have seen firsthand how walls confine some to lives of desperation and create an iron cocoon for those born in El Norte. On these trips we have crisscrossed the border, passing back and forth, acts that others can only perform by risking death in the blazing desert. Walls kill: both the physical walls and the multiple social barriers that divide us. But human beings find ways to transgress. In chapter 6, I told the story of a card game in Altar, Mexico, between DePaul University students and migrants from Central America and southern Mexico as an experience analogous to what John Dominic Crossan calls "open commensality," Jesus' practice of table fellowship that deliberately transgressed social barriers. In the teeth of war, Daniel Berrigan and Thich Nhat Hanh transgressed multiple walls dividing American Christians and Vietnamese Buddhists. They forged the bonds of friendship. If we really want to create solidarity, we, too, will need to transgress whatever illusions of purebred truths and practices wall us apart.

It is the common business of prophets to envision and to inspire. Throughout this book, I have tried to be faithful in presenting Berrigan's and Thich Nhat Hanh's visions. It is not part of either person's intent to formulate a social ethics. So, I have extrapolated from their ideas and actions in chapters 3, 4, and 5 by offering three different approaches to develop a more formal ethics. It has also not been Berrigan's or Thich Nhat Hanh's intent to offer a theory and praxis of social change.

6. Knitter, *Without Buddha*, 214.

In chapter 4, we explored how one's social location affects one's social ethics. I acknowledged that my own social location is within the *institution* of the university whereas we can see the Berrigan brothers as at the cutting edge of a *movement* and Thich Nhat Hanh as a builder of *community* through the creation of engaged Buddhist sanghas. I also told the story of my conversation with Daniel Berrigan about why I had worked in higher education administration to help create an engaged university and his stony silence. In chapter 4, we explored Berrigan's challenge at length, looking at his conversation with psychiatrist Robert Coles. "How does one really raise ethical and political questions," Berrigan asked, "and explore those questions in a real way—as contrasted to an academic or intellectual way? Can someone question gross and blatant injustice from a life-situation that is tied in dozens of ways, often subtle ways to that injustice?"[7] I said then and I repeat it now that these two questions take us to the heart of my endeavor in this book. Whether or not this book meets the challenge of the first question I leave to the reader to decide. My response to the second question is what other kind of situation is there—at least for a middle-class American? Certainly the Plowshares activists do not claim to be liberated from any complicity with injustice. For Berrigan there is only a very narrow possibility of a positive resolution to his two questions and that is if we can "move our professional life to the edge."[8] In the face of this challenge I have taken a stance: institutions matter, and my university has been both a home base and a launching pad for me.

In various chapters I have presented examples of institutions playing a critical role in supporting movements for social change and communities of hope: the NAACP during the civil rights era; the OAS, the US State Department as well as the papacy in supporting the Madres movement during the Argentinian "dirty war" against its own people; the Roman Catholic Church in support of Christian base communities in Latin America and the Solidarity movement in Poland; the Lutheran Church's similar support of the freedom movement in East Germany; the divestiture movement among US universities in opposition to transnational corporations doing business in apartheid South Africa; the International Committee of the Red Cross providing crucial support to the International Campaign to Ban Landmines leading to the Landmine Ban Treaty. The list could go on. These examples also illustrated my contention that social change can be facilitated by "working the linkages" among such institutions, spiritual communities, and social movements. Global civil society, I believe, offers a matrix in which all three

7. Berrigan and Coles, *Geography of Faith*, 78.

8. Ibid., 80–81.

can emerge, flourish, and exert pressure on the prevailing political and economic institutions.

One does not generally think of, say, Canada as a countervailing institution and, certainly, in many respects it is not, but in the case of the Landmine treaty that is how it functioned as one of the nations that negotiated with the ICBL and its TAN. Our understanding of what constitutes a countervailing institution needs to be enlarged. At the same time the example of Canada makes it abundantly clear that an institution may act in a countervailing way to support efforts to create peace and justice in some areas but fail to do so in many other ways. To work within an institution is to forsake the illusion of moral purity. Consequently in chapters 6 and 7, I juxtaposed alongside the positions of the prophet and the bodhisattva other models of social ethics and praxis. I was suggesting that no single model would suffice in treating the twin challenges of America's militarism and imperial overstretch, on the one hand, and the challenges of environmental justice and climate change on the other. Of course, you, the reader, will create your own juxtaposition of models of social ethics and praxis to grapple with these complex and dangerous issues.

In chapter 4, I argued that for an institution to become countervailing in any respect some professionals within it would have to engage in the praxis of institutional transformation. In other words they would need to work at the edges to push the institution forward. In the process some individuals have reinvented their institutions. Muhammad Yunus is a key example of working at the edges leading to reinvention. Initially a professor of economics before becoming Bangladesh's "banker to the poor," Yunus would have seemed an improbable candidate for a professional at the edge. His saving virtue was that he practiced what Thich Nhat Hanh calls "deep listening." He spent time in the village of Jobra trying to discern the barriers that kept villagers trapped in poverty and discovered that it was their inability to secure even the tiniest of loans except at extortionist rates from local moneylenders. He tried to no avail to talk established banks into engaging in what became known as microcredit lending. In response he created the Grameen Bank and revolutionized the way in which poor people could gain small amounts of capital to fund their own businesses. This economic revolution became a social revolution as small groups of mostly village women empowered and supported themselves. By 2006, over one hundred million poor people had been reached by financing institutions modeled on the Grameen Bank.[9]

9. Yunus, *World without Poverty*, 43–67.

As we saw in chapter 5, in Sri Lanka, A. T. Ariyaratne, a high school teacher who wanted to provide a service opportunity for his students, ended up creating the Sarvodaya movement which, based on Buddhist principles, has organized over fifteen thousand villages in self-determined, self-resourced programs of rural development.[10] But my own favorite example of a professional with an edge is an American, Dr. Paul Farmer, who is both a physician in a rural clinic in Haiti and a professor at the Harvard School of Medicine. As founder of Partners in Health, Farmer has revolutionized the way in which health care is delivered to poor people across the globe, especially those suffering from resistant strains of tuberculosis and AIDS. To do so he has had to battle major international institutions whose fixed policies about who receives what level of treatment discriminate against poor people.[11]

There are, in other words, more professionals with an edge than Daniel Berrigan might acknowledge. Certainly the prophet's warning about how institutions "ingest" human beings is sobering and, at best, we are still entangled in webs of complicity with injustice. However, these and other examples of professionals with an edge offer a number of traits that we can emulate. First, they have had direct contact with those who suffer and this contact has been transformative. Once you have held a child in your arms in a Hanoi bomb shelter, Berrigan might say, you will never be the same. Second, they listened to the voices of the poor and the suffering rather than imposing a predetermined model. Third, they started small; they worked with local communities in evolving a new model. As Thich Nhat Hanh would put it, community building is their practice. Fourth, they did need to resist and challenge major institutions with their inflexible procedures that place barriers to the alleviation of suffering. Fifth, they have stayed focused on the work. Hope, as Rebecca Solnit suggests, is not dreaming of a better future; it is an ax wielded in the present to break through barriers.

A professional engages in a practice for the long haul. In *Educating Citizens*, Anne Colby and her colleagues comment that people dedicated to service and social change "rarely asked themselves whether they were making actual progress towards their goals." To do so, given the magnitude of the issues that we face, would only invite despair. Instead, Colby compares their efforts at social transformation "to the cathedral builders, chipping away at social problems, the way stone masons of the Middle Ages inched

10. Bond, *Buddhism at Work*.

11. Kidder, *Mountains beyond Mountains*.

along in building cathedrals, knowing that the massive churches would not be finished for three or four hundred years."[12]

To affirm that there is a role for professionals working to create countervailing institutions is not to assert that the moral challenge of the prophet or the bodhisattva has been surpassed. To the contrary, a professional keeps her edge and continues to work at the edges of her institution only if she repeatedly hearkens to the challenge of moral exemplars. Daniel Berrigan and Thich Nhat Hanh in their lives and writings are genuine moral classics. *Testimony: The Word Made Fresh* includes Berrigan's intimate recollections of those persons, moral classics all—King, Romero, Merton—whose lives and work he finds unsurpassable. Of Philip Berrigan he writes, "I put on / like glasses / on a squinting soul— / your second sight." Of Rabbi Abraham Heschel: "The weight of one such life, or of a few, is of such vast import in God's sight as to restore, to recoup, to adjust the scales of moral creation into balance once more." And of Dorothy Day: "I wish to remember her . . . , to keep her life before me, to make that life available to those I love, to feel its moral tug and urgency, to explore her way."[13] What Daniel Berrigan affirms of these moral giants I affirm of Berrigan and equally of Thich Nhat Hanh.

It has been forty years since Berrigan and Thich Nhat Hanh held their conversations in Paris which were published as *The Raft Is Not the Shore: Conversations toward a Buddhist-Christian Awareness*. It is obvious that since then work on the cathedral of peace and justice has gone perilously slow, when it has gone at all. But these two master craftsmen have never given up. "Redeem the times," Berrigan, the prophet proclaims. "The times are inexpressibly evil. . . . And yet and yet the times are inexhaustibly good."[14] Thich Nhat Hanh, the bodhisattva replies: "The work of building will take ten thousand lives / But dear one, look— / that work has been achieved ten thousand lives ago."[15] Hope offers the possibility of passing back and forth between the prophet's stern demand and the bodhisattva's paradoxical reply.

12. Colby et al., *Educating Citizens*, 123.

13. Berrigan, *Testimony*, 96, 130, 142.

14. Berrigan, *Trial of the Catonsville Nine*, 93–95.

15. Nhat Hanh, *Opening the Heart*, 80–81.

BIBLIOGRAPHY

WRITINGS BY DANIEL BERRIGAN

Prose

Consequences: Truth And . . . New York: Macmillan, 1967.
The Dark Night of Resistance. New York: Bantam, 1971.
Exodus: Let My People Go. Eugene, OR: Cascade, 2008.
Ezekiel: Vision in the Dust. Maryknoll, NY: Orbis, 1997.
Foreword to *Love in Action: Writings on Nonviolent Social Change*, by Thich Nhat Hanh, 3–8. Berkeley: Parallax, 1993.
Isaiah: Spirit of Courage, Gift of Tears. Minneapolis: Fortress, 1996.
Jeremiah: The World, the Wound of God. Minneapolis: Fortress, 1999.
Job: And Death No Dominion. Franklin, WI: Sheed & Ward, 2000.
The Kings and Their Gods: The Pathology of Power. Grand Rapids: Eerdmans, 2008.
"Letter to Ernesto Cardenal." In *Poetry, Drama, Prose*, edited by Michael True, 166–70. Maryknoll, NY: Orbis, 1988.
"Life at the Edge." *Christian Century*, June 24, 1970, 787–90.
Minor Prophets, Major Themes. Marion, SD: Fortkamp, 1995.
No Bars to Manhood. New York: Bantam, 1970.
No Gods but One. Grand Rapids: Eerdmans, 2009.
Sorrow Built a Bridge: Friendship and AIDS. Baltimore: Fortkamp, 1989.
Testimony: The Word Made Fresh. Maryknoll, NY: Orbis, 2004.
To Dwell in Peace. New York: Harper & Row, 1987.
Trial of the Cantonsville Nine. Boston: Beacon, 1970.
"The Whale's Tale." In *Poetry, Drama, Prose*, edited by Michael True, 325–30. Maryknoll, NY: Orbis, 1988.
"Where Death Abounded, Life: St. Rose's Home." In *Poetry, Drama, Prose*, edited by Michael True, 171–76. Maryknoll, NY: Orbis, 1988.

Poetry

"Children in the Shelter." In *And the Risen Bread: Selected Poems, 1957–1997*, edited by John Dear, 114–15. New York: Fordham University Press, 1998.

"Eucharist." In *And the Risen Bread: Selected Poems, 1957–1997*, edited by John Dear, 124–25. New York: Fordham University Press, 1998.

"Hope, That Intransitive Being." In *Testimony: The Word Made Fresh*, 226–27. Maryknoll, NY: Orbis, 2004.

"Not Feeling Poetic." In *Poetry, Drama, Prose*, edited by Michael True, 343–44. Maryknoll, NY: Orbis, 1988.

"Peacemaking Is Hard." In *And the Risen Bread: Selected Poems, 1957–1997*, edited by John Dear, 100–101. New York: Fordham University Press, 1998.

"Prophecy." In *And the Risen Bread: Selected Poems, 1957–1997*, edited by John Dear, 230–31. New York: Fordham University Press, 1998.

"Vision (after Juliana of Norwich)." In *And the Risen Bread: Selected Poems, 1957–1997*, edited by John Dear, 220. New York: Fordham University Press, 1998.

WRITINGS BY THICH NHAT HANH

Prose

"Ahimsa: The Path of Harmlessness." In *Love in Action: Writings on Nonviolent Social Change*, 65–71. Berkeley: Parallax, 1993.

Anger: Wisdom for Cooling the Flames. New York: Riverhead, 2001.

The Art of Power. New York: HarperCollins, 2007.

Being Peace. Berkeley: Parallax, 2005.

Calming the Fearful Mind: A Zen Response to Terrorism. Berkeley: Parallax, 2005.

Creating True Peace: Ending Violence in Yourself, Your Family, Your Community, and the World. Berkeley: Parallax, 2003.

Cultivating the Mind of Love. Berkeley: Parallax, 2008.

Fragrant Palm Leaves: Journals, 1962–1966. Translated by Mobi Warren. New York: Riverhead, 1998.

"Go as a Sangha." In *Friends on the Path: Living Spiritual Communities*, edited by John Lawlor, 17–48. Berkeley: Parallax, 2002.

The Heart of the Buddha's Teachings: Transforming Suffering into Peace, Joy, and Liberation. New York: Broadway, 1999.

The Heart of Understanding: Commentaries on the Prajnaparamita Heart Sutra. Berkeley: Parallax, 1988.

Interbeing: Fourteen Guidelines for Engaged Buddhism. 3rd ed. Berkeley: Parallax, 1998.

Living Buddha, Living Christ. New York: Riverhead, 1995.

"A Lone Pink Fish." In *The Moon Bamboo*, 57–105. Berkeley: Parallax, 1989.

Love in Action: Writings on Nonviolent Social Change. Berkeley: Parallax, 1993.

The Miracle of Mindfulness: A Manual on Meditation. Rev. ed. Translated by Mobi Ho. Boston: Beacon, 1987.

My Master's Robe: Memories of a Novice Monk. Berkeley: Parallax, 2002.

Opening the Heart of the Cosmos: Insights on the Lotus Sutra. Berkeley: Parallax, 2003.

"The Path of Return Continues the Journey." In *Love in Action: Writings on Nonviolent Social Change*, 9–36. Berkeley: Parallax, 1993.

Peace Is Every Step: The Path of Mindfulness in Everyday Life. New York: Bantam, 1992.

"Spirituality in the Twenty-First Century." In *Friends on the Path: Living Spiritual Communities*, edited by John Lawlor, 9–16. Berkeley: Parallax, 2002.

"The Sun My Heart." In *Love in Action: Writings on Nonviolent Social Change*, 127–38. Berkeley: Parallax, 1993.

The Sun My Heart: From Mindfulness to Insight Contemplation. Rev. ed. Berkeley: Parallax, 2010.

Transformation and Healing: Sutra on the Four Establishments of Mindfulness. Berkeley: Parallax, 2006.

Vietnam: Lotus in a Sea of Fire. New York: Hill & Wang, 1967.

The World We Have: A Buddhist Approach to Peace and Ecology. Berkeley: Parallax, 2008.

Zen Keys. New York: Doubleday, 1995.

Poetry

"Condemnation." In *Call Me by My True Names: The Collected Poems of Thich Nhat Hanh*, 37. Berkeley: Parallax, 1993.

"Defuse Me." In *Call Me by My True Names: The Collected Poems of Thich Nhat Hanh*, 142. Berkeley: Parallax, 1993.

"Experience." In *Call Me by My True Names: The Collected Poems of Thich Nhat Hanh*, 10–14. Berkeley: Parallax, 1993.

"The Fire That Consumes My Brother." In *Call Me by My True Names: The Collected Poems of Thich Nhat Hanh*, 48–49. Berkeley: Parallax, 1993.

"The Good News." In *Call Me by My True Names: The Collected Poems of Thich Nhat Hanh*, 169. Berkeley: Parallax, 1993.

"Mudra." In *Call Me by My True Names: The Collected Poems of Thich Nhat Hanh*, 8–9. Berkeley: Parallax, 1993.

"Night of Prayer." In *Call Me by My True Names: The Collected Poems of Thich Nhat Hanh*, 16–17. Berkeley: Parallax, 1993.

"Our Green Gardens." In *Call Me by My True Names: The Collected Poems of Thich Nhat Hanh*, 6–7. Berkeley: Parallax, 1993.

"Please Call Me by My True Names." In *Call Me by My True Names: The Collected Poems of Thich Nhat Hanh*, 72–73. Berkeley: Parallax, 1993.

"Recommendation." In *Call Me by My True Names: The Collected Poems of Thich Nhat Hanh*, 18–19. Berkeley: Parallax, 1993.

"Those That Have Not Exploded." In *Call Me by My True Names: The Collected Poems of Thich Nhat Hanh*, 22–23. Berkeley: Parallax, 1993.

JOINT WRITINGS

Berrigan, Daniel, and Robert Coles. *The Geography of Faith*. Woodstock, VT: Skylight Paths, 2001.

Berrigan, Daniel, and Thich Nhat Hanh. *The Raft Is Not the Shore: Conversations toward a Buddhist-Christian Awareness*. Maryknoll, NY: Orbis, 2001.

GENERAL WORKS

Ackerman, Peter, and Jack Duvall. *A Force More Powerful: A Century of Nonviolent Conflict*. New York: St. Martin's, 2000.

Ahmed, Shamima, and David M. Potter. *NGOs in International Politics*. Bloomfield, CT: Kumarian, 2006.

Arendt, Hannah. *On Violence*. New York: Harcourt Brace, 1970.

Bacevich, Andrew J. *The Limits of Power: The End of American Exceptionalism*. New York: Holt, 2009.

———. *The New American Militarism: How Americans Are Seduced by War*. Updated ed. New York: Oxford University Press, 2013.

———. *Washington Rules: America's Path to Permanent War*. New York: Holt, 2010.

Beebe, Shannon D., and Mary H. Kaldor. *The Ultimate Weapon Is No Weapon: Human Security and the New Rules of War and Peace*. New York: Public Affairs, 2010.

Bernstein, Richard J. *Praxis and Action: Contemporary Philosophies of Human Activity*. Philadelphia: University of Pennsylvania Press, 1971.

Bond, George D. "A. T. Ariyaratne and the Sarvodaya Movement in Sri Lanka." In *Engaged Buddhism: Buddhist Liberation Movements in Asia*, edited by Christopher S. Queen and Sallie B. King, 121–46. Albany, NY: State University of New York Press, 1996.

———. *Buddhism at Work: Community Development, Social Empowerment and the Sarvodaya Movement*. Bloomfield, CT: Kumarian, 2004.

———. "Sarvodaya Shramadana's Quest for Peace." In *Action Dharma: New Studies in Engaged Buddhism*, edited by Christopher Queen et al., 128–35. New York: Routledge, 2003.

Boulding, Elise. *Cultures of Peace: The Hidden Side of History*. Syracuse, NY: Syracuse University Press, 2000.

Branch, Taylor. *Parting the Waters: America During the King Years, 1954–63*. New York: Simon & Schuster, 1988.

Brubaker, Pamela, et al. "Just Peacemaking as the New Ethic for Peace and War." In *Just Peacemaking: Ten Practices for Abolishing War*, edited by Glen H. Stassen, 1–40. Cleveland: Pilgrim, 2008.

Brueggemann, Walter. *The Prophetic Imagination*. 2nd ed. Minneapolis: Fortress, 2001.

Bstan-dzin-rgya-mtsho, Dalai Lama XIV. *Ethics for a New Millennium*. New York: Riverhead, 2001.

Butler, Judith. *Frames of War: When is Life Grievable?* New York: Verso, 2009.

Cahill, Lisa Sowle. *Love Your Enemies: Discipleship, Pacifism, and Just War Theory*. Minneapolis: Fortress, 1994.

Call, Charles. "A Human Rights Practitioner's Perspective." In *Restructuring World Politics: Transnational Social Movements, Networks, and Norms*, edited by Sanjeev Khagram et al., 123–27. Minneapolis: University of Minnesota Press, 2002.

Callicott, J. Beard. "The New New (Buddhist?) Ecology." *Journal for the Study of Religion Nature and Culture* 2 (2008) 166–82.

Chan Khong, Sister. *Learning True Love: Practicing Buddhism in a Time of War*. 2nd ed. Berkeley: Parallax, 2007.

Cherry, Conrad, ed. *God's New Israel: Religious Interpretations of American Destiny*. Englewood Cliffs, NJ: Prentice-Hall, 1971.

Clairmont, David A. "Persons as Religious Classics: Comparative Ethics and the Theology of Bridge Concepts." *Journal of the American Academy of Religion* 78 (2010) 687–720.

Clark, John. "UN-Civil-Society Interactions: Working Together for Peace." In *People Building Peace II: Successful Stories of Civil Societies*, edited by Paul van Tongeren et al., 59–69. Boulder, CO: Rienner, 2005.

Cleary, Thomas. *Entry into the Inconceivable*. Honolulu: University of Hawaii Press, 1982.

———. *No Barrier: Unlocking the Zen Koan*. London: Aquarian, 1993.

Coate, Roger A. "Growing the 'Third UN' for People-Centered Development—The United Nations, Civil Society, and Beyond." *Global Governance* 15 (2009) 153–68.

Cobb, John B., Jr. Foreword to *Resistance: The New Role of Progressive Christians*, vii–xviii. Louisville: Westminster John Knox, 2008.

Coetzee, J. M. *Age of Iron*. New York: Penguin, 1990.

Colby, Anne, et al. *Educating Citizens: Preparing America's Undergraduates for Lives of Moral and Civic Responsibility*. New York: Jossey-Bass, 2003.

———. *Education for Democracy: Preparing Undergraduates for Responsible Political Engagement*. New York: Jossey-Bass, 2007.

Cortright, David. *Gandhi and Beyond: Nonviolence for an Age of Terrorism*. Boulder, CO: Paradigm, 2009.

Crossan, John Dominic. *God and Empire: Jesus against Rome, Then and Now*. San Francisco: HarperSanFrancisco, 2007.

———. *Jesus: A Revolutionary Biography*. San Francisco: HarperSanFrancisco, 1994.

Darlington, Susan M. "Good Buddha and Fierce Spirits." *Contemporary Buddhism* 8 (2007) 169–85.

Devall, Bill, and George Sessions. *Deep Ecology: Living as if Nature Mattered*. Salt Lake City: Smith, 1985.

Dickinson, Emily. *Final Harvest: Emily Dickinson's Poems*. Edited by Thomas H. Johnson. Boston: Little, Brown, 1961.

Dogen, Eihei. "Actualizing the Fundamental Point." In *Moon in a Dew Drop: Writings of Zen Master Dogen*, edited by Kazuaki Tanahashi, 69–73. San Francisco: North Point, 1985.

———. "Guidelines for the Study of the Way." In *Moon in a Dew Drop: Writings of Zen Master Dogen*, edited by Kazuaki Tanahashi, 131–43. San Francisco: North Point, 1985.

———. "Mountains and Waters Sutra." In *Moon in a Dew Drop: Writings of Zen Master Dogen*, edited by Kazuaki Tanahashi, 97–107. San Francisco: North Point, 1985.

Doran, Chris. "Environmental Curses and Blessings through the Eyes of the Biblical Prophets." *Worldviews* 15 (2001) 291–301.

Douglass, James. "Civil Disobedience as Prayer." In *Swords into Plowshares: Nonviolent Direct Action for Disarmament*, edited by Arthur Laffin and Anne Montgomery, 93–97. San Francisco: Harper & Row, 1982.

Eckel, Malcolm David. "Is There a Buddhist Philosophy of Nature." In *Buddhism and Ecology: The Interconnection of Dharma and Deeds*, edited by Mary Evelyn Tucker and Duncan Ryuken Williams, 327–49. Cambridge: Harvard University Press, 1997.

Eilperin, Juliet, and Steve Mufson. "Activists Arrested at White House Protesting the Keystone Pipeline." *Washington Post*, February 13, 2013. http://articles.

washingtonpost.com/2013-02-13/national/37072748_1_keystone-xl-climate-change-southern-leg.

Farmer, Paul. *Pathologies of Power: Health, Human Rights, and the New War on the Poor.* Berkeley: University of California Press, 2005.

Fasching, Darrell J., and Dell Descant. *Comparative Religious Ethics: A Narrative Approach.* Malden, MA: Blackwell, 2001.

Feller, Ben. "Obama's Libya Speech Strongly Defends Intervention." *Huffington Post*, March 28, 2011. http://www.huffingtonpost.com/2011/03/28/obama-libya-speech-_n_841311.html.

Folke, Carl. "Resilience: The Emergence of a Perspective for Social-Ecological Systems Analysis." *Global Environmental Change* 16 (2006) 253–67.

Forest, James. "Thich Nhat Hanh's Seeing with the Eyes of Compassion." In *The Miracle of Mindfulness*, by Thich Nhat Hanh, translated by Mobi Ho, 101–8. Rev. ed. Boston: Beacon, 1987.

Friesen, Duane K. "Encourage Grassroots Peacemaking Groups and Voluntary Associations." In *Just Peacemaking*, edited by Glen H. Stassen, 201–14. 2nd ed. Cleveland: Pilgrim, 2008.

Gadgil, Madhav, and Ramachandra Guha. *Ecology and Equity: The Use and Abuse of Nature in Contemporary India.* London: Routledge, 1995.

Gardiner, Stephen M. *A Perfect Moral Storm: The Ethical Tragedy of Climate Change.* New York: Oxford University Press, 2011.

Gathje, Peter Ronald. "The Cost of Virtue: The Theological Ethics of Daniel and Philip Berrigan." PhD diss., Emory University, 1994.

Giddens, Anthony. *The Politics of Climate Change.* 2nd ed. Cambridge, UK: Politics, 2011.

Glassman, Bernie. *Bearing Witness: A Zen Master's Lessons in Making Peace.* New York: Random House, 1998.

Goodhart, Sandor. "'A Land That Devours Its Inhabitants': Midrashic Reading, Emmanuel Levinas, and Prophetic Exegesis." *Shofar: An Interdisciplinary Journal of Jewish Studies* 26 (2008) 13–35.

Green, Barbara, and Glen Stassen. "Reduce Offensive Weapons and Weapons Trade." In *Just Peacemaking*, edited by Glen H. Stassen, 177–200. 2nd ed. Cleveland: Pilgrim, 2008.

Gross, Rita. *Soaring and Settling: Buddhist Perspectives on Contemporary Social and Religious Issues.* New York: Continuum, 1998.

"Growing Group of Countries Speaking Out against Investments in Cluster Munitions." *StopExplosiveInvestments.org*, April 17, 2013. http://www.stopexplosiveinvestments.org/news/24/59/growing-group-of-countries-speaking-out%E2%80%93against-investments-in-cluster-munitions.

Guha, Ramachandra. "The Paradox of Global Environmentalism." *Current History* (2000) 367–70.

———. "Toward a Cross-Cultural Environmental Ethic." *Alternatives: Global, Local, Political* 15 (1990) 431–47.

Guha, Ramachandra, and Juan Martinez-Alier. "The Environmentalism of the Poor." In *Earthcare: An Anthology in Environmental Ethics*, edited by David Clowney and Patricia Mosto, 297–313. Lanham, MD: Rowman & Littlefield, 2009.

Hadsell, Heidi. "Profits, Parrots, Peons: Ethical Perplexities in the Amazon." In *Ecological Resistance Movements*, edited by Bron Raymond Taylor, 70–86. Albany: State University of New York Press, 1995.

Hamid, Mohsin. *The Reluctant Fundamentalist*. Orlando: Harcourt, 2007.

Hansen, James. *Storms of My Grandchildren: The Truth about the Coming Climate Catastrophe and Our Last Chance to Save Humanity*. New York: Bloomsbury, 2009.

Harris, Ian. "Buddhism and the Discourse of Environmental Concern." In *Buddhism and Ecology*, edited by Mary Evelyn Tucker and Duncan Ryuken Williams, 377–402. Cambridge: Harvard University Press, 1997.

Hedges, Chris. *War Is a Force That Gives Us Meaning*. New York: Anchor, 2002.

Heeley, Laicie. "U.S. Defense Spending vs. Global Defense Spending." Center for Arms Control and Non-Proliferation, April 24, 2013. http://armscontrolcenter.org/issues/securityspending/articles/2012_topline_global_defense_spending.

Heneghan, Liam. "Out of Kilter." *Aeon*, October 9, 2012. http://www.aeonmagazine.com/nature-and-cosmos/liam-heneghan-balance-of-nature/.

Herby, Peter, and Kathleen Lawand. "Unacceptable Behavior: How Norms Are Established." In *Banning Landmines: Disarmament, Citizen Diplomacy, and Human Security*, edited by Jody Williams et al., 199–216. Lanham, MD: Rowman & Littlefield, 2008.

Hershock, Peter. *Liberating Intimacy: Enlightenment and Social Virtuosity in Ch'an Buddhism*. Albany: State University of New York Press, 1996.

Heschel, Abraham. *The Prophets*. New York: Harper & Row, 1962.

Hoffman, Martin L. *Empathy and Moral Development: Implications for Caring and Justice*. Cambridge: Cambridge University Press, 2000.

Holder, John. "A Suffering (but Not Irreparable) Nature: Environmental Ethics from the Perspective of Early Buddhism." *Contemporary Buddhism* 8 (2007) 113–30.

Hollenbach, David. *Claims in Conflict: Retrieving and Renewing the Catholic Human Rights Tradition*. New York: Paulist, 1979.

———. *The Common Good and Christian Ethics*. New York: Cambridge University Press, 2002.

———. *The Global Face of Public Faith: Politics, Human Rights, and Christian Ethics*. Washington, DC: Georgetown University Press, 2003.

Hondagneu-Sotelo, Pierrette. *God's Heart Has No Borders*. Berkeley: University of California Press, 2008.

Hubert, Don. "The Landmine Ban: A Case Study in Humanitarian Advocacy." Occasional Paper no. 42, Thomas J. Watson Institute for International Studies, Boston University, 2000.

Ives, Christopher. "Deploying the Dharma: Reflections on the Methodology of Constructive Buddhist Ethics." *Journal of Buddhist Ethics* 15 (2008) 23–43.

Jasper, James M. *The Art of Moral Protest: Culture, Biography, and Creativity in Social Movements*. Chicago: University of Chicago Press, 1997.

John Paul II. *Sollicitudo Rei Socialis*. In *Catholic Social Thought: The Documentary Heritage*, edited by David J. O'Brien and Thomas A. Shannon, 395–436. Maryknoll, NY: Orbis, 1992.

Johnson, Chalmers. *Blowback: The Costs and Consequences of American Empire*. New York: Holt, 2000.

———. *Dismantling the Empire: America's Last Best Hope*. New York: Holt, 2010.

———. *Nemesis: The Last Days of the American Republic*. New York: Holt, 2007.

———. *The Sorrows of Empire: Militarism, Secrecy, and the End of the Republic.* New York: Holt, 2004.

Johnson, Mark. *The Moral Imagination.* Chicago: University of Chicago Press, 1993.

Jones, Ken. *The New Social Face of Buddhism: A Call to Action.* Boston: Wisdom, 2003.

Joyce, James. *Ulysses.* New York: Penguin Classics, 2000.

Juergensmeyer, Mark. *Terrorism in the Mind of God: The Global Rise of Religious Violence.* Berkeley: University of California Press, 2003.

Kaldor, Mary. *Global Civil Society.* Cambridge: Cambridge University Press, 2003.

Keane, John. *Global Civil Society?* Cambridge: Cambridge University Press, 2003.

Keck, Margaret E., and Kathryn Sikkink. *Activists Beyond Borders.* Ithaca, NY: Cornell University Press, 1998.

Keown, Damien. *The Nature of Buddhist Ethics.* New York: Palgrave, 2001.

Khagram, Sanjeev, et al. "From Santiago to Seattle: Transnational Advocacy Groups Restructuring World Politics." In *Restructuring World Politics: Transnational Social Movements, Networks, and Norms*, 3–23. Minneapolis: University of Minnesota Press, 2002.

Kidder, Tracy. *Mountains Beyond Mountains: The Quest of Dr. Paul Farmer.* New York: Random House, 2004.

King, Martin Luther, Jr. "Letter from a Birmingham Jail." In *A New Testament of Hope: The Essential Speeches and Writings of Martin Luther King, Jr.*, edited by James M. Washington, 289–302. San Francisco: Harper SanFrancisco,1990.

King, Robert H. *Thomas Merton and Thich Nhat Hanh: Engaged Spirituality in an Age of Globalization.* New York: Continuum, 2001.

King, Sallie B. *Being Benevolence: The Social Ethics of Engaged Buddhism.* Honolulu: University of Hawaii Press, 2005.

———. *Buddha Nature.* Albany, NY: State University of New York Press, 1991.

———. *Socially Engaged Buddhism.* Honolulu: University of Hawaii Press, 2009.

———. "Thich Nhat Hanh and the Unified Buddhist Church." In *Engaged Buddhism: Buddhist Liberation Movements in Asia*, edited by Sallie B. King and Christopher Queen, 321–63. Albany, NY: State University of New York Press, 1996.

Knitter, Paul F. *Without Buddha I Could Not Be a Christian.* Oxford: Oneworld, 2009.

Landmine and Cluster Munitions Monitor. "Cluster Munitions Monitor, 2013: Major Findings." http://www.the-monitor.org/index.php/publications/display?url=cmm/2013/CMM_Major_Findings_2013.html.

Lederach, John Paul. *The Moral Imagination: The Art and Soul of Building Peace.* New York: Oxford University Press, 2005.

Lederach, John Paul, and R. Scott Appleby. "Strategic Peacebuilding: An Overview." In *Strategies of Peace*, edited by Daniel Philpott and Gerard F. Powers, 19–44. New York: Oxford University Press, 2010.

Leighton, Taigen Daniel. *Faces of Compassion: Classic Bodhisattva Archetypes and Their Modern Expression.* Boston: Wisdom, 2003.

———. "Now the Whole Planet Has Its Head on Fire." In *A Buddhist Response to the Climate Emergency*, edited by John Stanley et al., 187–93. Somerville, MA: Wisdom, 2009.

Levine, Daniel. *Popular Voices in Latin American Catholicism.* Princeton: Princeton University Press, 1992.

Lipschutz, Ronnie. *Global Civil Society and Global Environmental Governance.* Albany, NY: State University of New York Press, 1996.

Loy, David R. *Money, Sex, War, Karma: Notes for a Buddhist Revolution*. Boston: Wisdom, 2008.

MacFarquhar, Neil. "U.N. Treaty Is First Aimed at Regulating Global Arms Sale." *NYTimes.com*, April 2, 2013. http://www.nytimes.com/2013/04/03/world/arms-trade-treaty-approved-at-un.html?_r=0.

MacIntyre, Alasdair. *After Virtue: A Study in Moral Theory*. Notre Dame: University of Notre Dame Press, 1981.

Macy, Joanna. *Despair and Personal Empowerment in the Nuclear Age*. Philadelphia: New Society, 1983.

———. Foreword to *Buddhism at Work: Community Development, Social Empowerment and the Sarvodaya Movement*, by George Doherty Bond, xi–xiii. Bloomfield, CT: Kumarian, 2004.

———. *Mutual Causality in Buddhism and General Systems Theory*. Albany, NY: State University of New York Press, 1991.

———. "Our Life as Gaia." In *Thinking Like a Mountain: Towards a Council of All Beings*, edited by John Seed et al., 57–65. Philadelphia: New Society, 1988.

Marlow, Hilary. *Biblical Prophets and Contemporary Environmental Ethics*. New York: Oxford University Press, 2009.

Marris, Emma. *Rambunctious Garden: Saving Nature in a Post-Wild World*. New York: Bloomsbury, 2011.

Martin, Julia. " Coyote Mind: An Interview with Gary Snyder." *Triquarterly* 79 (1990) 148–72.

Martin-Schramm, James. *Climate Justice: Ethics, Energy, and Public Policy*. Minneapolis: Fortress, 2010.

Massaro, Thomas. *Living Justice: Catholic Social Teaching in Action*. 2nd ed. Lanham, MD: Rowman & Littlefield, 2012.

McCann, Dennis P., and Charles R. Strain. *Polity and Praxis: A Program for an American Practical Theology*. Minneapolis: Winston, 1985. Reprint, Lanham, MD: University Press of America, 1990.

McKibben, Bill. *Eaarth: Making a Life on a Tough New Planet*. New York: St. Martin's Griffin, 2011.

———. "Global Warning's Terrifying New Math." *Rolling Stone*, July 19, 2012. http://www.rollingstone.com/politics/news/global-warmings-terrifying-new-math-20120719.

McMahan, David L. *The Making of Buddhist Modernism*. New York: Oxford University Press, 2008.

Meister, Richard J., and Charles R. Strain. "DePaul University: Strategic Planning and Service Learning." In *Public Work and the Academy: An Academic Administrator's Guide to Civic Engagement and Service-Learning*, edited by Mark Langseth and William M. Plater, 101–23. Boston: Anker, 2004.

Mekata, Motoko. "Waging Peace: Transnational Peace Activism." In *Transnational Civil Society: An Introduction*, edited by Srilatha Batliwala and L. David Brown, 181–203. Bloomfield, CT: Kumarian, 2006.

Miles, Tom. "US Defeated in Bid on Cluster Bomb Accord." *Reuters*, November 25, 2011. http://www.reuters.com/article/2011/11/25/us-weapons-clusterbombs-idUSTRE7AO1LF20111125.

Montgomery, Anne. "Divine Obedience." In *Swords into Plowshares: Nonviolent Direct Action for Disarmament*, edited by Arthur Laffin and Anne Montgomery, 25–31. San Francisco: Harper & Row, 1982.

Morrow, Avery. "Tree Ordination as Invented Tradition." *AsiaNetwork Exchange* 19 (2011) 53–60.

Moyn, Samuel. *The Last Utopia: Human Rights in History*. Cambridge: Harvard University Press, 2010.

Myers, Ched. Foreword to *Exodus: Let My People Go*, by Daniel Berrigan, ix–xiv. Eugene, OR: Cascade, 2008.

———. "The Way the Book Invites." In *Apostle of Peace: Essays in Honor of Daniel Berrigan*, edited by John Dear, 81–86. Maryknoll, NY: Orbis, 1996.

Naess, Arne. "The Deep Ecology Movement: Some Philosophical Aspects." In *Environmental Ethics: An Anthology*, edited by Andrea Light and Holmes Rolston III, 262–74. Malden, MA: Blackwell, 2003.

Nelson, Paul J. "Agendas, Accountability, and Legitimacy among Transnational Networks Lobbying the World Bank." In *Restructuring World Politics: Transnational Social Movements, Networks, and Norms*, edited by Sanjeev Khagram et al., 131–54. Minneapolis: University of Minnesota Press, 2002.

Nepstad, Sharon Erickson. *Culture and Agency in the Central American Solidarity Movement*. New York: Oxford University Press, 2004.

———. *Religion and War Resistance in the Plowshares Movement*. New York: Cambridge University Press, 2008.

Neusner, Jacob, ed. *Dictionary of Judaism in the Biblical Period*. Vol. 2. New York: Macmillan, 1996.

"New Credit Suisse Policy Furthers Swiss Disinvestment in Cluster Bombs." *StopExplosiveInvestments.org*, February 3, 2011. http://www.stopexplosiveinvestments.org/news/15/59/New-Credit-Suisse-policy-furthers-Swiss-disinvestment-in-cluster-bombs.

Niebuhr, H. Richard. *Christ and Culture*. New York: Harper, 1951.

Niebuhr, Reinhold. *The Irony of American History*. New York: Scribner, 1952.

———. *Moral Man and Immoral Society*. New York: Scribner, 1960.

Nixon, Rob. *Slow Violence and the Environmentalism of the Poor*. Cambridge: Harvard University Press, 2011.

Nussbaum, Martha Craven. "Compassion and Terror." *Daedalus* 132 (2003) 10–26.

———. *Creating Capabilities: The Human Development Approach*. Cambridge: Harvard University Press, 2011.

———. *Cultivating Humanity: A Classical Defense of Reform in Liberal Education*. Cambridge: Harvard University Press, 1998.

———. *Frontiers of Justice: Disability, Nationality, Species Membership*. Cambridge: Harvard University Press, 2006.

———. *Hiding from Humanity: Disgust, Shame, and the Law*. Princeton: Princeton University Press, 2004.

———. *Upheavals of Thought: The Intelligence of the Emotions*. Cambridge: Cambridge University Press, 2001.

———. "Virtue Ethics: A Misleading Category?" *Journal of Ethics* 3 (1999) 163–201.

———. *Women and Human Development: The Capabilities Approach*. Cambridge: Cambridge University Press, 2000.

Nussbaum, Martha, and Carla Faralli. "On the New Frontiers of Justice: A Dialogue." *Ratio Juris* 20 (2007) 145–61.

O'Brien, Julia M. *Challenging Prophetic Metaphor: Theology and Ideology in the Prophets.* Louisville: Westminster John Knox, 2008.

Odin, Steve. "The Japanese Concept of Nature in Relation to the Environmental Ethics and Conservation Aesthetics of Aldo Leopold." In *Buddhism and Ecology*, edited by Mary Evelyn Tucker and Duncan Ryuken Williams, 89–109. Cambridge: Harvard University Press, 1997.

Palmer, Claire. "An Overview of Environmental Ethics." In *Environmental Ethics: An Anthology*, edited by Andrea Light and Holmes Rolston III, 15–37. Malden, MA: Blackwell, 2003.

Palmer, Murray, and Jim O'Grady. *Disarmed and Dangerous: The Radical Lives and Times of Daniel Berrigan and Philip Berrigan.* New York: Basic, 1997.

Parenti, Christian. *Tropic of Chaos: Climate Change and the New Geography of Violence.* New York: Nation, 2011.

The Path of Compassion: The Bodhisattva Precepts; The Chinese Brahma's Net Sutra. Translated by Martine Batchelor. Lanham, MD: AltaMira, 2004.

Pixley, George. "The Bible's Call to Resist." In *Resistance: The New Role of Progressive Christians*, edited by John B. Cobb Jr., 3–31. Louisville: Westminster John Knox, 2008.

Richmond, Oliver P. "Conclusion: Strategic Peacebuilding beyond the Liberal Peace." In *Strategies of Peace*, edited by Daniel Philpott and Gerard F. Powers, 353–68. New York: Oxford University Press, 2010.

Schell, Jonathan. *The Unconquerable World: Power, Nonviolence, and the Will of the People.* New York: Holt, 2003.

Scheper-Hughes, Nancy. *Death without Weeping: The Violence of Everyday Life in Brazil.* Berkeley: University of California Press, 1992.

Schirch, Lisa. *The Little Book of Strategic Peacebuilding.* Intercourse, PA: Good Books, 2004.

———. *Ritual and Symbol in Peacebuilding.* Bloomfield, CT: Kumarian, 2008.

Schreiter, Robert J. *The New Catholicity: Theology between the Global and the Local.* Maryknoll, NY: Orbis, 2004.

Schroeder, Paul. "Work with Emerging Cooperative Forces in the International System." In *Just Peacemaking*, edited by Glen H. Stassen, 154–65. 2nd ed. Cleveland: Pilgrim, 2008.

Sen, Amartya. *Development as Freedom.* New York: Random House, 1999.

Shakespeare, William. *Richard II.* New York: Signet Classics, 1999.

Sharp, Gene. *Waging Nonviolent Struggle: 20th Century Practice and 21st Century Potential.* Boston: Porter Sargent, 2005.

Sikkink, Kathryn, and Jackie Smith. "Infrastructures for Change: Transnational Organizations, 1953–93." In *Restructuring World Politics: Transnational Social Movements, Networks, and Norms*, edited by Sanjeev Khagram et al., 24–34. Minneapolis: University of Minnesota Press, 2002.

Silko, Leslie Marmon. *Ceremony.* New York: Penguin, 1977.

Sivaraksa, Sulak. "Buddhism with a Small 'b.'" In *Dharma Rain*, edited by Stephanie Kaza and Kenneth Kraft, 117–24. Boston: Shambhala, 2000.

———. *Seeds of Peace: A Buddhist Vision for Renewing Society.* Berkeley: Parallax, 1992.

Smith, Jackie. "Economic Globalization and Strategic Peacebuilding." In *Strategies of Peace: Transforming Conflict in a Violent World*, edited by Daniel Philpott and Gerard F. Powers, 247–69. New York: Oxford University Press, 2010.

Smith, Michael Joseph. "Strengthen the United Nations and International Efforts for Cooperation and Human Rights." In *Just Peacemaking: Ten Practices for Abolishing War*, edited by Glen H. Stassen, 166–76. Cleveland: Pilgrim, 2008.

Snyder, Gary. *A Place in Space: Ethics, Aesthetics, and Watersheds*. Berkeley: Counterpoint, 1998.

———. *The Practice of the Wild: Essays*. San Francisco: North Point, 1990.

———. *The Real Work: Interviews and Talks, 1964–1979*. Edited by William Scott McLean. New York: New Directions, 1980.

Solnit, Rebecca. *Hope in the Dark: Untold Histories, Wild Possibilities*. New York: Nation, 2006.

Stanley, John. "Global Warming Science: A Buddhist Approach." In *A Buddhist Response to the Climate Emergency*, edited by John Stanley et al., 35–73. Boston: Wisdom, 2009.

Stark, Jerry A. "Postmodern Environmentalism: A Critique of Deep Ecology." In *Ecological Resistance Movements*, edited by Bron Raymond Taylor, 259–81. Albany: State University of New York Press, 1995.

Stassen, Glen H. "Take Independent Initiatives to Reduce Threat." In *Just Peacemaking*, edited by Glen H. Stassen, 57–70. 2nd ed. Cleveland: Pilgrim, 2008.

Strain, Charles R. "In Service of Whom? The Impact of Vincentian Universities' Investment Practices on Global Poverty." *Vincentian Heritage Journal* 28 (2008) 167–81.

———. "Moving Like a Starfish: Beyond a Unilinear Model of Student Transformation in Service Learning Classes." *Journal of College and Character* 8 (2006) 1–12.

———. "The Pacific Buddha's Wild Practice: Gary Snyder's Environmental Ethic." In *American Buddhism: Methods and Findings in Recent Scholarship*, edited by Duncan Ryuken Williams and Christopher S. Queen, 143–67. Richmond, Surrey, UK: Curzon, 1999.

———. "Sapiential Eschatology and Social Transformation." In *Jesus and Faith*, edited by Jeffrey Carlson and Robert Ludwig, 115–31. Maryknoll, NY: Orbis, 1994.

Sweeney, Marvin. *The Prophetic Literature*. Nashville: Abingdon, 2005.

Tannenbaum, Nicola. "Protest, Tree Ordination, and the Changing Context of Political Ritual." *Ethnology* 39 (2000) 109–27.

Taylor, Bron. "Deep Ecology and Its Social Philosophy: A Critique." In *Earthcare: An Anthology in Environmental Ethics*, edited by David Clowney and Patricia Mosto, 217–39. Lanham, MD: Rowman & Littlefield, 2009.

———. "Popular Ecological Resistance and Radical Environmentalism." In *Ecological Resistance Movements: The Global Emergence of Radical and Popular Environmentalism*, edited by Bron Raymond Taylor, 334–54. Albany: State University of New York Press, 1995.

Thalhammer, Kristina, et al. *Courageous Resistance: The Power of Ordinary People*. New York: Palgrave Macmillan, 2007.

Tocqueville, Alexis de. *Democracy in America*. Edited by J. P. Mayer. Garden City, NY: Doubleday, 1969.

Topmiller, Robert J. *The Lotus Unleashed: The Buddhist Peace Movement in South Vietnam, 1964–1966*. Lexington: University of Kentucky Press, 2002.

Tracy, David. *The Analogical Imagination: Christian Theology and the Culture of Pluralism*. New York: Crossroad, 1981.

———. "Catholic Classics in American Liberal Culture" In *Catholicism and Liberalism*, edited by R. Bruce Douglass and David Hollenbach, 196–213. New York: Cambridge University Press, 2002.

Turner, Victor. *Drama, Fields, and Metaphors: Symbolic Action in Human Society*. Ithaca, NY: Cornell University Press, 1974.

Tuveson, Ernest Lee. *Redeemer Nation: The Idea of America's Millennial Role*. Chicago: University of Chicago Press, 1968.

Twain, Mark. *The Adventures of Huckleberry Finn*. Edited by Sculley Bradley et al. New York: Norton, 1962.

Tweed, Thomas A. "Night-Stand Buddhists and Other Creatures: Sympathizers, Adherents, and the Study of Religion," In *American Buddhism: Methods and Findings in Recent Scholarship*, edited by Duncan Ryuken Williams and Christopher S. Queen, 71–90. Richmond, Surrey, UK: Curzon, 1999.

"UK Banks Blacklist Cluster Bomb Producers." *StopExplosiveInvestments.org*, May 11, 2012. http://www.stopexplosiveinvestments.org/news/20/59/UK-banks-blacklist-cluster-bombs-producers.

Waal, Frans de. *The Age of Empathy: Nature's Lessons for a Kinder Society*. New York: Three Rivers, 2009.

Walker, Brian, and David Salt. *Resilience Thinking: Sustaining Ecosystems and People in a Changing World*. Washington, DC: Island, 2006.

Walzer, Michael. *Exodus and Revolution*. New York: Basic, 1985.

Warner, Koko, et al. "In Search of Shelter: Mapping the Effects of Climate Change on Human Migration and Displacement." Policy paper in preparation for the 2009 climate negotiations, Bonn, Germany: United Nations University, CARE, and CIESIN-Columbia University and in close collaboration with the European Commission Environmental Change and Forced Migration Scenarios Project, the UNHCR, and the World Bank. http://www.careclimatechange.org/publications/global-reports/41-%20in-search-of-shelter.

Weiner, Matthew. "Maha Ghosananda as a Contemplative Social Activist." In *Action Dharma: New Studies in Engaged Buddhism*, edited by Christopher Queen et al., 110–27. New York: RoutledgeCurzon, 2003.

White, Lynn. "The Historic Roots of Our Ecologic Crisis." *Science* 155 (1967) 1203–7.

Whitman, Walt. "Song of Myself." In *Walt Whitman: The Complete Poetry and Selected Prose*, edited by James E. Miller, 25–68. Boston: Houghton Mifflin, 1972.

Williams, Jody. "New Approaches in a Changing World: The Human Security Agenda." In *Banning Landmines: Disarmament, Citizen Diplomacy and Human Security*, edited by Jody Williams et al., 281–97. Lanham, MD: Rowman & Littlefield, 2008.

Williams, Jody, and Stephen Goose. "Citizen Diplomacy and the Ottawa Process: A Lasting Model?" In *Banning Landmines: Disarmament, Citizen Diplomacy, and Human Security*, edited by Jody Williams et al., 181–98. Lanham, MD: Rowman & Littlefield, 2008.

Williams, Rhys. "Religious Social Movements in the Public Sphere." In *Handbook of the Sociology of Religion*, edited by Michele Dillon, 315–30. Cambridge: Cambridge University Press, 2003.

Wills, Garry. *Bomb Power: The Modern Presidency and the National Security State*. New York: Penguin, 2010.

———. "Entangled Giant." *New York Review of Books*, October 8, 2009. http://www.nybooks.com/articles/archives/2009/oct/08/entangled-giant/.

Wilson, Jeff. "'Deeply Female and Universally Human': The Rise of Kuan-yin Worship in America." *Journal of Contemporary Religion* 23, No. 3 (October, 2008) 285–306.

Wilson, Robert R. *Prophecy and Society in Ancient Israel*. Minneapolis: Fortress, 1980.

Wink, Walter. *Jesus and Nonviolence: A Third Way*. Minneapolis: Fortress, 2003.

Winthrop, John. "A Modell of Christian Charitie." In *God's New Israel: Religious Interpretations of American Destiny*, edited by Conrad Cherry, 39–43. Englewood Cliffs, NJ: Prentice-Hall, 1971.

Worster, Donald. *Nature's Economy: A History of Ecological Ideas*. 2nd ed. New York: Cambridge University Press, 1994.

Wylie-Kellermann, Bill. "Taking the Book with Life and Death Seriousness." In *Apostle of Peace: Essays in Honor of Daniel Berrigan*, edited by John Dear, 87–91. Maryknoll, NY: Orbis, 1996.

Yunus, Muhammad. *Creating a World without Poverty: Social Business and the Future of Capitalism*. New York: PublicAffairs, 2007.

"Zen Master Hakuin's Chant in Praise of Zazen." In *Zen: Dawn in the West*, by Philip Kapleau, 181–83. Garden City, NY: Doubleday, 1979.

PERMISSIONS

Excerpts from the following poems reprinted from Thich Nhat Hanh, *Call Me By My True Names: The Collected Poems of Thich Nhat Hanh* (1993) with permission of Parallax Press, Berkeley, CA: "Condemnation," "Defuse Me," "Experience," "The Fire That Consumes My Brother," "The Good News," "Mudra," "Our Green Gardens," "Please Call Me by My True Names," "Recommendation," "Those That Have Not Exploded."

Excerpt from untitled poem reprinted from Thich Nhat Hanh, *Opening the Heart of the Cosmos* (2003) with permission of Parallax Press, Berkeley CA. www.parallax.org.

"Eucharist" reprinted from Daniel Berrigan, *Trial Poems* (1970) with permission of Beacon Press, Boston.

Excerpts from untitled poems reprinted from Daniel Berrigan, *Isaiah: Spirit of Courage, Gift of Tears* (1996) with permission of AugsburgFortress.

Excerpts from "Not Feeling Poetic" reprinted from Daniel Berrigan, *Poetry Drama Prose*, ed. Michael True (1988) with permission of Orbis Books, Maryknoll, NY.

Excerpts from untitled poem reprinted from Daniel Berrigan, *Ezekiel: Vision in the Dust* (1997) with permission of Orbis Books, Maryknoll, NY.

Excerpts from "Hope, That Intransitive Being" reprinted from Daniel Berrigan, *Testimony: The Word Made Fresh* (2004) with permission of Orbis Books, Maryknoll, NY.

"Vision (after Juliana of Norwich)" reprinted from Daniel Berrigan, *And the Risen Bread: Selected Poems: 1957 –1997*, ed. John Dear. (1998) with permission of Fordham University Press, Bronx, NY.

Excerpts from the following poems reprinted from Daniel Berrigan, *And the Risen Bread: Selected Poems: 1957 –1997*, ed. John Dear (1998) with permission of Fordham University Press, Bronx, NY: "Children in the Shelter," "Peacemaking is Hard," "Prophecy."

Excerpt from Daniel Berrigan *The Trail of the Catonsville Nine* (1970) reprinted with permission of Fordham University Press, Bronx, NY.

INDEX

Made in the USA
Lexington, KY
20 November 2018